MEDIA, FEMINISM, CULTURAL STUDIES

Steven Spielberg: God-light
by Jeremy Mark Robinson

The Poetry of Cinema
by John Madden

The Sacred Cinema of Andrei Tarkovsky
by Jeremy Mark Robinson

Jean-Luc Godard: The Passion of Cinema / Le Passion de Cinéma
by Jeremy Mark Robinson

Liv Tyler: Star In Ascendance
by Thomas A. Christie

Disney Business, Disney Films, Disney Lands
The Wonderful World of the Walt Disney Company
Daniel Cerruti

The Cinema of Hayao Miyazaki
by Jeremy Mark Robinson

The Cinema of Richard Linklater
by Thomas A. Christie

Stanley Kubrick
by Jeremy Mark Robinson

Walerian Borowczyk
by Jeremy Mark Robinson

Stepping Forward: Essays, Lectures and Interviews
by Wolfgang Iser

Wild Zones: Pornography, Art and Feminism
by Kelly Ives

Global Media Warning: Explorations of Radio, Television and the Press
by Oliver Whitehorne

'Cosmo Woman': The World of Women's Magazines
by Oliver Whitehorne

Andrea Dworkin
by Jeremy Mark Robinson

Cixous, Irigaray, Kristeva: The Jouissance of French Feminism
by Kelly Ives

*The Erotic Object: Sexuality in Sculpture
From Prehistory to the Present Day*
by Susan Quinnell

Sex in Art: Pornography and Pleasure in Painting and Sculpture
by Cassidy Hughes

Women in Pop Music
by Helen Challis

Detonation Britain: Nuclear War in the UK
by Jeremy Mark Robinson

Feminism and Shakespeare
by B.D. Barnacle

Julia Kristeva: Art, Love, Melancholy, Philosophy, Semiotics
by Kelly Ives

Luce Irigaray: Lips, Kissing, and the Politics of Sexual Difference
by Kelly Ives

Helene Cixous I Love You: The Jouissance *of Writing*
by Kelly Ives

Jeremy Robinson has written many critical studies, including *Steven Spielberg, Arthur Rimbaud,* and *The Sacred Cinema of Andrei Tarkovsky,* plus literary monographs on: William Shakespeare; Samuel Beckett; Thomas Hardy; André Gide; Robert Graves; and John Cowper Powys.

It's amazing for me to see my work treated with such passion and respect. There is nothing resembling it in the U.S. in relation to my work.

Andrea Dworkin (on *Andrea Dworkin*)

This model monograph – it is an exemplary job, and I'm very proud that he has accorded me a couple of mentions... The subject matter of his book is beautifully organised and dead on beam.

Lawrence Durrell (on *The Light Eternal: A Study of J.M.W. Turner*)

His poetry is very good deep moving stuff.

Cloud Nine magazine

Jeremy Robinson's poetry is certainly jammed with ideas, and I find it very interesting for that reason. It's certainly a strong imprint of his personality.

Colin Wilson

Sex-Magic-Poetry-Cornwall is a very rich essay... It is a very good piece... vastly stimulating and insightful.

Peter Redgrove

BLADE RUNNER
AND THE CINEMA OF PHILIP K. DICK

BLADE RUNNER
AND THE CINEMA OF PHILIP K. DICK

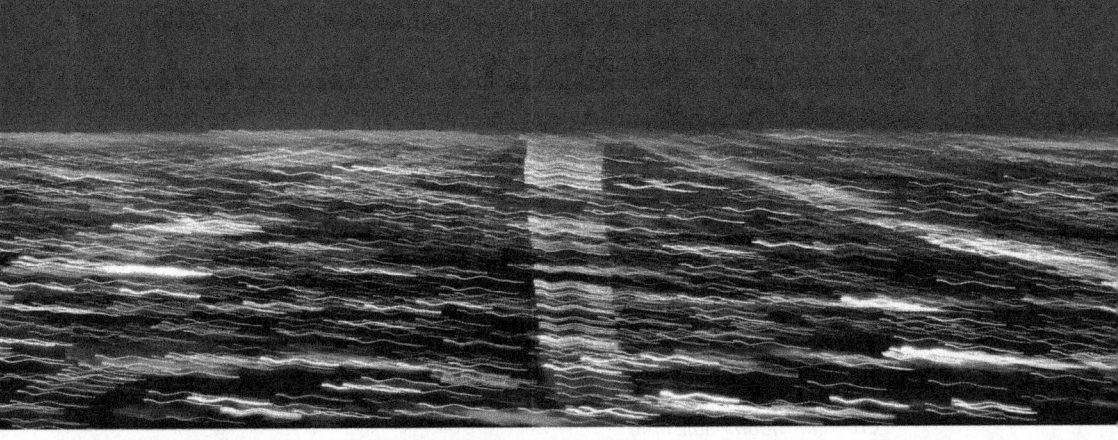

Jeremy Mark Robinson

Crescent Moon

First published 2008. Second edition 2012.
© Jeremy Mark Robinson 2008, 2012.

Printed and bound in the U.S.A.
Set in Rotis SemiSans, 10 on 14pt.
Designed by Radiance Graphics.

The right of Jeremy Mark Robinson to be identified as the author of this book has been asserted generally in accordance with sections 77 and 78 of the Copyright, Designs and Patents Act 1988.

All rights reserved. No part of this book may be reprinted or reproduced, stored in a retrieval system, or transmitted, in any form or by any means, electronic, mechanical, photocopying, recording or otherwise, without permission from the publisher.

British Library Cataloguing in Publication data available for this title.

ISBN-13 9781861713568 (Pbk)

ISBN-13 9781861713575 (Hbk)

Crescent Moon Publishing
P.O. Box 1312
Maidstone
Kent
ME14 5XU, Great Britain
www.crmoon.com

CONTENTS

Acknowledgements   *11*
Abbreviations   *12*
Foreword   *15*
Introduction   *18*

1   The Cinema of Philip K. Dick   *20*
2   *Blade Runner*   *30*
     Illustrations   *125*
3   *Total Recall*   *159*
4   Steven Spielberg Meets Philip K. Dick: *Minority Report*   *178*
5   *A Scanner Darkly*   *203*
6   Other Philip K. Dick Movies   *212*

Bibliography   *225*
Filmographies   *229*

ACKNOWLEDGEMENTS

To the authors and publishers quoted.
To the copyright holders of the illustrations.
To Warner Brothers. The Blade Runner Partnership.

Other images courtesy of Universal; 20th Century Fox; Carolco; Warner Brothers; Warner Independent; Lion's Gate; DreamWorks; Paramount; MGM; Miramax; Lucasfilm; Sony/ Columbia; and Columbia/ TriStar.

Many thanks to Thomas Christie for his chapter on *A Scanner Darkly*.
Many thanks to Sheena Duggal for the foreword.

ABBREVIATIONS

FN   *Future Noir* by Paul Sammon
MR   *Minority Report* by Philip K. Dick
PV   *Paul Verhoeven* by Paul Verhoeven

This is for Sheena

One of the cities of the future that influenced the film *Blade Runner*: the caption reads:

**LOS ANGELES
2008**

Some of the movies based on the fiction of Philip K. Dick

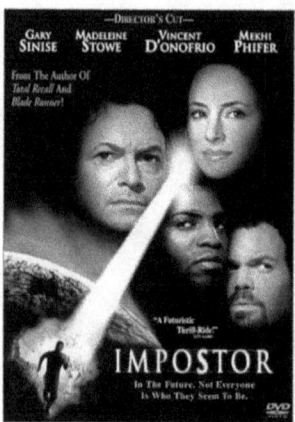

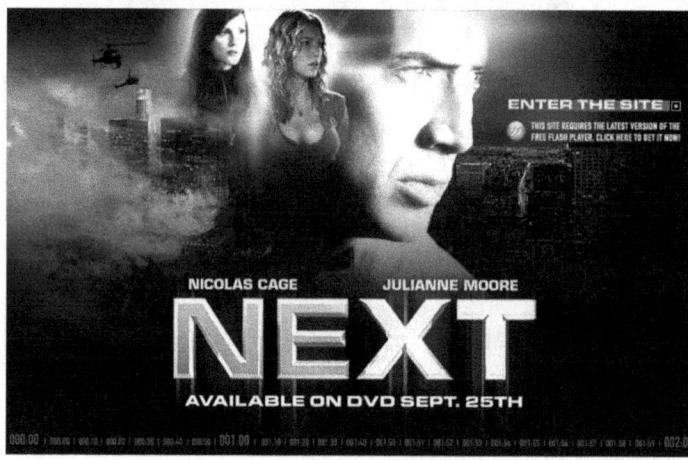
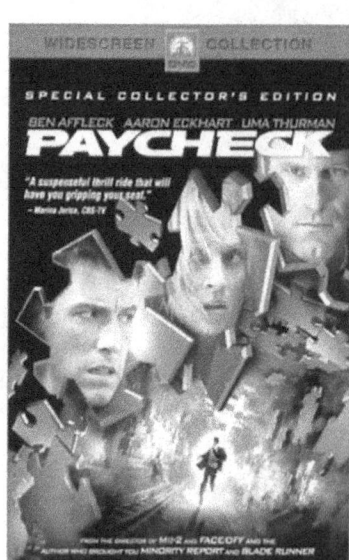

(© 20th Century Fox, Carolco, DreamWorks, Dimension Films, Paramount, Columbia TriStar, Lion's Gate)

FOREWORD

by Sheena Duggal

Jeremy and I went to school together in England. When I sat down to write this foreword for Jeremy's book on *Blade Runner*, I had not written a foreword before. I realised that while writing a foreword is a great privilege, it is also an introduction to the author and the subject. I pondered what you, the reader, would find interesting enough that you didn't flip hastily past the foreword to the meat of the book. So while I would like to tell you anecdotes about what went on behind the bike shed at King Charles 1st School in Kidderminster, I will confine my remarks to the literary topic at hand.

Jeremy has asked me to write the foreword for this book because I am currently working with Sir Ridley Scott in my capacity as a visual effects supervisor at Sony Pictures Imageworks (in Los Angeles), where we recently worked on the *Blade Runner* film, utilizing visual effects to enhance certain visual aspects of the original film, for the release of the 25th anniversary digitally re-mastered definitive *Final Cut*.

The effects included the refurbishment of several sequences in the film including the Zhora chase sequence, Deckard/ Abdul Ben-Hassan sequence and the newly created opening eye shot composites.

❦

I loved *Blade Runner* when I first saw it in 1982. I was a young woman studying design at art school. I already appreciated David Lynch's *Eraserhead* and *Elephant Man*, so the two films that stood out to me in 1982 were Peter Greenaway's *The Draftman's Contract* and Ridley Scott's *Blade Runner*. Perhaps what I was captivated by was the fact that these particular films broke the mold, that they weren't the typical commercial Hollywood-style movie that we grew up with; the moral of the story wasn't wrapped up neatly for us at the end of the film. The story-telling was complimented with images that were visually stunning and music tracks that were emotionally compelling.

I felt inspired, I wanted to see films that made me think, to see films that left me with more questions than answers, to feel that same feeling of ambiguity that you get from reading John Fowles' *The Magus*, to delve into psychoanalysis and mystical philosophy, to be a voyeur in what I can only describe as a mind game.

❦

In my role as a visual effects supervisor in Hollywood, I have worked with many big name directors such as Robert Zemekis, (*Contact, Cast Away, Polar Express, The Prize Winner of Defiance Ohio*), Peter Segal (*Anger Management, Fifty First Dates*), Barry Sonnenfeld (*Men In Black 2*), Sam Raimi (*Spiderman 3*), and Ridley Scott (*Matchstick Men, Body of Lies*), to mention a few.

Ridley stands out as being uniquely talented. He is a visionary storyteller; he is smart, skilled, gracious, collaborative and enormously visual. When he isn't focused on the visual narrative of film making, he is telling a story about his life experience; in essence he loves to tell stories and this is part of what makes him an amazing filmmaker. When he combines this storytelling skill with his fertile imagination and great sense of humour amazing things happen. Working with Ridley is a privilege and despite his success he remains humble and focused.

While shooting on-set in Morocco with Ridley for his latest film *Body of Lies*, I commented on the beautiful natural lighting of a particular shot. He began to tell me a story about how he used to be very concerned about setting up a beautiful shot when he was making films like *Alien* and *Blade Runner* – how he would wait hours for the perfect light. But now he likes to see things that are more realistic, so he shoots raw and gritty juxtaposed with natural beauty. He doesn't wait for nature, he keeps moving forward.

When I pondered what he was saying I think he was telling me is that there is more to life than perfection, that perfection and the fundamentally flawed go hand in hand, a theme I can relate to many of his films (although I could be over-thinking it and perhaps he simply doesn't have the patience to wait for the 'right' light anymore?). (While shooting in the central Sahara desert in December the natural light was beautiful and it was impossible to not point the camera in any one direction and have gorgeous backlighting.)

In this comprehensive book, Jeremy explores the themes of *Blade Runner* with his usual insight and knowledge of visual and narrative film. Jeremy presents a critical and objective outside viewpoint. He tries to be balanced, and to offer criticism as well as praise. It is ultimately important to note that he is writing about art, not the artist, and he admires Ridley Scott as much as I do.

Blade Runner has been analyzed, debated, dissected and discussed extensively over the last 25 years and I hope you find Jeremy's exploration into Ridley Scott's seminal sci-fi *film noir* masterpiece to be innovative and glowing with new ideas that stimulate your imagination and jump start your synapses.

Sheena Duggal

Visual Effects Supervisor
Sony Pictures Imageworks

INTRODUCTION

This book is about the films made from the fiction of Philip K. Dick, not a study of Dick's fiction, or Dick himself, or the relations between Dick's fiction and science fiction, or world literature.

Philip Kindred Dick (1928-1982) was a key figure in 20th century science fiction, famous for embracing drugs and the counter-culture in his work. Dick's themes included perception and reality, drug-taking, state control, global capitalism, surveillance, and paranoia.[1] Dick's fiction includes *The Man In the High Castle, Flow My Tears, The Policeman Said, A Scanner Darkly, The Game Players of Titan, Clan of the Alphane Moon, The Three Stigmata of Palmer Eldritch, Do Androids Dream of Electric Sheep?, Valis, The Divine Invasion, Martian Time-Slip, The Minority Report,* and *We Can Remember It For You Wholesale.*

---

[1] For John Baxter, Phil Dick was 'the one sf author that people outside of the sf readership tend to know about, in the same way that Tolkien is the one fantasy author that people have heard of. In the case of Dick I think he's not regarded as a sf writer by many people because he never wrote hard, technological sf, it was more sociological, state-of-consciousness sort of stuff. He had a cult following that extended beyond the purely sf crowd' (in J. Brosnan, 1991, 384).

Born on December 16, 1928 in Chicago, Philip Kindred Dick lived most of his life in California. He studied at Berkeley High School, and for a short period in 1949 at the University of California. He was married five times, and had three children (Laura Archer, Isa Dick Hackett and Christopher Kenneth). He died on March 2, 1982 in Santa Ana. Dick mainly worked in the science fiction zone. He wrote 121 short stories and 44 novels.

Four films are studied here: *BladeRunner, Total Recall, Minority Report* and *A Scanner Darkly* (in a chapter by Thomas Christie). The other pictures based on Phil Dick's fiction include *Confessions d'un Barjo* (a French movie based on *Confessions of a Crap Artist*), a Canadian film, *Screamers*, based on Dick's *Second Variety* story, *Paycheck*, directed by John Woo, *Next* (Lee Tamahori, 2007), based on *The Golden Man*, and *Impostor* (Gary Fleder, 2002).

The more recent cycle of Philip Kindred Dick movies began with *Minority Report* and *Impostor* in 2002 – *Paycheck* and *Next* followed in 2003 and 2007, and *The Owl In Daylight*, a movie about Dick (rumoured in 2009), and *Radio Free Alemuth* (2008). A sequel to *Screamers* (*Screamers 2: The Bloodening* – no, sorry, it was subtitled *The Hunting*) was in released in 2009 (again shooting in Canada, with Peter Weller starring). In 2011 *The Adjustment Bureau* (George Nolfi) with Matt Damon appeared. *King of the Elves* was in the works from the Walt Disney Company, an animated feature to be released in 2012.[2]

---

[2] Stage and radio productions have included an opera based on *VALIS*, and plays of *Do Androids Dream of Electric Sheep?* and *Flow My Tears, the Policeman Said*.

1

THE CINEMA OF PHILIP K. DICK

PHILIP K. DICK AT THE GLOBAL BOX OFFICE

A striking aspect of the films made from the fiction of Philip K. Dick is how many are very high budget movies (*Paycheck, Minority Report, Blade Runner, Next* and *Total Recall*), and just how many high profile filmmakers have been attracted to Dick's stories: Ridley Scott, Paul Verhoeven, John Woo and the most successful film director of recent times, Steven Spielberg. Those four directors together have generated billions globally.

The high budget films produced from Philip K. Dick's stories come in at $102 million (*Minority Report*), $28 million (*Blade Runner*) and 60 million bucks for *Total Recall* (in contemplating budgets there are numerous factors to take into account – not least the period in which the film was produced: *Blade Runner* costing in the region of $28 million was not unknown for a big budget movie made in 1981-82; by the end of the decade, budgets had escalated enormously. But in 1990 the year of *Total Recall*, many of the most successful films financially were more modestly budgeted.)[3]

The average negative cost for a Hollywood movie rose from $9.4 million in 1980 to $26.8 million in 1990 (and $39 million in 1995). The average cost for domestic P & A (prints and advertizing) rose from $4.3 million in 1980 to $11.6m in 1990 to $20 million in 1995.

Total Recall grossed £261 million worldwide; *Blade Runner* took $27m gross at the US box office; *Paycheck* pulled in $95m globally; *Screamers* made $5.8 million in the U.S.A.; *Impostor* about $6m (its budget was $40 million); and the Tom Cruise-Steven Spielberg film took $342 million.

Filmmakers came to Philip K. Dick at different stages in their careers, too: by the time Steven Spielberg took up Dick's short story, he was a veteran of some of the most successful films in cinema history, and was particularly known for his science fiction and fantasy movies (*Jurassic Park, Close Encounters, E.T., Hook*, etc).

John Woo was another veteran, who produced *Paycheck* with his regular producer Terence Chang after making the move to Hollywood from China, and turning in a series of big actioners: *Broken Arrow, Face-Off* and *Mission Impossible 2*. Paul Verhoeven was another veteran of many features, who moved to America for *RoboCop*. Ridley Scott was also a visitor: *Blade Runner* was his third film (after a successful career in TV commercials), and his third Hollywood movie (although his previous two films, *Alien* and *The Duellists*, had been shot in Europe). Richard Linklater, meanwhile, is one of the few independent filmmakers to take on Philip K. Dick (although Linklater became more mainstream and establishment over the years).

---

[3] 1990 was a bumper year for medium budget films that did well: Disney's *Pretty Woman* cost $18 to make and distribute but made $82 million domestically; Fox's *Home Alone* cost $18 million and made $120 million domestic; Paramount's *Ghost* cost $28 million and made $95 million; Warners' *Driving Miss Daisy* cost $8 million and generated $50 million. These are domestic (i.e., US) grosses, not rentals, always the more accurate figure.

SCI-FI CINEMA AND PHILIP K. DICK'S CINEMA

> I was beginning to sense that what we perceived was not what was actually there. I was interested in Jung's idea of projection – what we experience as external to us may really be projected from out of the unconscious, which means of course that each person's world has to be somewhat different from everybody else's, because the contents of each person's unconscious will be to a certain extent unique.
>
> Philip K. Dick[4]

BladeRunner, Total Recall, Minority Report and other Philip K. Dick movies were part of a general trend in Hollywood cinema towards fantasy and the fantastic: after the success of *Star Wars*, space opera, sci-fi, and fantasy became staples in Hollywood A-list output: *E.T.* (1982), *The Black Hole* (1979), the *Superman* series (1978 onwards), the *Alien* series (+1979 onwards), the *Star Trek* films (1979 onwards), the *Mad Max* series (1979 onwards), *Ghostbusters* (1984), *The Last Starfighter* (1984), *Gremlins* (1984), *RoboCop* (1987), *Total Recall* (1990), *Tron* (1982), *Brainstorm* (1983), *The Abyss* (1989), *Escape From New York* (1981), *The Thing* (1982), the *Terminator* films (1984 onwards), the *Back to the Future* films (1985 onwards), and the sword-and-sorcery fantasies: *The Beastmaster* (1983), *Ladyhawke* (1985), *Willow* (1988), *Krull* (1983), *Conan the Barbarian* (1982), *Dragonslayer* (1981), *The Dark Crystal* (1983), *The Sword and the Sorcerer* (1982), and *Labyrinth* (1987).

The successes of the pictures of the late 1970s and early 1980s, the highpoint of the Lucas-Spielberg era, with their heavy sci-fi and fantasy content, would lead towards the more recent Philip K. Dick adaptions, including *Minority Report, Screamers,* and *A Scanner Darkly*.

For John Baxter, sci-fi films became increasingly superficial and visual in the 1980s, with fewer ideas and science fiction in them. It was all about action and visuals, made by people with no feeling or understanding for sci-fi. *BladeRunner*, Baxter said, was 'ravishingly visual – a wonderful film to look at', but its ideas were 'really aboriginal'.[5]

---

4 Quoted in C. Platt, 149.
5 Quoted in J. Brosnan, 1991, 382.

Blade Runner, Minority Report, Total Recall and other Philip K. Dick adaptions tend towards the 'intellectual', 'thoughtful' or 'philosophical' type of sci-fi movie (although both *Minority Report, Next, Impostor, Paycheck* and *Total Recall* are very much also firmly part of the action genre). One of the more intriguing of Dick's concerns was the role of spirituality and religion in contemporary society, and the links between the spiritual and alternate realities (such as drug states).

In some respects, science fiction and fantasy films have replaced the religious movies of the 1950s and 1960s. The move is embodied by the shift from the 1950s *The Ten Commandments* to the 1970s *Close Encounters of the Third Kind*. Cinema's space aliens are the new gods, the divine beings who live in the sky and come down from Heaven.

Blade Runner buys into that view in a number of ways, from its evocations of religious awe at the spectacle of the city of Los Angeles of the future, to its depiction of the replicants as rebel angels (to reinforce that allusion, Roy Batty quotes from British religious poets John Milton, Percy Bysshe Shelley and William Blake). In *Minority Report*, meanwhile, the pre-cogs are worshipped as modern-day saints, with a cult building up around them. The sequel to *BladeRunner*, had it appeared, would have explored the spiritual aspects of the replicants.

It's not remarkable that aliens, UFOs and science fiction and fantasy should comprise the new religious element in movies. In a secular, technological age, old-fashioned deities would no longer hold sway; instead, beings with enhanced technological capabilities would be worshipped. The new frontier in the contemporary world is not the American West, but outer space, as the space race demonstrated.[6] The sky, as Mircea Eliade said, is one of the origins of the sacred, of the feeling for the holy: the sky is the ultimate Other, infinite and awe-inspiring. Gods have since earliest times inhabited celestial realms.

꽃

The typical Philip K. Dick film has some McGuffin or narrative hook that's used as the basis for the story: in *Paycheck* and *Minority Report* it's seeing into the future, in *Blade Runner* it's androids, in *A Scanner Darkly* it's

---

[6] The frontier is now outer space, as sci-fi fiction and films have often explored: Mars in Dick's fiction, or the mining and industrial colonies and outposts in films such as *Starship Troopers, Serenity, Screamers* and *Alien*.

drugs, and in *Total Recall* it's memory implants (also used in *Blade Runner*).

Philip K. Dick's fictions are often but not always set in America. Most of the Dick adaptions have been set in the U.S.A., with *Screamers* and *Total Recall* going to other planets.[7] (Maybe it's significant that four of the key Phil Dick films have been helmed by people who came to Hollywood already established in their home countries as filmmakers: Ridley Scott, Paul Verhoeven, Lee Tamahori and John Woo. Maybe Dick's fiction requires the viewpoint of a visitor or outsider to tease out the potential in the texts).

But only *A Scanner Darkly* and *Next* take place in a world very similar to present-day America (although *A Scanner Darkly* is meant to be a few years in the future): *Minority Report, Blade Runner, Impostor, Total Recall* and *Paycheck* are set in the future (*Minority Report* is fifty years hence; *Screamers* and *Impostor* are set in the late 2070s; *Paycheck* is a few years off; *Blade Runner* is 37 years after 1982, when the film was released, though 2019 ain't so far away now). Of course, all of Dick's stories, like all future sci-fi stories, are always about right now (or about when they were written).

The Phil Dick films are stuffed with hardware – with computers, cameras, screens, digital billboards, cool flying machines, cool cars, time machines, scanners, lie detectors, guns, and endless cities. Those cities may have their dark underbellies, but they are still amazing places to live.

Blade Runner was partly a picture about all-pervading technology (as with *2001: A Space Odyssey* and *Star Wars*). In *Blade Runner*, however, technology was viewed ambiguously and anxiously, as well as rapturously. While the filmmakers celebrated the sublime aspects of technology (the spinners flying over a sprawling metropolis, for example, or the video phones), the characters within the piece struggle with technology. *Blade Runner* is like many a science fiction picture in seeing advanced technology as highly problematic – the emphasis on surveillance, the invasion of privacy and the breakdown of identity, for instance, are recurring themes in sci-fi cinema.

Philip K. Dick adaptions tend to be conceived as star vehicles for male stars: Tom Cruise, Arnold Schwarzenegger, Nic Cage, Keanu Reeves and Harrison Ford. And because they are star vehicles for major stars, with the

---

[7] *Second Variety*, on which *Screamers* is based, was set on Earth.

stars in most every scene, they become a particular kind of movie: big budget and big action.

Apart from *Blade Runner* and *A Scanner Darkly*, most Philip K. Dick movies tend to be conceived as action-adventure films, usually within a thriller narrative. So the chases are longer and more action-packed, the fight scenes are louder and more violent, and the stunts are more grandiose. They are very formulaic: the hero's heroic and leads the narrative, there's a buddy (who turns into a rival or enemy), there's love interest, etc.

The movies are also very macho, with the emphasis completely on masculinity, on guys with guns, with the hero trying to defend their masculine identities from all sorts of social and psychological as well as physical attacks.

Finally, interpretations of Phil Dick's fiction are not really adaptions, because they add so much to the stories (especially the short stories), altering them nearly beyond recognition. They have the kudos of being Dick adaptions, but, like so much of contemporary Hollywood's approach to literary properties, they take the story elements only as a starting-point: then they do what the hell they like.

Nothing wrong with that: it's what a movie should do, Orson Welles reckoned. A movie isn't a book or a piece of literature. Welles' approach to adapting books was to treat the text as part of the collaboration, but not something to be treated reverentially. Often, Welles used the text as a starting-point, a source of inspiration, but wound up departing from it (as in *The Lady From Shanghai*). Welles did not stick reverentially to the letter, the word and the text; he said he felt free to go in any direction he wished.[8]

Orson Welles railed against those critics who demanded that a film be 'faithful' to the original text by reproducing it in its entirety. Welles used the example of Giuseppe Verdi making operas out of William Shakespeare's plays many times as an illustration: 'when Verdi wrote *Falstaff* and *Otello*, nobody criticized *him* for radically changing Shakespeare' (2002, 132). Unfortunately, the additions and alterations to some of the Philip K. Dick movies are so extreme, they might as well not bother buying the rights to the material in the first place.[9]

---

[8] 'I don't believe in an essential reverence for the original material. It's simply part of the collaboration', Welles asserted (2002, 201).

[9] The rights to Phil Dick's material have risen sharply from the 2,000 bucks that Brian Kelly paid for *Do Androids Dream of Electric Sheep?* in the 1970s.

RECIPE FOR A PHILIP K. DICK MOVIE

The typical Philip Kindred Dick movie contains the following ingredients:

> a hero who's hunted down for reasons he doesn't wholly understand;

> he has a loving wife/ girlfriend who stands by him, but he can't get back to her (the Dick films are always thoroughly heterosexual – and white American, too);

> there's a stern father figure;

> a mean villain;

> a sidekick or buddy;

> the government is corrupt and all-pervasive, close to fascist;

> the society is more brutal, the police more sadistic;

> a bunch of misfits or rebels band together to oppose the regime;

> even when the government and its agents seem to be on the side of what's good and right, they are still portrayed as suspect;

> and the hero gets the girl at the end and saves the world, but there's a price.

Other rules for a Philip K. Dick adaption include:

> there's always a scene with the hero on the run at night in rainswept city streets, backlit in blue;

> there's always an interrogation scene (with some hi-tech device);

> there's always a scene where a building or person is scanned or x-rayed;

> there's always some strange new drug;

> there're always some hi-tech environments which're contrasted with poor districts;

> there're always scenes with vidphones, screens, and surveillance;

> there's always a scene where some friend or colleague betrays the hero;

> there's always a scene where the hero has some crazy mind-reading, brain-altering machine strapped to his head;

> there are always machines which become like humans, and technology which goes awry.

A Scanner Darkly is the exception amongst most Philip K. Dick films: although it starred Keanu Reeves, best known prior to *A Scanner Darkly* for action flicks like the *Matrix* movies and *Speed*, it wasn't conceived and delivered as an action-adventure movie. In the hands of another team of filmmakers, *A Scanner Darkly* might've contained the same high number of action sequences as the other recent Dick adaptions. Richard Linklater and his team aren't known for action movies, though, and they clearly wanted to try for a different kind of Dick adaption.

Many Phil Dick movies are taken from short stories, and few from full-length novels – that inevitably means thousands of elements are added, such as new characters, action beats, gadgets, more back-story, more exposition, etc. Sometimes the films of Dick's fiction bear only a meagre resemblance to the original texts: the filmmakers will retain some key scenes, but go off in many different directions.

Finally, Philip K. Dick movie adaptions tend to be mounted as visual effects extravaganzas. *Blade Runner* began all that, with some extraordinary visual effects,[10] and films such as *Total Recall* and *Screamers* continued to put vfx at the centre of the movie. If you've got those sorts of visual effects in a film, that automatically increases the budget considerably. By the time of the pictures of the 2000s – *Minority Report, Paycheck, Next* – the visual effects budgets ran into tens of millions. And even more modest films, such as *Screamers* or *A Scanner Darkly*, are packed with visual effects.

So Philip K. Dick movies share many elements, from the big star parts for men, to the futuristic settings, to the elaborate look and design, to the visual effects. There are numerous ways of adapting a science fiction text, or of adapting Phil Dick's fiction, but, thus far, the Dick adaptions produced have been within a narrow set of formal, economic and cultural boundaries.

---

10 Originally budgeted by EEG at $5.5 million, the effects were cut down to $2 million.

THE DYSTOPIAS OF PHILIP K. DICK'S CINEMA

> If I can make you see the world the way I see it, then you will automatically think the way I think. You will come to the conclusions that I come to. And the greatest power one human being can exert over others is to control their perceptions of reality, and infringe on the integrity and individuality of their world.
>
> Philip K. Dick[11]

Dystopian or apocalyptic visions of the future in sci-fi films, many of them post-nuclear or post-holocaust films, are so commonplace they're practically the default setting for sci-fi cinema. *Blade Runner* is a key movie of the dystopian type (but did dystopia ever look so compelling with its neons, skyscrapers, rain and post-punk design?). Dystopian sci-fi films include: *THX-1138* (1970), *Ice* (1970), *Glen and Randa* (1971), *The Ultimate Warrior* (1975), *A Boy and His Dog* (1975), *Damnation Alley* (1977), from Robert Zelazny's 1969 book, *Logan's Run* (1976), *The Final Programme* (1975), based on Michael Moorcock's Sixties James Bond parody, *The Last Battle* (1984), *Waterworld* (1995), *The Terminator* (1984), *A Clockwork Orange* (1972), based on Anthony Burgess's early Sixties novel, *The Lathe of Heaven* (1980), based on Ursula K. Le Guin's 1971 novel, *Millennium* (1989), *The Handmaid's Tale* (1990), based on Margaret Atwood's novel, *Sleeper* (1973), *Zardoz* (1974), *The Man Who Fell to Earth* (1976), *Escape From New York* (1981), *Escape From L.A.* (1996), *The Postman* (1997), *Westworld* (1973), *Deathrace 2000* (1975), *Rollerball* (1975), *Judge Dredd* (1995), *Twelve Monkeys* (1995), *Warlords* (1986), *Mutant Hunt* (1987), *Crime Zone* (1988), *Tin Star Void* (1989), *Welcome To Oblivion* (1990), *Roller Blade* (1986), *Cyborg* (1989), *MindWarp* (1992), *Ultra Warrior* (1993) and the *Mad Max* movies. Japanese *anime* movies and TV shows have delivered the most amazing dystopian fantasies: *Akira* (1988), *Ghost In the Shell* (1995, 2004), and *Legend of the Overfiend* (1989 onwards).

Films such as *A Scanner Darkly* and *Minority Report* are not as dystopic as *Blade Runner*, but there are serious things wrong with the contemporary American societies depicted in them. In *A Scanner Darkly*

---
11 Quoted in C. Platt, 150.

much of contemporary America is addicted to mind-altering drugs, while in *Minority Report* the government is covering up corruption that begins inside the legal and criminal system but by implication involves the wider society.

The animal subplot of *Blade Runner*, which was part of Hampton Fancher's script but is included only in the edges of *BladeRunner*, is part of science fiction's long-standing exploration of ecological issues (Philip K. Dick has explored ecological themes). Ecological concerns in sci-fi films include *The Omega Man* (1971), about biological warfare, *Z.P.G.* (1972) and *Soylent Green* (1973), about over-population,[12] and *No Blade of Grass* (1970), based on John Christopher's *The Death of Grass* (1956). Concerns about the environment and ecology recurred in the 1990s, with films such as *Outbreak* (1995), *Twelve Monkeys* (1995), *The Stand* (1994), and *Princess Mononoke* (1997), and also some of the cycle of disaster movies of the same mid-1990s period.

---

12 Based on Harry Harrison's *Make Room! Make Room!*

2

BLADE RUNNER

BLADE RUNNER, STAR WARS AND *ALIEN*

I found *Star Wars* totally amazing when I saw it with friends in the English Midlands way back when. Beginning with the opening crawl and the view of the giant spaceship... Wow! Of course, scale and size ain't nuttin' new in movies: go back to 1916 and have a look at *Intolerance*, possibly the biggest American movie ever.[13] The scale of the imagery in *Intolerance* is so stupendous you *simply can't believe it.*

Many filmmakers, as well as fans and audiences, have raved about *Star Wars* and the effect it had on them when they first saw it in 1977. Ridley Scott, director of *Blade Runner*, recalled the impression that *Star Wars* had on him: 'frankly I couldn't believe it... this film was massive. It

---
[13] But not the grandest spectacle internationally – that is probably the Russian *War and Peace* of 1967.

actually changed my mind about what I would do next'.[14] Scott said that seeing *Star Wars* was one of the reasons he decided to make *Alien* instead of the more highbrow *Tristan and Isolde*, to go for entertainment instead of something esoteric. Scott's version of *Dune*, he admitted, would be *very* much in the *Star Wars* vein.

> *Star Wars* is a great movie [enthused Scott]. It's absolutely extraordinary. Completely turned me around. I thought, "What the hell am I doing?" It's just the idea of taking that as a subject and doing it in a particular way was absolutely incredible. I never go to a film twice but I saw *Star Wars* four times, and I just thought that all the detail was incredible.[15]

As *Star Wars* influenced *Blade Runner* (and *Alien*), so *Blade Runner* would in turn influence the later *Star Wars* films. The downtown area of Coruscant in 2002's *Star Wars: Attack of the Clones*, for instance, with its neons and Asians, resembles *Blade Runner* (as well as the cities in *Total Recall* and *Fifth Element*).[16]

Cultural theory critics seriously discussed the use of the replicants in *BladeRunner* in relation to racial and minority issues, but *Star Wars* was not given the same hallowed treatment, and was thought to be on the wrong side of racism. *BladeRunner* might be just as reactionary and right-wing (and plain dumb) as *Star Wars*, but for some cultural critics, *Star Wars* just wasn't as 'cool' as *Blade Runner*. *Blade Runner* had a cool, post-punk, postmodern sheen which snooty, snobby cultural theorists adore (plus it was a lesser-known movie, with its own cult of followers). But *Star Wars* was loud, silly, superficial entertainment for the masses.

ALIEN.

Alien was essentially a 1950s horror B-movie given an A-list sci-fi treatment, with hi-tech visual effects masking the fact that it was just another horror film about a monster terrorizing a group of people, as Ridley Scott admitted. This was true of other genre reworkings by the New Hollywood 'movie brat' filmmakers: *Close Encounters* updated the 1950s

---

14 In T. Shone, 86.
15 R. Scott, *Cinefantasique*, 12, 5-6, 1982.
16 *Attack of the Clones* shows off the new digital technology, though: instead of layers of film compiled in the optical printer as in *BladeRunner*, the second film of the second *Star Wars* trilogy shows off the ability of computerization to create three-dimensional images, enabling the high speed chase through the skyscrapers of Coruscant.

UFO and Cold War paranoia movie; *Jaws* was simply a Roger Corman monster flick with a bigger budget; and *Star Wars* was *Flash Gordon*. *Jaws* was definitely an influence on *Alien* – *Alien* was dubbed '*Jaws* in space', and Scott and his team often referred to *Jaws*, such as not showing the monster too much. David Giler called *Alien* 'a nasty *Star Wars*'.[17]

The *Alien* films were made by 20th Century Fox, and had the continuity of being sci-fi adventures set in space or on distant planets, with a central character, Ellen Ripley, battling against evil alien creatures. However, each picture was created by a different team, and each was conceived to stand on their own (like most sequels). *Alien* looked back to Fifties sci-fi movies such as *It! The Terror From Beyond Space* (1958), *Them*, and also the low-budget *Planet of the Vampires* (Mario Bava, 1965).

BLADE RUNNER IN THE MARKETPLACE

The previews of *Blade Runner* were disastrous. The film was deemed too confusing, too slow, with too much going on visually.[18] The story really is straightforward, but director Ridley Scott acknowledged that there were too many distractions in the look of the piece.[19] So *Blade Runner* was another of thousands of movies which have been altered after previews.

Blade Runner grossed $27 million in the United States, placing it no. 16 in that year's box office chart (it was released on June 25, 1982, in 1,290 theatres in the U.S.A.). 1982 was the year, of course, of *E.T.*[20] The films that

---

17 Some of the production team on *Alien* had worked on *Star Wars* (such as John Mollo, wardrobe, and designers Roger Christian and Les Dilley). *Alien* was also made at Fox, with Alan Ladd, Jnr OK-ing the film, the same executive who had green-lit *Star Wars*. The Ladd company invested $7.5m in *Blade Runner*.
18 The head honchos of Tandem didn't like the film at all: 'this movie gets worse with every screening,' they complained (M. Deeley, 2008, 251). They didn't like the voiceover, the stick figures, the slow pace, scenes that went on too long, and the weird bits.
19 One of the reasons for adding a voiceover was to clarify things for the audience (FN, 388).
20 Michael Deeley reckoned that audiences might be ready for something darker and less lightweight after *E.T.* (FN, 317), but that Summer was totally dominated by *E.T.* Indeed, *E.T.* took 10% of the total market share in 1982.
I don't agree that *E.T.* is lightweight and sentimental – *Blade Runner* is easily as sentimental, as conservative, as silly. But it has that 'dark', stylish veneer which seduces cultural critics into thinking they're looking at something Important and Worthy.

came in way behind Steven Spielberg's Universal fantasy were *Tootsie* at no. 2, *An Officer and a Gentleman* third, and *Rocky 3* in fourth place. Other sci-fi and fantasy flicks in 1982 included *Star Trek 2, Conan the Barbarian, Mad Max 2* and *The Thing. Blade Runner* is often trotted out as another big, important picture that flopped on its theatrical release. That isn't quite true, but it certainly wasn't a hit movie by any standards. The opening weekend was pretty good, but the movie seemed to fade away rapidly after that.

Many reviewers and critics came out against *Blade Runner* on its first release, including Roger Ebert, Pauline Kael, Sheila Benson, and Janet Maslin. 'Muddled', 'gruesome', 'pretentious' and 'overheated' were some of the words used to describe it.

RIDLEY SCOTT

As well as hundreds of commercials,[21] Ridley Scott (born in 1937 in South Shields in Tyne & Wear, Northern England) had also directed TV shows such as BBC's *Z-Cars* and *The Informer*. 'I was a designer trained as a painter, then an art director, and then from art direction drifted into graphic design', Scott explained (in H. Lightman, 1982). Scott has married twice (Felicity Heywood, 1964-1975, and Sandy Watson, 1979-1989). and has three children (Jake, Luke and Jordan).[22] More recently his partner has been actress Giannina Facio.

The movies directed by Ridley Scott can be grouped into genres: contemporary thrillers (*Black Rain, Someone To Watch Over Me, Hannibal, Body of Lies*); prestige historical films (*Gladiator, 1492, Robin Hood*); sci-fi and fantasy (*Alien, Legend* and *BladeRunner*); and the military is the *milieu* for many movies: *G.I. Jane, Black Hawk Down, Kingdom of Heaven, The*

---

[21] Ridley Scott filmed the famous Hovis bread ad of the 1970s (in Shaftesbury in Dorset), and the pricey commercial for Apple, drawing on *1984* and Big Brother, in the 1980s.
[22] Jake and Luke Scott have worked in dad's business, and all three Scott kids are commercials directors (which's *very* unusual - for one kid to follow in a parents' footsteps is quite common, but not all three). Jake has directed a movie, *Plunkett & Macleane* (1999).

Duellists and others. Scott's films tend to be masculine and macho and rather grim,[23] headed up by big male stars: Harrison Ford, Michael Douglas, Denzel Washington, Leonardo di Caprio, Nic Cage, Gérard Depardieu and Russell Crowe (Crowe's now practically Scott's alter ego on screen). The involvement of Hollywood stars like that inevitably shapes the scripts. Both Dustin Hoffman and Harrison Ford changed the screenplay for *Blade Runner*, for instance.

Going to Hollywood has been common among British filmmakers from the 1910s onwards. Britain and Australia constituted the largest portion of filmmakers going to Hollywood (Charlie Chaplin, Alfred Hitchcock, and James Whale are famous examples in the classic Hollywood era). Since the decline of the British film industry in the late 1960s (partly due to American companies withdrawing their investment in British movies), British directors have been the most numerous imports into Hollywood: Guy Hamilton, J. Lee Thompson, John Schlesinger, Karel Reisz, Tony Richardson, Peter Yates and John Boorman in the 1960s; in the 1980s, Alan Parker, Ridley and Tony Scott, Michael Apted, Ken Russell, Mick Jackson, John Mackenzie, Jonathan Lynn, Stephen Frears, Neil Jordan, Adrian Lyne and Hugh Hudson.[24]

Filmmakers such as Alan Parker, Hugh Hudson, Adrian Lyne, Roland Joffé, Ridley Scott and Tony Scott had no qualms about going 'commercial', about aiming for big budget feature filmmaking in the American style. Parker, Lyne, Hudson and the Scotts were the film directors that did much of their groundwork in making TV adverts. Whether they made their movies in Britain (such as Ridley Scott's *Alien* or Alan Parker's *The Wall*), the product was distinctly American. Virtually all of Tony Scott's films are American, in either feel, theme, location, finance or actors.

Some went to Hollywood earlier than others: Ridley Scott, for instance, went the Hollywood route right from the beginning, from his first film, *The Duellists* (1977), which, although some of it was shot in the UK, had American stars (Keith Carradine and Harvey Keitel), and American money. Scott didn't make any movies with a 'British' subject for decades. Tony

---

23 Comedy and humour are not Ridley Scott's strong points in movies, but that's also true of many pictures by his contemporaries. Scott's signature pics – *Alien, Gladiator, Thelma & Louise* and *Blade Runner* – tend to be rather serious and dour.

24 Australian directors in Hollywood include Peter Weir, Bruce Beresford, George Miller, Philip Noyce and Fred Schepisi.

Scott followed his brother to Hollywood, producing American-style films from the beginning: *The Hunger, Beverly Hills Cop, Days of Thunder, Top Gun* and *The Last Boy Scout*. (The Scotts have a company, Scott Free, and have invested in British film studios – Shepperton, as well as producing TV shows such as *Numb3rs* and *The Good Wife*).

Ridley Scott followed up *Blade Runner* with his 20th Century Fox fairy tale film *Legend* (1985), a truly dreadful movie starring Tom Cruise, Mia Sara and Tim Curry. In *Legend*, Scott's, Assheton Gordon's and Alex Thomson's elaborate visuals this time really do smother the story, and *Legend*'s difficult to watch even once.[25] Go and rent *The Wizard of Oz* or anything by Hayao Miyazaki instead. ('I'll never want to do another movie like that again,' remarked Tom Cruise).[26]

Until 2000, Ridley Scott's biggest box office successes had been *Alien* and *Thelma & Louise*; he has his place assured in cinema history, by making two cult films: *Alien* and *Blade Runner*. Then, in 2000, *Gladiator* was released, and became no. 27 in a list of top grossing films at the worldwide box office (up until 2000), generating $440.9m. Made in conjunction with DreamWorks and Universal, it was the no. 2 earner of 2000 (behind *Mission: Impossible 2*).[27]

If Ridley's Scott's star languished somewhat in the mid-1990s (remember *1492: Conquest of Paradise* and *G.I. Jane* anybody?),[28] it was revived big time with 2000's *Gladiator*, a reworking by David Franzoni, John Logan and William Nicholson of the ancient world historical epic (and virtually a remake of both *The Fall of the Roman Empire* and *Spartacus*). No Oscar for best director, but *Gladiator* won best film.

And from *Gladiator* onwards, Ridley Scott has been amazingly productive: *Black Hawk Down, A Good Year, Hannibal, Body of Lies, Kingdom of Heaven, American Gangster, Matchstick Men* and *Robin Hood*. Hell, that's about a movie a year! And by this time Scott wasn't young (he was 63 in 2000).

---

25 The best thing about *Legend* is the soundtrack by German electronic gurus Tangerine Dream; in Europe *Legend* has a music track by Jerry Goldsmith.
26 T. Cruise, in C. Connelly, *Rolling Stone*, June 19, 1986.
27 Aside from being produced by DreamWorks, there are other links between *Gladiator* and Steven Spielberg: it was co-written by David Franzoni, who had authored *Amistad*; and it starred *Amistad*'s Djimon Hounsou, who played one of Russell Crowe's gladiator buddies.
28 *G.I. Jane* is one of those films you forget instantly as soon as you've seen it. Demi Moore with a shaved head doing press-ups I remember, but little else.

Following *Blade Runner*, Ridley Scott didn't make another movie as influential or as passionately admired as the 1982 Warners flick: his biggest success post-*Blade Runner* was probably *Thelma & Louise* and *Gladiator*. Certainly, films such as *White Squall*, *Black Rain*, *1492* and *Someone to Watch Over Me* had some of the impressive Ridley Scott visual style, but lacked the power of *Blade Runner*.

1996's *White Squall* is among my favourite of the movies that Ridley Scott has directed. It was an adventure film (based on a true story), concerning a group of teenage boys, part of the Ocean Academy, who set sail in 1961 around the world in the *Albatross*, a square-rigged Brigantine, accompanied by an English teacher (John Savage) who spouts lines of William Shakespeare (the opening of *The Tempest* being the inevitable first bit of the Bard quoted in the film), and the tough, determined, charismatic skipper, Christopher Sheldon (Jeff Bridges).

The themes here were the relations between fathers and sons, men and boys, with Jeff Bridges as the 'good father' (strong, dynamic, but also fair), and the 'bad father', the rich man who overwhelms his child with a possessive love. Uneasy relations between fathers and sons are recurring themes in Scott's cinema.

White Squall was a strangely reactionary and simplistic film, the characters easily recognizable stereotypes: the tough, silent captain; the ship bully who hides an insecurity about his lack of education; the boy scared of heights (his brother died when falling from a tree). The speech made by the film's narrator, the youth at the centre of the teenage group of boys, summarized the movie's thrust: it was about boy's and men's stuff, yet another Hollywood film about fathers and sons, with sons doing the things they had to do, and fathers doing the things they had to do. The film ended with a group hug, the boys surrounding the weeping captain in the courtroom (these scenes were overlong).

In the portraits of the captain and his relation with the boys who admired him and would have followed him anywhere, one sensed the relation Ridley Scott himself is said to have had with his film crews, actors and even his own children (Scott's son Jake spoke of elements of his father in his film characters in a BBC TV *Omnibus* interview). But for all its faults, *White Squall* is still an engaging and enjoyable piece.

Black Hawk Down (2001) I find disturbing for its unashamedly gung-ho and uncritical pro-American, rightwing politics (and it's also ridiculously, grotesquely violent).29 I have friends like James Smith who disagree with me completely about *Black Hawk Down*. For me, *Black Hawk Down* is virtually an advert for the American military machine, and could not have been made, like *Top Gun* (which Scott's brother Tony directed for Don Simpson and Jerry Bruckheimer), without the full co-operation of the US military. Talk about increasing co-operation between Washington and Hollywood: *Black Hawk Down* was a movie as a war machine.

Hannibal (2001), part of the *Silence of the Lambs/* Thomas Harris franchise, was overseen by film legend Dino de Laurentiis (1919-2010), for whom Ridley Scott had worked on the abandoned *Dune* project. *Hannibal* was a pitifully bad thriller, woefully misjudged in tone and substance. It's difficult to believe that Ridley Scott directed it, and that David Mamet and Steve Zallian worked on the screenplay (*Steve Zallian*! He wrote *Schindler's List*! Much-celebrated playwright *David Mamet*!).30

According to Wikipedia, the budget for *Hannibal* was $87 million. 87,000,000 bucks! You have GOT to be kidding! For a routine thriller that would cost less than a million on TV!

For everyone concerned, *Hannibal* is lamentable.31 But we should remember that *Hannibal* wasn't Ridley Scott's concept, or franchise, or characters, or script: the producers on *Hannibal* were L. Franco, B. Melniker, C. Roven and E. Thomas.

And the less said about *Kingdom of Heaven* (2005) the better. Some people enjoyed the film,32 but have a look at *Hero, The House of Flying Daggers, The Curse of the Golden Flower* or *Seven Swordsmen*, big Chinese movies, to see how action-oriented historical films should be done in the contemporary era. Sure, the battles and the action were terrific in *Kingdom*

---

29 Of *Black Hawk Down*, Joe Morgenstern wrote: 'Functions mainly as an action extravaganza, and a numbingly depersonalized one at that' (*Wall Street Journal*). 'It's every bit as harrowing – and also every bit as pointless and misguided – as the botched military mission it depicts', remarked Andrew O'Hehir in Salon.com.
30 Some critics agree with me: 'very likely the worst film of this year and quite possibly the next', commented Charles Taylor in Salon.com, while Ella Taylor in *L.A. Weekly* called it 'the flabbiest of cop-outs'. Mick LaSalle in the *San Francisco Chronicle* found *Hannibal* 'wilfully gross, fundamentally stupid and in no way worth the discomfit of watching it.'
31 The stars were Anthony Hopkins, Julianne Moore, Ray Liotta and Gary Oldman.
32 And some critics didn't: 'muddled and oppressive storytelling' (Stephen Zacharek, Salon.com); 'a frustratingly thin epic' (Ian Nathan, *Empire*); 'fails to arouse any passion' (David Denby, *Newsweek*).

of Heaven, but Orlando Bloom in the lead role had the charisma of a soggy cardboard box. Orlando Bloom! You gotta be kidding! Where's Arny?!

Simply dreadful: *Kingdom of Heaven* was completely a *producer's* movie, like almost every movie that comes out of Hollywood. Despite the enshrinement of the *auteur*, still at work in the marketing and PR of movies (and Ridley Scott is regularly trumpeted as an *auteur*), the American film industry is wholly producer-dominated. And you can see the involvement of producers and studio executives everywhere in *Kingdom of Heaven*. It's all so cynically calculated, like the rejuvenation of Warners' *Batman* franchise (with *Batman Begins*) in the same year, 2005: 'OK, we have a bit of martial arts business for this section of the audience, some romance, a mentor figure who dies', and so on.

One critical view of the films directed by Ridley Scott is that they are slick, professional, beautiful to look at, but lacking in substance, with shallow characters.[33] Another criticism is that Scott spends so much time on his visuals he ignores narrative; Scott, though, always stresses the script and the story. The most important part of his movies, Scott said, was the script. 'Yet the toughest part is also always the screenplay, every time. Movie-making is really all story, story, story' (P. Sammon, 1999, 132). Getting the script right first before shooting began was Scott's goal: sci-fi demands rigorous planning and pre-production, Scott said.

> Sci-fi presents a wonderful opportunity, because if you get it right, anything goes. But you'd better have drawn up your rule book for the world you've created first. Then you'd better stick to it. (FN, 380)

---

[33] Others have accused Scott's films of a sometimes misanthropic worldview, and a dubious portrayal of women. For a tiny fraction of further negative criticism of Scott's cinema, see M. Garrone, Salon.com; Jim Moran, Lost In Negative Space, 2006, and Joshua Tyler, Cinema-Blend.com, 2006.

RIDLEY SCOTT AND *DUNE*

> I think that self-limitation is the major limiting factor for most people in the world. People could do far more things than they believe they can.
>
> Frank Herbert[34]

In 1975, financier Michael Seydaux and writer Dan O'Bannon (who worked on *Alien*) were developing an 11-hour *Dune* for Alejandro Jodorowsky (Jodorowsky's big claim to fame at this time was the bizarre religious Western *El Topo*, 1971). Jodorowsky commissioned influential graphic designer Moebius to provide the storyboards (he went on to design the spacesuits for *Alien*, and influenced the look of *Blade Runner*). H.R. Giger was to design the Harkonen's planet: 'my planet would be ruled by evil. Violence would run free. Perversion would be the order of the day. In a word, it was my speciality.' But the Jodorowsky *Dune* became another of many might-have-been films. Prior to that, in 1972, the film rights to *Dune* had been bought by Arthur P. Jacobs (who produced *Planet of the Apes*). David Lean and Charles Jarrott were considered as directors, and Robert Greenhut wrote a script, with Rospo Pallenberg later writing a script.[35]

After the success of *Star Wars*, Ridley Scott was commissioned to make *Dune* for Dino de Laurentiis, and had developed a screenplay in 1981 with Rudy Wurlitzer (a former Sam Peckinpah collaborator, who had written *Pat Garret and Billy the Kid* and the novel *Quake*). H.R. Giger was brought in again. Preparations commenced at Pinewood studios. (Scott had initially declined making *Blade Runner*, because of *Dune*).

But Ridley Scott took on *Blade Runner*, when the budget for *Dune* escalated to $50m (and the script was rumoured to be exploring the theme of incest). Scott worked later for de Laurentiis on the sequel to *The Silence of the Lambs, Hannibal.*

Dune was again filmed, for a TV mini-series, in 2000, adapted and directed by John Harrison. *Frank Herbert's Dune* was divided into three 95-minute episodes, corresponding to the parts of the novel (*Dune, Muad'Dib* and *The Prophet*), and starred William Hurt as Duke Leto, Ian McNiece as Baron Harkonnen (another over-the-top performance), Saskia Reeves as

---
[34] Quoted in C. Platt, 204.
[35] A good website for *Dune* information is duneinfo.com.

Lady Jessica, and newcomer Alec Newman as Paul. Shot by renowned cinematographer Vittorio Storaro, one of the top two or three DPs in the world at the time, *Dune* was made by Victor Television, Intesa, Evison, the Sci-Fi Channel and Fox. It designed by the Czechs Theodor Pistek and Miljen Kljakovic, and shot largely in the Barrandov Studios in Prague.

The 2000 *Dune* was far more satisfying than the 1984 version, as a film in itself, and as a version of the novel. The 1980s movie had been a disaster in many ways, memorable for the wrong reasons (such as its incomprehensible plot, its cast of international stars who looked as confused as the audience, and its camp extravagance).

While there was plenty to enjoy in the 1984 *Dune*, it wasn't a very accomplished adaption of the novel. Which was a pity, because Frank Herbert's book was a classic of science fiction literature (and a best-seller, with sales of 12 million by 2011). The 2000 *Dune* put back lots more of the story, and had enough time to be able to explore some of the issues deeper.[36] There were numerous scenes which fleshed out the world of Arakis further: the scenes between Kynes and Paul, and Paul and Chani, in the fremen's garden; more of the fremen's rituals; and a terrific scene where a baby worm is captured in a pool (in order to extract the 'waters of life').

The 2000 *Dune* was also clearer about the complex plot of warring factions and planets. There are so many levels to *Dune*, from the messiah plot to the battle over spice and Arakis, to the many groups (the Bene Gesserit, the Harkonens, the Atreides, the Fremen, the Landsraad, the Mentats, the trade guild, the guild navigators, and so on). A significant part of *Dune* the novel was about complex political manœuvres, about back-stabbing, betrayal, spying, secret alliances, etc, very reminiscent of ancient Rome or mediæval feuds or William Shakespeare's plays (the political intrigue, the plots and prophecies recall *Macbeth* and *Richard III*, while Duke Leto appearing to Paul in a vision is pure *Hamlet*; there are numerous other parallels between *Dune* and Shakespeare). That was the part that was hopelessly muddled in de Laurentiis's film, which the 2000 *Dune* was able to clarify.

The 2000 version of *Dune* managed to convey a deeper sense of the

---

[36] Yet another version of *Dune* was due to go into production in 2008, helmed by Peter Berg. Came to nothing. Other directors were attached then left. The problem is simple: to do *Dune* in the action-adventure manner of Hollywood, it's gonna cost plenty.

political machinations of Frank Herbert's novel, which was far more mediæval or Shakespearean than futuristic or sci-fi (the fights and battles, for example, were not carried out with ray-guns but with knives, and even the climactic final battle featured a lot of hand-to-hand combat). The social structures of the different peoples in *Dune* were mediæval or Renaissance (or ancient Roman) rather than modern (*Dune* has kings, queens and princes, blood lines, palaces and guards, poisons and prophecies, family and tribal feuds, and fights to the death). Ridley Scott would explore similar territory in *1492*, *Gladiator* and *Kingdom of Heaven*.

BLADE RUNNER AND 2001: A SPACE ODYSSEY

For many, including myself, *2001: A Space Odyssey* is *the* great sci-fi movie (other classics or favourites might include *Solaris*, *Forbidden Planet*, *Metropolis*, *Alien*, *Ghost In the Shell*, *Akira*, *Nausicäa of the Valley of the Wind*, *Close Encounters of the Third Kind* and *Star Wars*).

2001: A Space Odyssey was an immensely influential film; the 1968 picture, with its combination of technology and the mystical, the future and otherness, did not just influence most of the sci-fi movies that followed (such as *Dark Star*, *Silent Running*, *Logan's Run*, *Black Hole*, the *Star Trek* TV series, *Star Trek: The Motion Picture*, *Contact*, the *Star Wars* series, *Close Encounters of the Third Kind*, the *Terminator* films, *The Abyss*, the *Alien* series and some of the *James Bond* outings [such as *Moonraker*]), it also influenced the way science was presented on TV and radio.

MGM's epic film inaugurated the era of wonder and awe at the universe, which directly led to some of the most lucrative (sci-fi) movies – *Close Encounters*, *E.T.*, *Star Trek*, *Star Wars* – and the way space and sci-fi would be depicted with slow or grand music, or in long, meditative shots (yup, including the opening sequence of *Blade Runner*). Twenty years later, during the anniversary celebrations of the moon landings, the space scenes were still being accompanied by mysterious music (this time by Brian Eno and Harold Budd); thirty years later, for the BBC's *The Planets* TV series, this sort of approach was still being employed (this time with swathes of post-Vangelis synthesizer).37

References to *2001: A Space Odyssey* popped up in odd places: in pop promos by Lenny Kravitz, the Thompson Twins and Michael Jackson (John Landis, who directed the *Thriller* music video, liked to include the line 'see you next Wednesday', spoken by Poole's parents, in all his films). Woody Allen's movies alluded to *2001: A Space Odyssey* – *Sleeper* and *Manhattan*, for example (Allen had at first disliked the film, then came round to appreciating it). Jan de Bont put Kubrick films in his own films: *2001: A Space Odyssey* is seen in *Speed*, and *The Shining* in *Twister*.

Some filmmakers after *2001: A Space Odyssey* deliberately designed their films in opposition to the clean, efficient world it depicted: movies such as *Alien*, *Blade Runner* and *Star Wars* went the other way, creating a messy, disorganized future world. George Lucas said he didn't want his spaceships to look like the ones in *2001: A Space Odyssey*, too neat and tidy, while the *Nostromo* in *Alien* went even further in designer chaos and shadows.

An important aspect of *2001: A Space Odyssey* is the relation it re-established (and developed) between movies and the concept of the 'sublime'. In painting, that means the sublime in landscape painters such as J.M.W. Turner and John Martin, with their grand visions of mountains and ancient civilizations, up to the 'Abstract Sublime' of the Abstract Expressionists, in particular Barnett Newman and Mark Rothko, who made huge canvases of single colours, or two or three hues combined. Theirs was a self-consciously religious art, deliberately mythic and heroic, with transcendent, timeless and tragic subject matter. Their art culminated in the enormous, austere and very dark paintings in the Rothko Chapel in Houston, and Newman's ascetic *Stations of the Cross* series. The more 'sublime' reaches of Abstract Expressionism have a melodramatic, operatic quality, which seems to be reaching for something it is not equipped either to grasp or to put to use. It is an art of striving or Nietzschean 'becoming', and this journey towards transcendence sometimes produces paintings that

---

37 Even thirty years and more after its release its influence could still be discerned – in *Mission To Mars*, for example, directed by one-time 'movie brat' Brian de Palma, or the *Solaris* remake of 2002.

are so self-consciously 'sublime', 'epic' and 'heroic' that they fall into bathos or fascism (criticisms that have been made of Stanley Kubrick and *2001: A Space Odyssey*).

The sublime had always been a part of cinema (from early films such as *Intolerance* onwards), but after *2001: A Space Odyssey*, it became an essential ingredient of sci-fi and fantasy films (think of *Star Wars, Close Encounters of the Third Kind, Blade Runner, Total Recall, Independence Day* and *The Fifth Element*). *2001: A Space Odyssey* set the precedent for the sublime in sci-fi films, for gigantic scale, infinite distances, mysteries, long, elaborate shots, and complex special effects.

A sense of wonder is one of the hallmarks of science fiction, and *2001: A Space Odyssey* trades on producing awe throughout many sections: every time the monolith appears (in prehistory, at the Tycho site, in Jupiter space and in the 18th century room); during the whole end section (from the Jupiter space scenes, through the Stargate, to the 18th century room and the final Star Child images); and in most of the space flight scenes.

For at least half of *2001: A Space Odyssey*, then, the filmmakers are reaching towards the manufacture of amazement, with the viewer required to be in a state of awe. *2001: A Space Odyssey* is literally meant to be one of sci-fi's 'amazing stories', emphatically 'astounding' (to use two famous sci-fi magazine titles). And *Blade Runner*, although super-cynical with its crime/ detective/ hard-boiled genre elements, also works hard to evoke awe and wonder.

2001: A Space Odyssey doesn't take place in a future dystopia, with society falling apart; rather, *2001: A Space Odyssey* offers a rare example of a democratic, functioning future society (or, at least, in America, and America's outposts in space and on the moon). However, from the late 1960s onwards, there were far more films portraying a dystopian vision of the future, of societies in the process of crumbling, from the ecological and disaster films of the 1970s, to the post-apocalyptic nuclear wastelands of the 1980s.

Again, one sees how *2001: A Space Odyssey* is born out of the optimism, politically, socially and technologically, of the early-to-mid-1960s. If *2001: A Space Odyssey* had been conceived in the late 1960s or early 1970s, it would probably have shown a different picture of the future. Sci-fi films of disasters, viruses and ecological failures started appearing from the late 1960s (and especially the early 1970s) onwards (*The Andromeda Strain, Westworld, The Omega Man, Planet of the Apes, Silent Running, Soylent Green, Rollerball* and *THX-1138*, for example).[38] Indeed, Stanley Kubrick's next film would be about this very subject – *A Clockwork Orange* – with the familiar dystopian themes of a totalitarian state, urban wastelands, brainwashing, ultra-violence, alienation, and so on.

Politically, *Blade Runner* wants to have it both ways, both utopian and dystopian: it wants to be a cool, distanced look at contemporary America, with cynical characters and hard-boiled attitudes, an America where the idealism of the 1960s is long forgotten. Yet *Blade Runner* is also, like *Star Wars* and many sci-fi and fantasy films of the period, distinctly rightwing and pro-American (the term often used is 'Reaganite').[39]

Blade Runner depicts the late capitalist society of the Eighties exaggerated: the 'haves' are fewer and have more, while the 'have nots' are poorer and more numerous (and are of non-white, Western origin). The middle-classes have migrated to the suburbs (the Off-world colonies), while the poor and immigrants live in over-crowded streets and apartment blocks, right next to derelict or empty buildings (such as J.F. Sebastian's).

STANLEY KUBRICK.

The number of film directors who've been influenced by Stanley Kubrick, or who acknowledge him as one of the masters, is many: Ridley Scott (*2001: A Space Odyssey*'s influence can be seen in *Alien* and *Blade Runner, Spartacus* in *Gladiator,* and *Barry Lyndon* on Scott's first film, *The Duellists*; Scott even made his own version of *Paths of Glory,* in the early 1960s); John Carpenter's *Dark Star* was (partly) a *2001* spoof; James Cameron claimed that *2001* was one of the reasons he became a director; François Truffaut's *Vivement Dimance!* featured *Paths of Glory*; Michael Mann said he would have loved to have made *Dr Strangelove* (if he remade it, he wouldn't change a thing); and Quentin Tarantino's *Reservoir Dogs* (1992) reworks *The Killing*.

---
[38] The look of George Lucas's first feature film, *THX 1138,* derived very much from *2001: A Space Odyssey.*
[39] Most of Ridley Scott's films tend to be pro-military and pro-America.

BLADE RUNNER AND SOLARIS

Russian filmmaker Andrei Tarkovsky (1932-86) produced a version of Stanislaw Lem's novel *Solaris* in 1972 for Mosfilm. Often referred to as the 'Russian *2001*' (Tarkovsky wasn't keen on the 1968 Hollywood film), *Solaris* explores similar territory to *Blade Runner*, but in a much more impressive way in many respects.

There are obvious affinities between the replicas in *Solaris* and the replicants in *Blade Runner*. *Blade Runner*'s replicants have been likened by film critics to different ethnic minorities; marginalized, they have to live off the planet; the police boss Bryant refers to them as 'skin jobs', evoking the racist policemen in other films referring to 'niggers'.[40] The replicants are slaves, and work in the 'Off-World colonies', recalling the slave trade of the West. For some critics, the replicants are at the centre of *Blade Runner*'s exploration of reality and dream, the imagined and the real past, real and implanted memories, themes which are reflected in the tensions between the modernist and postmodern look of the film, its 'retrofitting', the evocation of the future using elements of the past.

The themes of time, mortality, memory and reality/ artifice are taken up in the photographs the replicants collect (in *Solaris*, as in most of Andrei Tarkovsky's films, paintings, rather than photographs, are the psychic touchstone, indicating Tarkovsky's more traditional modernism, preferring painting over photography. But Tarkovsky does use photographs of Kris's mother, and of Hari, at key moments).

For Deckard in *Blade Runner*, the photos are fakes provided by genetic engineering boss Tyrell to aid the implanted memories of the replicants, and thus control them (in a way, Kris in *Solaris* uses the home videos he shows Hari as a way of humanizing her, of helping her to become more 'human'. It's as if he's educating her, rebuilding her).

Deckard also collects photographs, which are 19th and 20th century images, of people he could not have known personally, suggesting that these too are fakes. The photos are little pieces of history and the world, whether faked or not, and they are needed by humans or cyborgs to fill in missing gaps in their lives (in *Solaris*, one of the first things the mimoid

---
[40] In subsequent years, the term 'nigger' would assume even greater strength as a term of racial hatred, while also being taken up hip-hop artists as a positive word.

Hari does is to study closely a photograph of the real Hari that Kris has brought with him).

In a totally postmodern world, where surface is everything, photographs (or home movies) may stand in for memories, may have as much weight and resonance as real memories. Much of *Blade Runner* concerns a nostalgia for 'real life', for something beyond mere image and surface, for something beyond the flashing, swivelling lights, the layers of rain and smoke, the huge wedding cake of artifice, an escape into reality; and always with the sense that time is running out – for Rachel as well as for the murderous replicants. 'Too bad she won't live', says Gaff at the end of the film, 'but then again, who does?'[41]

Like Deckard in *BladeRunner*, Kris in *Solaris* finds himself falling in love with a replica of a woman, something synthetic (half-human, half-cyborg in *Blade Runner*, and a woman made of neutrinos in *Solaris*), manufactured by a higher intelligence (the Tyrell Corporation and the Ocean). And, importantly, both Deckard and Kris begin not to care if the women they love are not 'real'; the *feelings* they have for them, the bonds between them, have more significance than their flesh-and-blood materiality. Also, both Rachel and Hari begin to ask questions about their origins and real selves, and Deckard and Kris muse on what is real and what isn't. The journey of both Deckard and Kris is to learn to become more human, more humane and compassionate.

Thus, although *Blade Runner* is a piece of mainstream Hollywood entertainment, it is also in the category of the metaphysical sci-fi film (of which *2001: A Space Odyssey* is the obvious example), though it is nowhere near as meditative and introspective as Andrei Tarkovsky's Soviet classic.

---

41 Bryant was going to appear and say the line, but it made more sense to have Gaff do that, Katy Haber remarked, because Gaff had left the paper unicorn, and had been following Deckard around (FN, 198).

THE SCRIPT AND PRE-PRODUCTION

I don't regard *BladeRunner*[42] as 'a Ridley Scott film', or a film which relies entirely for its success on one person, Ridley Scott. I've mentioned Scott a lot here, but *Blade Runner* is more a Philip K. Dick film, or a Hampton Fancher film, than it is a Ridley Scott film, in so many respects. Oh, of course Scott's involvement was critical to *Blade Runner*, but many of the things viewers love about the movie – the design, the *mise-en-scène*, the music, the romance – come from other sources: the design work of Lawrence Paull, Syd Mead, David Snyder, Moebius *et al*, Vangelis Papathanassiou's music, the cinematography of Jordan Cronenweth[43] and his team. And then there's the script, the script, the script – and that was by Hampton Fancher and David Peoples (and Daryl Ponicsan and Roland Kibbee).[44]

Although most people credit Ridley Scott with creating much of the final film, Scott himself says the movie is really Fancher's ('my final impression was of how much of *Blade Runner* was Hampton Fancher's movie', Scott said when he saw the film on the BBC in 1995 [FN, 393]); most of the key personnel on the production rated Fancher's script highly ('the most driving and interesting and original piece of writing I'd ever seen', said Michael Deeley [FN, 34]). Fancher introduced a number of elements into the script, including an ecological slant (in the rarity of real animals).

Martin Scorsese had considered filming Philip K. Dick's novel *Do Androids Dream of Electric Sleep?* in 1969; he was going to buy it for Jay Cocks to write the script. Robert Jaffe (son of the producer Herb Jaffe) wrote the first script, in the mid-70s. Dick didn't like Jaffe's script at all: 'so terribly done I couldn't believe it was a shooting script', Dick remarked (FN, 23). Dick was suspicious of Hollywood, and the way it operated. He loved movies, but found Hollywood's way of doing things difficult to take.

The project passed to Hampton Fancher and producer Brian Kelly, who

---

42 I went to see *BladeRunner* at the ABC cinema in Bournemouth in October 1982, when I was studying at film school, and loved it, of course.
43 Prior to *Blade Runner*, Jordan Cronenweth had lit *Altered States*, a $15m sci-fi extravaganza directed by England's great visionary director, the utterly extraordinary Ken Russell.
44 The DVD release of *The Final Cut* of *Blade Runner* is worth having solely for the audio commentary by Fancher and Peoples, as they discuss the script in detail, and wonder who wrote what.

completed a screenplay in 1974, which Philip K. Dick disliked. Fancher had turned his book into a bunch of clichés about private detectives, Dick thought. (Fancher has few writing credits, and was mainly known as an actor: it's one of the amazing things about *Blade Runner* that this cult classic movie loved by millions wasn't penned by a Hollywood veteran, but by a young newcomer).

It wasn't *BladeRunner*, though, that made Philip Kindred Dick one of the cool writers in sci-fi for Hollywood, but the success of 1990's *Total Recall*. Screenwriter Ron Shusett had paid $1,000 for the option on Dick's "We Can Remember It For You Wholesale" in the 1970s, which *Total Recall* was based on; after *Total Recall*, Dick's estate was asking for $500,000 for stories of the same length. By 2002, a Dick story (*Minority Report*) was the basis for a picture made by two of Hollywood's biggest talents – Steven Spielberg and Tom Cruise.

Barbara Hershey had helped to persuade Hampton Fancher to write the screenplay[45] (Hershey had also tested for the part of Rachel).[46] Producer Brian Kelly bought the rights to the 1968 book (for $2000!) and commissioned Fancher to write the script; Fancher had wanted to act as a producer, not writer, at first. Kelly persuaded him to have a go at writing the screenplay. Fancher preferred some of Dick's other stories to *Do Androids Dream of Electric Sheep?* But he did admire the paranoid, Kafkaesque quality of *Electric Sheep*, and liked the idea of doing the book as 'a chase movie, with a detective after androids in a dystopic world' (FN, 26).

Brian Kelly took the project to British producer Michael Deeley (who turned it down twice before being convinced).[47] Deeley's producer credits included *The Italian Job, Murphy's War, The Wicker Man, Nickelodeon,*

---

[45] Fancher said 'it was really Barbara Hershey who convinced me that writing a script was the only way to get this project off the ground' (FN, 31).

[46] For me, Barbara Hershey would've been much more satisfying than Sean Young, who is, how to put it kindly, not the most compelling of actresses. Maybe it helped in *BladeRunner* that Young was playing a robot – her rather blank, uninvolved style suited the part (Young was 22 at the time of filming, and had appeared in *Jane Austen In Manhattan* and *Stripes*).

Three actresses were screentested, including Young and Hershey (some say there were more). The filmmakers auditioned about 50 actresses for the part. Scott wanted Monique van den Ven, who had appeared in Paul Verhoeven's eccentric Seventies film *Turkish Delight*. One reason for not casting Hersey, for Deeley and Scott, was that she was too well-known.

For Pris the casting team screentested four actors, including Stacey Nelkin, who was cast as Mary, the mother android.

[47] Fancher commented later that Kelly had kept the project alive, for the year it took to write the first draft (FN, 32).

Convoy, The Deer Hunter, and *The Man Who Fell to Earth* (some of these became, like *BladeRunner*, cult films). Deeley said he had been attracted by the 'marvellous blending of a thriller with a romance,' in Hampton Fancher's script, and the moral drama of a cop falling for his quarry. David Peoples was called in by Scott and Deeley to revise Fancher's screenplay.[48] Bringing in Peoples was very upsetting for Fancher at first, although he later appreciated Peoples' contribution to the piece. It was one of those situations where the writers hadn't met before Peoples started to revise Fancher's scripts. And after he'd been replaced, Fancher said he'd not kept up with the production, and stayed away (FN, 318).

Robert Mulligan was the first director attached to the project (for a time it looked like the film would be made with Mulligan and Universal). Later CBS Films were in the running to make the movie, but they dropped out when the budget grew too big (partly due to Ridley Scott expanding the film's scope).

Dangerous Days (as *Blade Runner* was called then) had already been in the development stage for months before Ridley Scott came on board. Scott turned down *Blade Runner* when he was first offered it, despite Michael Deeley and Ivor Powell persuading him to do it. One reason was that Scott had recently finished a sci-fi flick (*Alien*), and wanted to explore other subjects. Another reason was he was already committed to Dino di Laurentiis' *Dune.*

Personnel on *Blade Runner* included producers Michael Deeley, Bud Yorkin, Jerry Perenchio and Brian Kelly; writers Hampton Fancher, David Peoples, Daryl Ponicsan and Roland Kibbee (Yorkin also contributed to the script); associate/ assistant producers Ivor Powell and Katy Haber; director Ridley Scott; DP Jordan Cronenweth; editors Terry Rawlings, William Zabala and Marsha Nakashima; hair by Shirley Padgett; make-up by Marvin Westmore and Bridget O'Neill; production managers C.O. Erickson and John Rogers; assistant director Newt Arnold; props by Terry Lewis; art directors

---

[48] Peoples was then working for Scott's brother Tony, at Filmways. After *Blade Runner*, writer David Peoples went on to script *Ladyhawke* (Richard Donner, 1985), a sword-and-sorcery romp with Rutger Hauer, Matthew Broderick and Michelle Pfeiffer, *Leviathan* (George Pan Cosmatos, 1989), a lame sci-fi film, *Predator* (John McTiernan, 1987), an Arnold Schwarzenegger action movie, *The Salute of the Jugger* (1990, a.k.a. *The Blood of Heroes*), which starred Rutger Hauer, and *Twelve Monkeys* (1995), one of the best post-*BladeRunner* sci-fi movies.

Stephen Dane and David Snyder; production designers Larry Paull and Peter Hampton; casting by Mike Fenton, Jane Feinberg and Marci Liroff; illustrators Tom Southwell and Syd Mead; sound by Bud Alper and Peter Pennell; script supervisor Ana Maria Quintana; visual effects by Doug Trumbull, David Dryer, and Richard Yuricich; matte paintings by Matthew Yuricich; stunts by Gary Combs and his team; wardrobe by Michael Kaplan and Charles Knode, with additional design by Moebius a.k.a. Jean Giraud (plus Winnie Brown, Bob Horn, James Lapidus, Linda Matthews, Jan Ferris and Jenny Herrin); and performers such as Harrison Ford, Rutger Hauer, Sean Young, Daryl Hannah, William Sanderson, Joe Turkel, M. Emmet Walsh, James Hong, Brion James, Morgan Paull, Joanna Cassidy and Edward Olmos James.

The initial budget of *Blade Runner* was $13.5 million; producer Michael Deeley negotiated a more expensive deal after Filmways (the original producers) pulled out: Warners and the Ladd Company put in $7.5 million; Tandem put in $7 million, for ancillary rights (including providing the completion bond);[49] Sir Run Run Shaw (of the famous Shaw Brothers in Hong Kong) put in $7.5 million, for foreign rights; the final budget of $21.5 million was raised to $28 million.[50] The effects cost $3.5 million for 90 shots. Paul Sammon called it the 'first $28 million mainstream science fiction art film' (1996, 7).[51] (While some have drawn attention to the high budget of *BladeRunner*, *Legend*, 3 years later, cost $30 million, and was a much bigger flop at the box office. $30 million bucks! What a shocking waste of $$$$$).

The title, *BladeRunner*, came from William Burroughs, who was a fan of Philip K. Dick's fiction (his *Blade Runner: A Movie* had reworked Alan Nourse's novel). The title was bought for a small fee; the production team also wanted to get rid of calling Deckard a detective, and of using the well-worn concept of androids (it was David Peoples and his daughter Risa who came up with the name replicants [FN, 61]).[52]

Katy Haber was one of the key personnel on *Blade Runner*; it was

---

[49] Including TV, home entertainment, cable, etc. Tandem also owned the negative.
[50] Thirteen Hollywood film companies turned *BladeRunner* down after Filmways bailed out, including Fox, United Artists and Universal (FN, 66).
[51] Maybe; actually, *Solaris* and *2001: A Space Odyssey* were big budget science fiction art movies before *Blade Runner*.
[52] For Dick, an android was a 'metaphor for people who are physiologically human but behaving in a nonhuman way' (FN, 16).

Haber who suggested casting Rutger Hauer, a vital decision (she recalled that she showed some of Hauer's movies which he'd made with Paul Verhoeven to the producers – *Turks Fruit, Keetje Tippel* and *Soldaat van Oranje* – and Hauer was cast, without meeting Ridley Scott [FN, 130]).

Jerry Perenchio and Bud Yorkin were part of Tandem, the production company; Tandem (linked to Embassy) was best-known for TV productions. Tandem is usually cast as the baddie in accounts of *Blade Runner*'s production, with the director Scott, producer Deeley, writers Fancher and Peoples, and some of the crew on the other side, the good side. Stories of *Blade Runner* pit the studio (Warners) and the production company (Tandem) against the filmmakers.53 It's never that simple, though.

The production needed Tandem and the $7 million they brought to the table. Without them, the film might not have been made at that time. The filmmakers probably would have preferred not to have given Tandem so much control, however, as Michael Deeley hinted in the documentary *Dangerous Days* (particularly of the complex post-production process).54

The film is set in 2019 because 2020 had connotations with vision ('20-20 vision'). After the awkward title *Do Androids Dream of Electric Sheep?* was shortened to *Android*,55 the film was called *Mechanismo*, then *Dangerous Days* for a long time. *Gotham City* was also considered by the filmmakers, but Bob Kane, the creator of *Batman*, wouldn't sell the name.

Incredibly, Ridley Scot admitted he hadn't been able to finish the book *Do Androids Dream of Electric Sheep?*. That's not going to endear an author to the people adapting their book, is it, if they haven't even bothered to read the thing all the way through? (and Dick's books aren't particularly long – certainly not compared to some fantasy and sci-fi authors, who seem to think that 'epic' and 'grand' means writing books that are 800-pages plus).

Philip K. Dick had come out publicly against the film (it started way

---

53 Everyone has a different views of events on a troubled picture like this – their own agendas, their own memories. For instance, Tandem fired Michael Deeley and Ridley Scott, but that lasted about two weeks, during which time Deeley and Scott continued to work on the movie anyway. Editor Terry Rawlings recalled how he delayed Tandem re-cutting the film, by telling them it was in pieces and wasn't ready to be worked on as a whole (FN, 209).

54 Scott said he didn't feel that he and Tandem were working on the same wavelength; they just couldn't quite understand the type of film he was trying to make. However, Scott also thought that the extra $3-4 million that Perenchio and Yorkin put into the movie on top of their $7 million, was probably 'a drop in the ocean for those guys' (FN, 386).

55 There's an odd, not particularly successful but kinda watchable movie called *Android*, which stars the inimitable Klaus Kinski (directed by Aaron Lipstadt in 1982).

back, when Hampton Fancher had done the first adaption of the book), but he was won over when he came to a screening in L.A. to see some of the footage.

THE DIRECTOR'S CUT OF *BLADE RUNNER*

There are apparently six versions of *Blade Runner*, the main three being the 1982 version, the 1992 *Director's Cut*, and the 2007 *Final Cut*; the main differences between the first two are the loss of the hard-boiled detective voiceover, and the 'happy' ending.

The voiceover had been in the original script, but was taken out, before being put back in by the studio's executives. Ridley Scott and Harrison Ford were not happy with the voiceover; Scott had been impressed by Martin Sheen's voiceover in *Apocalypse Now*, and wanted it in *Blade Runner*, but he and his writers hadn't been able to nail it. It was Scott who pushed for the voiceover, according to Hampton Fancher and others (FN, 292). 'We wrestled with it and wrestled with it', explained Scott, but they couldn't crack it (FN, 388). Voiceover, Scott reflected, 'is extremely difficult to pull off, because in a way it has to be totally internal and reflective' (ibid.). The voiceover was recorded three times in an effort to crack it (FN, 295).

As well as Peoples, Fancher, Yorkin and others, Daryl Ponicsan and Roland Kibbee also contributed to the voiceover. Some of the voiceovers were recorded after the picture was pretty much done and was being screened at sneak previews. A voiceover recording was added after the Dallas and Denver previews, for instance, overseen by Yorkin, Katy Haber and Kibbee.

The six versions are on video cassette, laser disc, DVD and theatrical release. Paul Sammon in *Future Noir*, the best book on *Blade Runner* (which I've drawn on a lot in my book), has made a detailed study of the differences between the versions.[56] Sammon defines the versions thus:

---

[56] In Appendix B.

(1) the domestic (US) cut,
(2) the international cut (both 1982),
(3) the TV version (1986),
(4) Ridley Scott's *Director's Cut* (1992),
(5) the San Diego preview print (shown only once, in May, 1982),
(6) the workprint, shown at sneak previews in Denver and Dallas,
(7) and what Paul Sammon calls the Fairfax cut, the UCLA cut, and the NuArt/ Castro cut.[57]

Paul Sammon's book also details the many differences between each of the television, laser disc and video cassette versions. The broadcast version (for CBS, 1986) cut some of the language (for example, Batty tells Tyrell before he kills him 'I want more life, father', instead of 'I want more life,fucker');[58] there are widescreen versions, panned and scanned versions, and ones with different aspect ratios.

The video version to have, Paul Sammon says, is the *Blade Runner Director's Cut* on Warners Home Video (1993), VHS, Dolby stereo, Surround Sound, widescreen, 116 minutes, R-rated, with an aspect ratio of 2.41:1 (later released on DVD, of course). The film was re-invented yet again for an 'ultimate' DVD box set, with another 'director's cut' in 2007. This was dubbed 'the final cut', and contained further additions and revisions.

The 1992 *Director's Cut* came about when film archivist Michael Arick found a a 70mm Workprint of *Blade Runner* in Warners' vaults; when Warners saw that this Workprint was doing good business when it was shown at special screenings,[59] with queues of Deckard lookalikes in long coats lining up around the block, they decided a *Director's Cut* release was possible.

Peter Gardiner began putting together an 'Enhanced Workprint', called

---

[57] On the 2007 home entertainment releases of the 'final cut' of *Blade Runner*, the deleted and alternate scenes were strung together with a voiceover by Harrison Ford, and constituted yet another version of *Blade Runner* (though not the entire story).
In this version of *Blade Runner*, the narration works nicely in relating Deckard's hunt for the replicants, enabling the deleted and alternative scenes to be put together in a logical sequence which's a satisfying alternative to the more well-known cuts of *Blade Runner*.
[58] Originally, Batty was going to kill Tyrell's family, a story point that Dustin Hoffman disagreed with when he was attached to the project. That scene was dropped, and subsequently stayed out of the film.
Oddly, 'father' was restored in the *Final Cut* of *Blade Runner*. Actually, 'father' has more philosophical and psychological resonance in the context than 'fucker'.
[59] Such as at the NuArt: Hampton Fancher said he was amazed to see kids turning up in long overcoats and smoking Boyards cigarettes (FN, 340).

'*Blade Runner*: The Final Director's Cut Version', in L.A., while Michael Arick was working on a different *Director's Cut* in London. There was a mix-up between London and L.A.; Warners wanted the *Blade Runner Director's Cut* to come out for a September, 1992 release, which they had organized. Consequently, Arick had to rush the job of putting together a *Director's Cut* for Warners, which he thought only approximated to Ridley Scott's ideas. The hospital scene, for example, didn't make it into the *Director's Cut*, partly because sound for the scene couldn't be found; additional violent footage didn't turn up; and there were various sound mistakes. (Arick had received a new set of instructions from Scott, when it was clear they couldn't complete the restoration in time – the new instructions included removing the narration, dropping the happy ending, and inserting the unicorn dream [FN, 365]).

Director Ridley Scott was very intent on putting his beloved unicorn dream into whatever *Blade Runner Director's Cut* was going to be released; however, the shots he wanted were also lost; so a positive outtake was used for a new negative (which meant the unicorn shot was poorer quality than the rest of the picture, which makes it stand out – but in the wrong way).[60]

For Ridley Scott, it seemed the three main aspects of putting together a *Director's Cut* were losing the voiceover and the 'happy ending', and putting in the unicorn dream. One or two other additions were made: a woman's voice coming from the advertizing blimp says 'this announcement has been brought to you by the Shimata-Dominguez Corporation, helping America into the New World'; a new piece of Vangelis music is heard over the 12 second unicorn shot; and the violence in the International Cut was left out.[61]

Michael Arick also created a digitally remixed soundtrack for the film, and cleaned up and colour corrected it. The *Director's Cut* of *Blade Runner* is therefore not exactly what the director wanted, because footage and sound could not be found. 'The so-called Director's Cut isn't, really. But it's close. And at least I got my unicorn', Scott remarked (FN, 368).

---

[60] The shot was an outtake that had been cast aside in favour of other footage of the unicorn, but it was the only piece of unicorn footage that could be found in the Rank vault in London.
[61] Scott also wanted the shot of the giant eye put back in, and dialogue corrections (FN, 352).

In 2007 the 'final cut' of *Blade Runner* was released. It followed the 1992 director's cut very closely, but included all sorts of additions, as well as altered elements (such as sound and dialogue). The additional elements to the 2007 cut included:
- dancers wearing hockey masks at Taffey's club;
- a new unicorn dream sequence;
- many new vistas of streets, buildings, panoramas;
- new or alternative close-ups;
- alternative or additional dialogue (no voiceover, though, of course);
- a new soundtrack including new dialogue, and new recordings of foley work.

The unicorn dream sequence in the *Final Cut* was now more of a montage, intercutting between Deckard at the piano and different images of the unicorn. And Deckard is awake, not asleep (although the differences between waking dreaming, day dreaming, remembering, imagining, fantasizing and other states are hazy).

The *Final Cut* also contained new filming – Joanna Cassidy was shot on a greenscreen stage, so that her face could be superimposed on that of stunt performer Lee Pulford during her death scene (for some that would be an insult to Pulford, who died of cancer in 1997, aged 57). And Harrison Ford's son Ben was filmed, so his mouth could be replaced over his father's mouth in the scene where Deckard encounters Ben-Hassan (Ben Astar).[62]

The *Final Cut* was developed between 2000 and 2002, led by restoration producer Charles de Lauzirika (who worked on other Ridley Scott movies), and was then abandoned for some years (while the legal situation was ironed out). It was taken up again in 2006, and finally released in 2007. As well as the 'final cut' itself, a bunch of new documentaries were commissioned (headed up by *Dangerous Days*), and the workprint was also released (these additional materials came about largely because of the enormous expansion of the DVD market – now big movies had not one short 'making of' featurette, which might have been fed once upon a time to TV channels, plus a trailer or two, but in-depth documentaries on many

---

[62] But why not Harrison Ford himself? Well, you can guess why! Ford sure ain't gonna appear in any subsequent *Blade Runner* outings, sequels, etc.

aspects of the production, plus archival material, plus the critical response, and input from fans too).

The *Final Cut* was a restoration job in the digital age – the film was restored using all sorts of digital technology, including being scanned at a high resolution. As well as cleaning up the print, many elements were added or subtracted with digital tools: for instance, the cables that held up the spinners. OK, blurring out the shadow of a camera operator or removing cables seems reasonable (but also can be seen as going too far – so there was a guy with a camera following the actor? So what? We *know* this is all fake!), but some of the additions and digital bits seemed too much (I think the teams involved in updating and reworking *Blade Runner* have missed the point about what a movie is, how movies work, why people watch movies, and why movies are valuable).

Other filmmakers, such as George Lucas and Steven Spielberg, have also gone back to some of their earlier films and restored them or altered them with digital technology. Spielberg and his team, for instance, inserted a computer generated alien into *E.T.* for the 20th anniversary release. And Lucas just can't leave any of his movies alone, going back over *THX-1138*, *Star Wars*, *The Empire Strikes Back*, *Return of the Jedi*, *The Phantom Menace*, etc.

For some, these re-issues and re-workings of existing movies are cynical and commercial, for others they are a chance to revisit pictures they enjoy. Hollywood is show *business*, and is *always* about money, but filmmakers such as Spielberg and Lucas don't *need* to drag earlier films from storage, dust 'em down, re-cut and rework 'em, and re-release 'em in theatres and on DVD. When you're worth $500 or $1 billion or whatever Lucas and Spielberg are worth, you certainly don't need to bother with goofing around with old celluloid from 1977 or 1982.

Thing is, if you keep revising and altering a movie, where does it end? A film is never 'finished', of course, but it does take up a place within people's memories. You shouldn't under-value how much viewers really like a movie, and they couldn't care less about so-called mistakes (it's the arists, of course, who see the flaws every time they look at their work. But that's a normal part of being an artist, you always see the mistakes first! And you always wanna go back and fix stuff).63 The purist's line would be to leave it all alone, blemishes included. They are part of the charm of the original film ('beloved mistakes'). If you start updating one part of an old movie for the digital age, you can keep going, updating every part. It gets silly (and very expensive).

Blade Runner is already very good – it's a masterpiece, for some fans. It doesn't need 'improving'. The ultimate is colorizing classic movies. No, no, no.

THE UNICORN DREAM

The slow-motion shot of the unicorn running towards the camera stands out so dramatically from the rest of the film (no other character is given a dream sequence – but that's standard in movies – only heroes get the dream scenes or the back-stories). In the 'final cut' of *Blade Runner*, the unicorn dream is slightly different, and includes additional footage. However, like most symbols, the unicorn is ambiguous and can be interpreted in many ways. (It was meant to be mysterious, Ridley Scott said, that was partly the point, it was meant to be something Other in among the dark urban world of the rest of the film.64 It was also intended to be an image that only Deckard would dream about [FN, 276]). And it wasn't an implanted memory, of course – when did Deckard see a unicorn running through a forest?

The unicorn dream was shot using a white stallion in Black Park, near Pinewood Studios, in January, 1982; it was generally seen as Ridley Scott's own idea – Deeley, Peoples and Fancher all state it was Scott's concept (FN,

---

63 Besides, I don't regard continuity errors and the like as 'mistakes'. They are part of the movie. Movies are *stories* (even ultra-abstract, *avant garde*, experimental movies). It's all about *storytelling*, and things like occasionally being able to see some wires in a shot are incredibly *minor* elements in a movie-going experience. And the dweebs and nerds who point out editing or continuity flubs in movies really do need to get a life.

64 And it wasn't the unicorn that was important for Scott, so much as the green landscape surrounding it (FN, 377). A unicorn had appeared in Fancher's script, however, as part of a robot menagerie that Deckard kept.

355). It wasn't a test, either, for Scott's follow-up film, *Legend*.

Other clues on Deckard's replicant status include the other blade runner (Holden) looking like him; both Tyrell's building and Deckard's apartment have Mayan designs; Deckard's eyes glow at one point, in the background of a shot, like the replicants' eyes do (there seems to be much more of that replicant glint in actors' eyes in the *Final Cut*).

Some of the hints that Deckard was a replicant were intentional,[65] others were simply mistakes, due to the many script revisions. Hampton Fancher hated the idea of Deckard's eyes glowing, such an obvious way of telling the audience Deckard was a replicant; Harrison Ford also disliked the idea, as did Michael Deeley (ibid.). Fancher wanted the idea to be more ambivalent (FN, 362). For Slavoj Zizek, *Blade Runner*, via Deckard, presents a meeting between people and their own 'replicant-status' (1993).

I don't think the issue of Deckard being a replicant is that interesting, really, and it doesn't alter the film that much. After all, can't even replicants hope to find the girl of their dreams and run away from it all to hole up in the countryside?

Maybe audiences aren't that bothered about the Deckard/ replicant issue. Maybe they just see a guy doing his job, who doesn't like doing his job, who has to kill robots, which he doesn't like to do, who meets a woman he likes.

If Deckard *isn't* a replicant, then *Blade Runner* becomes very odd indeed, on one level: *it's a story about a man who falls in love with a robot, and runs away with her at the end!* That makes Deckard a strange guy, who can't get a girlfriend, so ends up going out with a machine. It's a guy and a sex doll, really, a guy and a love machine. And that's very creepy.[66] Creepy, but we know the lengths some guys will go to for sex!

But if Deckard *is* a replicant, then it's even stranger: the audience is watching (and loving) *a movie about two robots who run away together*, trying to find a little peace and quiet before their sell-by date destroys

---

[65] David Peoples explained that the idea of Deckard being a replicant may have come out of the voiceover he wrote for Ridley Scott; or, rather, it was the way that Scott interpreted Peoples' metaphysical speculations about birth and God. Scott took up the notion that Deckard was a replicant and ran with it (FN, 361).

[66] There're also odd notions – like, why would a secretary robot be fitted by the Tyrell Corporation with sexual responses and even genitals? Oh, maybe it was so bosses could enjoy their secretaries.

them. Either way, it's very odd.[67]

But then, maybe it's not bizarre at all: cinema history is full of creatures who have love affairs who aren't human: Disney's films, for instance, are stuffed with characters who are inanimate or animals or mythical beasts. It's no big deal to see lions making love in *The Lion King*, for example, or centaurs in *Fantasia*.

❦

Back to unicorns.

In Western mediæval symbolism, unicorns symbolized purity, innocence, virginity, and also Christ. Unicorns were shown, in mediæval paintings and tapestries, in flowery enclosed gardens with virginal women, and with the Virgin Mary. The unicorn might thus be linked with Rachel, a passive, idealistic, virginal type, a Virgin Mary to Deckard's Christ. The unicorn was a mythical animal, hunted down, an outsider, like Deckard; but it could also refer to Deckard hunting down the replicants, including Rachel (unicorns also have obvious phallic connotations).

One doesn't insert a pale, strange, symbolic shot into an otherwise dark and melancholy movie without considering the implications carefully; Ridley Scott, a painter conscious of his Celtic heritage (FN, 390), would have known something of unicorn symbolism. Indeed, he later dived into Celtic and British mythology with William Hjortsbetg's fairy tale film *Legend*.

Other critics have related the unicorn to Rachel, associating it with *The Glass Menagerie* by Tennessee Williams, which used unicorn motifs, where a character is described as 'different to other horses'. For some critics,[68] having Deckard definitely a replicant (as the *Director's Cut* suggests) takes away the important ambiguity of the narrative.

---

[67] Rutger Hauer thought it was sick: 'Deckard loving replicants didn't make any sense to me. Frankly, I thought Deckard was a little sick, because he ran away with a vibrator that *looked* like a woman'. The moral of the book, for Hauer, was that robots do not love you.
  Ridley Scott, though, did not want to deal with the moral issues that the creation of the replicants raised. That would have made *BladeRunner* a different movie (in fact, it would be close to the 1972 *Solaris*).
[68] S. Bukatman, 1997, 82.

SCRIPT CHANGES AND PLOT HOLES

Due perhaps to the many script revisions, many glitches appeared in the plot of *Blade Runner* (such as Pris and Batty knowing that Leon and Zhora had been killed, though they were holed up in J.F. Sebastian's apartment). The testing of the replicant, at the beginning of the film, is redundant, because the Tyrell Corporation would have comprehensive records of all the replicants it manufactured, and would easily be able to identify their own products (and later, when the police chief Bryant introduces Deckard to the replicants, there are full records).

Another weak point in *Blade Runner* is where Sebastian gets through Tyrell's security via the chess game; Tyrell has no security, no guards, no assistants (no Rachel), and not even a camera in the elevator (in this world of surveillance). Hampton Fancher had wanted Sebastian to deliver a small unicorn automata to Tyrell at his country estate, but budgetary restrictions had persuaded Scott and Deeley to go for the chess game (FN, 171). It has to be said that an elevator ride and a conversation about chess, which's what the scene amounts to, isn't the most exciting part of the film (though everyone is trying their best to build up the suspense. And, once again, Vangelis Papathanassiou's perfect score helps out enormously).

It's also not made clear why Rick Deckard has to hunt down the replicants, when they're going to die anyway (well, actually they are killing a lot of people as they travel back to Earth – a more formulaic or traditional film script would probably have opted to show the replicants being nasty villains at the start). If Deckard was such a good blade runner, he would have probably worked out that the replicants would try to get to Tyrell; it would be simply a case of guarding Tyrell and waiting for the replicants to arrive.

Another scene that was in an early draft of the *Blade Runner* script, but was never shot, was Batty and Sebastian going up another floor in the Tyrell pyramid, after Batty has killed Tyrell, to see the 'real' Tyrell, frozen in a cryogenic chamber because he had a terminal illness and was waiting for a cure (FN, 176), a common science fiction notion, entering the popular imagination in figures such as Walt Disney, who was thought to have been frozen after death (he wasn't, but the Walt Disney Company was).

There were originally six replicants; when Captain Bryant (M. Emmet Walsh) briefs Deckard on the replicants, he says there are six. The sixth was originally intended to be Mary (played by Stacey Nelkin),[69] 'an American dream mom', but her part was cut due to financial restrictions. In one draft, Mary was going to be seen on her deathbed, surrounded by the other replicants (Mary's scenes were dropped around the 3rd week of shooting).

Leaving out Mary caused some plot confusions, the most famous being: is Deckard a replicant?, a much discussed question. The unicorn dream is taken by many to prove that Deckard is a replicant; the unicorn is part of his dreams, which no one else could know about, so when Gaff leaves a tinfoil unicorn outside his apartment, it shows that Gaff knows of Deckard's inner thoughts, the implants the replicants have.

Some other elements that were dropped from *Blade Runner* included:
- Rachel being morally superior to Deckard;
- Hampton Fancher's ecological ending;
- Deckard's dream of owning an electric sheep;
- Zhora's snake dance, cut because of budgetary restrictions (although the stage set had been built – a pity because it would have made sense to cut to the snake performance after the shot of Deckard at the bar with the MC announcing the act heard off-screen);[70]
- Zhora being hit by a bus, after Deckard's shot her;
- Leon hiding on a bathroom ceiling;
- Pris having rats crawling over her, when she's at Sebastian's apartment;
- Leon using a 'Black Hole Gun', which would emit a black beam;[71]
- Deckard entering L.A. on a train;
- three replicants escaping from a 'furnace asteroid';[72]
- Deckard and Pris fighting in a gym;
- two scenes of Deckard visiting the wounded Holden (Morgan Paull)

---

69 Nelkin had screentested for Pris. She was very disappointed when her part was cut. 'Stacey was devastated, poor thing. I still feel a bit badly about that', Scott admitted later (FN, 381).
70 It was another fight among the filmmakers – the director wanted to shoot the scene, but Tandem declined, because it would cost $200,000 (FN, 151).
71 Invented by David Dryer, but, again, dropped for budgetary reasons, though a little hint of it remains (FN, 239).
72 These were sequences heavy on visual effects, which made them especially expensive, so they were dropped during pre-production. EEG said they couldn't deliver the shots required any cheaper (FN, 224).

in hospital, where Holden is recovering in a metal sarcophagus, not used, because Ridley Scott thought they weren't necessary.[73]

NARRATIVE STRUCTURE AND THE HAPPY ENDING

Blade Runner opens narratively in simple, A-B-C terms: like ten thousand other films (such as *Citizen Kane, Star Wars, Aguirre: Wrath of God*, and so on), it shows the setting of the film then moves in closer to introduce some of the lead characters. *Blade Runner* also employs the time-honoured narrative device of a journey, to lead in to the characters and story (here the spinner approaching the Tyrell Corporation building).[74]

In other respects, *Blade Runner* is constructed along simple narrative lines: the oppositions of the two men and two women, for example (Batty and Deckard, Pris and Rachel); the blonde and the dark; the two couples; Deckard's fear and desire of both women, and so on. Also, despite being an influential science fiction thriller, *Blade Runner* contains a conventional Hollywood romantic plot, between Deckard and Rachel. There are familiar exchanges between them ('do you love me?', 'do you trust me?'). And they are together at the end of the film, in both the 1982 version and the *Director's Cut* (and *The Final Cut*). The *Director's Cut* has the more ambiguous and 'darker' ending, with Deckard finding the paper unicorn and Gaff's voice heard in Deckard's thoughts 'too bad she won't live', and Rachel and Deckard moving into the elevator at his apartment block and the door shutting; however, the lovers are still together (and framed in the same cinematic space in a two-shot).

Many critics were disappointed with the ending of *Blade Runner*, the

---

[73] These scenes crop up on the DVD of *The Final Cut*.
[74] It isn't specified who is travelling to the Tyrell pyramid, or who the eye belongs to. It could be Holden, or Leon, or Tyrell, the Big Brother of the piece.

re-shot 'happy ending', apparently ordered by the studio.75 The pressures of traditional Hollywood narrative cannot be avoided, and the 'bad' couple, Batty and Pris, are eliminated, enabling Deckard and Rachel to ride off into the sunset, to fly away... where? Nowhere: they have no place to go, because the planet has been ruined (the helicopter shots for this part of *Blade Runner* were taken from 1980's *The Shining*; another connection with *The Shining* was the use of Joe Turkel as the head of the Tyrell Corporation: he had been the bartender in the Overlook Hotel; Hampton Fancher had wanted Sterling Hayden; and both movies were Warner Bros' productions).

Using Stanley Kubrick's *Shining* outtakes was Ivor Powell's idea; landscape footage had been shot in Monument Valley, led by Katy Haber, but it hadn't worked.76 So Powell called Kubrick up, and two hours later 17 2000-foot rolls of helicopter film were delivered (FN, 389). When Fancher saw the 'happy ending' he was 'beyond shocked', he 'could not fucking believe it... [it] was like waking up from a nightmare – and then you didn't wake up!' (FN, 201).

Scott, Powell and a small crew shot the new ending with Ford and Young near Cedar Lake in California in late March, 1982.

But the happy ending was *planned* from early drafts of the script – it *wasn't* a case of the filmmakers being pressured into adding it after the sneak previews or due to the Ladd Company or Warners and production company Tandem. The filmmakers had run out of time and money to shoot the happy ending; and Ridley Scott had changed his mind about it, too, and preferred the tougher, ambiguous ending. But when the cards came from the previews in Denver and Dallas, the filmmakers decided that the happy ending might be a good idea to bolster the picture. So they were

---

75 The re-shoots lasted two weeks, in late March and early April, 1982. Inserts and additional photography also took place during post-production, into October, 1981, and January, 1982. Elstree and Pinewood studios in London were the base for the re-shoots. The filmmakers had requested a number of re-shoots, including the snake dance, Deckard looking down from Sebastian's apartment roof, a new giant eye shot, a new elevator roof shot, a cityscape, a beefed-up intro for Batty on the computer screen in the police station scene, etc. Tandem nixed most of the re-shoot requests (FN, 278f). The bathroom scene was shot, though: here stunt co-ordinator Vic Armstrong, who had doubled for Harrison Ford in *Raiders of the Lost Ark*, stood in for Deckard searching Leon's bathroom. (The office scene was re-shot during principal photography).

76 Haber had filmed in Utah over 5 days with doubles of the actors, Deckard's car and a helicopter, in March, 1982, but the footage had been unusable. That was when Powell thought of contacting Kubrick (FN, 302-3).

happy to shoot it.[77] One of Hampton Fancher's earlier drafts had Rachel asking Deckard to kill her; another idea was to have Rachel go off and kill herself.

Terry Gilliam was so appalled by the ending of *Blade Runner* he was determined not to allow his film *Brazil* (1985) to be messed with (T. Gilliam, 146). But at least the rest of *Blade Runner* was good enough, and the scene didn't ruin the rest of the piece because it came at the end. When he saw the film at an Academy screening, with various cast and crew in attendance, Fancher was very impressed:

> Man, when that first Vangelis music cue went *ka-BOOM!* and you saw that industrial landscape, people just sucked the breath out of that room. (FN, 319)

The happy ending isn't that big a deal, really. For a start, it's pretty short: there are big landscape helicopter shots and shots of Deckard and Rachel in the car, and some voiceover, and that's about it. The narration restates what Gaff has already said: who knows how long we'd have?

Anyhoo, this 'happy ending' ain't a 'happy ending': if you followed the dialogue in *Blade Runner*, you know the couple have a limited amount of time left. Plus, as fairy tales show, 'happy endings' of this kind (the holy couple of Western mythology re-united again), are not meant to be taken seriously. No one believes that everything's gonna be blissful just because the prince and princess get married (indeed, as some commentators have pointed out, that's the *start* of the problems!).

But the happy ending doesn't negate or let down the rest of the film that much, really. It's almost the sight of the lovely American landscape in full daylight more than the sentimentality of two lovers riding off into the sunset that jars, because the rest of *Blade Runner* is dark and rainy and always night and always urban. The sunlight and greenery and mountains is such a contrast with the rest of the picture, in feel and look, that it takes the viewer out of the previous 100 minutes, even more than the fact that the hero and heroine are riding off into the hills.

Because in both endings, of the director's cut and the US theatrical cut,

---

[77] One idea for the ending was to have Deckard's car driving through a forest into the desert. One idea for the ending used the visual rhyme of the L.A. skyscrapers dissolving into the famous silhouettes of Monument Valley (FN, 301). Ridley Scott later employed Monument Valley in *Thelma and Louise*

the couple are together at the end of the film: both versions have a Hollywood 'happy ending'. Whether they walk into an elevator or into a car, the hero and heroine are *together* (and, in the *Director's Cut,* presumably they're gonna go from the elevator to Deckard's car and get out of the city – like the end of *Alphaville* (1965), another dystopian futuristic thriller).[78] What's way more disturbing is that our hero, whom the audience's been rooting for, is running away with a robot! And if he's a robot too, that's even weirder!

MORE ON THE BOOK AND THE FILM

The 1982 movie dropped Philip K. Dick's novel's reference to a post-nuclear world, though the *mise-en-scène* of *BladeRunner* is that of a post-atomic bomb world (but a lot flashier and slicker than, say, the *Mad Max* or *Terminator* films, made around the same time). Deckard was turned from a petty bureaucrat (the typical Dick hero) to a world-weary private detective.

Another aspect of Philip K. Dick's novel that *Blade Runner* didn't develop was the importance of animal life, which humans have nearly wiped out (hence the significance of Tyrell's owl, the stripper Zhora's snake, and the mythical animal, the unicorn). Deckard dreams of owning a real sheep (ironically, in the mid-1990s, one of the first animals to be cloned was a sheep called Dolly). Rachel's Voight-Kampff test included questions about spiders (according to Hampton Fancher, taken from one of Barbara Hershey's childhood dreams); Leon Kowalski (Brion James) was asked about a tortoise; rats infest Sebastian's apartment; Batty prowls and howls like a wolf and holds a dove; and Pris makes herself up like a raccoon (and

---

[78] For once, in *Alphaville,* a Jean-Luc Godard film doesn't end with the heroes getting killed: Lemmy and Natacha manage to escape from Alphaville, driving away in a car at night. The movie closes with a – for Godard – very direct expression of love and tenderness: Natacha says the magic three words in a halting manner: 'je vous aime'. And she smiles. In close-up.

Who says Godard's cold and unfeeling? This is as soppy and gooey as the gooiest and sentimentalist Hollywood ending: the heroine saying 'I love you' as she drives away with the hero to a new life. It's cornball upon cliché upon gooiness in the extreme.

But it works.

rolls her eyes up, like a doll).

There was a short Animoid Row scene (on a $1 million set), as Deckard searches for the Egyptian manufacturer of Zhora's snake, and walks through a Middle Eastern-style *souk*, with different animals on show (a falcon, a donkey, an ostrich), accompanied by Vangelis's quasi-Arabic music.[79] The Animoid Row was a Cairo-style casbah, while Abdul Ben-Hassan was a stereotypical movie Egyptian, a Sydney Greenstreet type, fat, white suit, florid tie, in a fez (though with a futuristic optical device attached to his head).

It's a pity that the scene with 'the Egyptian', as he's called, is directed by numbers, without any flashes of inspiration. The visual design, though, is splendid, as everywhere in *Blade Runner*. Maybe it doesn't matter if the scene of a detective figure interrogating a guy in a store as he's on the trail of a mystery is so ploddingly done, because there's plenty of other stuff to be enjoying. A textbook example of how to really do those kind of common scenes in crime fiction is the work of Raymond Chandler (great as *Blade Runner* is, the detective elements ain't a patch on Chandler).

The Snake Pit sequence was suitably sleazy, with a crowded, smoky bar, people smoking opium with clay pipes, using long cigarette holders, drinking strange concoctions, and wearing high fashion. The Snake Pit was presided over by Hy Pyke's cynical sleazeball, Taffey Lewis. There's little build-up to Lewis, though, and his character makes little impression beyond being cynical and slimy. The scene concentrates more on Deckard's blurry state as he gets drunker.

---

[79] Vangelis has regularly incorporated musical styles from other cultures in his work – such as his album of Chinese-related themes, *China*, while his soundtrack for *1492* took on Spanish flavours (like his later album *Oceanic*), and for his brilliant score for *Alexander*, Vangelis took up Middle Eastern instrumentation and melodies.

MAKING *BLADE RUNNER*

Shooting began on March 9, 1981, at Warners' Burbank Studios in Los Angeles (pre-production had lasted about a year – that helped to make *BladeRunner* a better film. The longer the pre-production period the better, usually. Or, to put it another way, had *Blade Runner* been rushed into production, it probably wouldn't be so rich).

The production of *Blade Runner* was fraught with problems, most of which are typical for many Hollywood movies: Harrison Ford and Ridley Scott fell out with each other, nearly fighting at one point;[80] Ford did not get on with Sean Young, and ignored her on set; that bothered Young, a lot. In an interview, she said she wouldn't dish any dirt, but acknowledged: 'I wouldn't call Harrison Ford generous' (FN, 214).[81]

Harrison Ford was rough with Young during the love scene in *Blade Runner* (Michael Deeley called the 'kiss me, kiss me' scene 'the rape in the corridor', because it was so rough [FN, 164]);[82] the screenwriters disagreed with each other and with Scott; Philip K. Dick disagreed with Scott and his writers; the producers and Tandem didn't agree; the production company and studio disagreed about the film, and so on.

Harrison Ford was good casting for *BladeRunner*, which didn't require great acting chops, but more a certain look, attitude and style. Ford's short crewcut was one of the more memorable aspects of his performance. Apparently, the only other actor offered the role was Dustin Hoffman (other actors considered included Burt Reynolds, Nick Nolte, Al Pacino and Peter Falk). The filmmakers approached Hoffman partly because they needed a big star to keep the film afloat during pre-production. They worked with

---

80 Harrison Ford was fast becoming one of Hollywood's big stars at the time, appearing in two *Star Wars* films and *Raiders of the Lost Ark* immediately prior to *Blade Runner*. Ford remained an important Hollywood star, though he'd always tried to choose some 'serious' or prestige projects as well as the more routine Hollywood fare.

81 Sean Young was starting out in movies at the time of *Blade Runner*, and found it difficult to adjust to the multiple takes required of her. She said that the director shot 26 takes of her saying her introductory line in her first scene (FN, 214). Some in the crew dubbed the movie *Blood Runner*.

82 Hampton Fancher said the love scene was meant to be 'a very tender erotic moment. I was shocked and attracted by what turned up on the screen instead' (FN, 163). But Fancher hadn't wanted a sex scene at all in the film, and only wrote one reluctantly.

Apparently, there was more to the scene, too, with Rachel wrapping her legs around Deckard, and the lovemaking being less brutal (FN, 165). Parts of the unused footage appear on the DVDs of *Blade Runner*. Suffice to say, it's not one of the great love scenes or sex scenes in cinema history. Ridley Scott acknowledged that the scene was one of the least effective in *Blade Runner*.

Hoffman in New York for a long time,[83] so Hoffman has also influenced *Blade Runner*, although he's not in it.[84]

Some in the team, such as Hampton Fancher, didn't like the idea of using Dustin Hoffman at all. (In fact, Fancher had been writing partly with Robert Mitchum in mind, the Mitchum of 1940s and 1950s *film noir* classics such as *Build My Gallows High*, a.k.a. *Out of the Past* and *The Night of the Hunter*).

The filmmakers had been impressed with Harrison Ford when they visited London and saw the rushes of *Raiders of the Lost Ark*. Ridley Scott had liked the idea of using a hat in Deckard's look, which fitted in with the retro *film noir* look he was going for. The notion was dropped[85] (but both Gaff and Bryant sport hats).

Casting on *Blade Runner* was by one of the most significant casting directors in the business – Mike Fenton (aided by Jane Feinberg and Marci Liroff). You can't over-emphasize the importance of casting on a movie, although, with films such as *Blade Runner*, there are many other components which overshadow it, like the visual fx, the sets, the look. Someone, for instance, had to cast all of the extras, who add so much to the street scenes in *Blade Runner*, and other people had to dress them and make them up.

Harrison Ford and Ridley Scott argued about the look of Deckard's character, as well as his personality. Scott wanted the grizzled, shabby look of Indiana Jones. Ford, meanwhile, didn't agree, and didn't want to play up the Humphrey Bogart/ Philip Marlowe connection either. 'I played a detective who did no detecting. There was nothing for me to do but stand around and give some vain attempt to give some focus to Ridley's sets', Ford remarked in 1991 (FN, 211).

Harrison Ford found Ridley Scott as unforthcoming about performances and acting as Sigourney Weaver had done in *Alien*. Ford said he'd look up to see Scott thirty feet up on a camera crane composing his shots, leaving him with little direction. He wanted to be directed. When

---

[83] Dustin Hoffman is well-known for contributing a lot to the movies he makes, with negotiations over the script which can run on for months. Hoffman is a movie star who will have all sorts of ideas about the character he plays.

[84] Deeley recalled: 'we had wasted vital months trying to adjust the script to Dustin or vice versa' (2008, 214).

[85] Scott told Deeley, 'shit, I wanted that hat for Deckard!' Deeley replied that they'd lost a hat, but gained a star (M. Deeley, 215).

filmmaker Alan Raymond visited the set he noted that Ford never said a word to Scott (FN, 210).

Crew members as well as the actors found Ridley Scott's perfectionism trying: shooting would be stopped while some prop or extra was moved an inch.[86] Scott also liked to direct looking through the camera, but the union stopped him doing that. Some in the crew found Scott a 'megalomaniac' and 'dominating'. The pressure of the arduous shoot resulted in some walk-outs (and there were Tee shirt gags, such as discontent over an interview Scott had done remarking that crews in Blighty called the director 'guvnor': the Yanks responded with Tee shirts that read 'yes guvnor my ass'). It didn't help that the seven sprinklers employed to deliver the rain made shooting uncomfortable, plus the smoke, plus the night shoots. And Scott asking for take after take didn't help either.

David Peoples said sometimes he was writing scenes that would be shot the next day, and also 'just frantically trying to make certain changes to solve this particular thing or that particular thing'.[87] Again, normal for a movie.

From day one the Warners production was behind schedule. As Alan Ladd recalled: 'after the first day of shooting the production manager called me to say we were now five days behind. Ridley had shot smoke all day'.[88] Bud Yorkin and Jerry Perenchio at Tandem were impatient with the director's slow methods of working. As publicist Charles Lippincott put it, what Tandem saw coming from the set was 'rain, gloom, a woman being shot in the back, and a relentlessly perfectionist director who'd shoot the same sequence over and over again, all day long' (FN, 206).

The shoot was tense, as with *Alien*. Ridley Scott felt he was being questioned about every decision, which he was miffed about after making 2000 commercials and directing *The Duellists* and *Alien*. 'I was getting pissed off. Pissed off regularly. Every day', he recalled (T. Shone, 116). According to Katy Haber, the whole shoot was full of problems and tensions: 'it was just wretched awfulness, really; *Blade Runner* was a

---
[86] Art director David Snyder said that Scott wanted to change everything, that no set was shot just as it was built.
[87] T. Shone, 115.
[88] There was also the first day on the Tyrell office set, where Scott wanted the columns turned upside-down. Larry Paull said, err, OK, come back at two p.m. The columns were duly up-ended. But the set had to be largely reconstructed later, as a matte painting by Matthew Yuricich.

monument to stress' (FN, 202). Joanna Cassidy remembered that filming got 'brutal towards the end' (FN, 217) – particularly her death scene, which had to be achieved in one take, due to the pressure of time (i.e., money).

It's understandable that Warners and the producers would put pressure on the filmmakers, because this was a time when big films going over-budget and over-schedule were very much on their minds: *Blade Runner* was being shot not long after the very high budget productions of *Heaven's Gate, Raise the Titanic, Superman, Star Trek, Moonraker* and *Apocalypse Now*. The Hollywood studios weren't keen on letting film directors run away with productions. So a visual expert like Ridley Scott was at the time viewed suspiciously, even though *Alien* had been a big success. (Remember, though, that expensive movies such as *Superman, Star Trek* and *Moonraker* went on to make lots of money, but others didn't: *Raise the Titanic, Heaven's Gate* and *Honky Tonk Freeway*, for instance).[89] A movie like *Legend*, costing $30 million, which Scott directed 3 years later from William Hjortsberg's script, is a far, far greater disaster. (Incidentally, *Heaven's Gate* rivals *Blade Runner* for being shrouded in smoke, rain, fog and practical effects – it was a concern of United Artists about *Heaven's Gate* that you couldn't see what the hell was going on – for instance in the big battle at the end.)[90]

Philip K. Dick's response to the film was ambiguous and mixed; while impressed by what he saw,[91] there were many aspects he wasn't so keen on. He also didn't see the completed movie (or any of the subsequent adaptions of his fiction). Dick was asked to do a novelization of the film, but preferred to reissue his novel instead; he said he only made $12,500 from reprinting *Do Androids Dream of Electric Sheep*, but kept his integrity (FN, 282).

---

[89] While *Heaven's Gate* lost plenty of money, there were other films of the time that lost plenty too, and films that were similarly expensive but were nowhere near as good as *Heaven's Gate*: *Honky Tonk Freeway* and *Raise the Titanic*, to name a couple. (*Honky Tonk Freeway* recouped only 2.1% of its $24 million budget).

[90] *Heaven's Gate* was shot by one of the superstar cinematographers of the 'New Hollywood' era, Vilmos Zsigmond. He was DP on *Close Encounters of the Third Kind, McCabe and Mrs Miller, The Long Goodbye, Melinda and Melinda, The Deer Hunter, Heaven's Gate, Maverick* and *Deliverance* and would've been perfect for *Blade Runner*.

[91] It wasn't exactly what he'd seen when he was writing the book, Phil Dick told the filmmakers, but the environment was very close, and he was dazed by the movie, according to David Dryer (FN, 284).

LOCATIONS

Ridley Scott spoke (in a Warner Bros. press release) of his technique of 'layering', filling the frame with 'a kaleidoscopic accumulation of detail', so that 'every incident, every sound, every movement, every colour, every set, prop or actor' was significant. For Scott, a film was 'like a seven hundred layer cake' (FN, 47). That attention to detail had really impressed Scott about *Star Wars*, and he was determined to put it on screen with *Blade Runner*. But it took a lot of effort and concentration, and some of the cast and crew felt they weren't getting the attention they wanted (FN, 387).

Certainly *Blade Runner* looks fabulous, with an amazing amount of detail in nearly every composition. *Blade Runner* was shot at Warners, in Burbank, on the backlot, as well as several Los Angeles locations, such as Union Station and the Bradley Building, in downtown L.A., and the Second Street Tunnel.

The Old New York Street set (built in 1929) at Burbank Studios (now Warners) was dubbed 'Ridleyville' by the crew.[92] The Warners set was used for the Noodle Bar, the Animoid Row casbah, the nightclub and red light area, Chinatown, and the shopping arcade where Zhora (Joanna Cassidy) is gunned down. The set combined elements from Tokyo (the Ginza area), London (Piccadilly Circus), Hong Kong and New York (FN, 101). The streets were littered with wet newspapers and other junk; electronic 'Trafficators' controlled the movement of people (made mainly from parts of aeroplanes); shops were built out into the street; VidPhons; graffitied walls and booths; a newsstand displayed fictitious magazines (such as *Krotch*, showing a nude woman's torso on the cover, *Creative Evolution, Droid, Bash,Kill*, with a crazed dog on the cover, and a porn mag, *Horn,* featuring a scantily-clad woman on the cover, with cover-lines such as 'The Cosmic Orgasm', 'Scratch and Sniff Centerspread' and 'Hot Lust in Space').

After scouting locations such as London, Atlanta, Boston[93] and New York, the production team decided to film on the Warners' Burbank lot,

---

[92] David Snyder recalled he and Larry Paull and their team had 'bought every piece of pipe, plastic, steel and wood in a five-thousand mile radius' to get the street looking right (FN, 216).
It's actually quite a small backlot – compared, say, to the Universal backlot. Most of the backlots in L.A. are now shadows of what they used to be, of course, having been sold off for land.
[93] An abandoned housing estate in Boston was considered.

where shooting could be controlled. Much of the film was made at night and in rain and smoke for the simple practical reason that it hid the limitations of the Burbank set (many a movie has followed the same procedure).[94] Ridley Scott didn't want *Blade Runner* to look as if it had been shot in a studio or a backlot, with the low hills not far away.[95] Smoke, rain and night shoots helped to push up the budget quite a bit, but they also added to the look and feel of the film. And I don't think, ultimately, that audiences care that much whether a movie was made in a studio, a backlot, the script girl's cousin's aunt's daughter's bedroom or a plane circling the planet at 1,000 mph – they just want to enjoy a movie.

Scriptwriter Hampton Fancher was wholly against using the Bradley Building in downtown L.A., at 304 South Broadway, because it's far too well-known, and had been seen on TV many times; he tried to persuade Ridley Scott not to use it. However, the production team transformed the Bradley Building into something new.

The exterior of Deckard's apartment was the 'Ennis-Brown house' at 2655 Glendower Avenue in L.A., a Frank Lloyd Wright building of 1924.[96] The apartment was intended to be one floor in a block of hundreds of storeys (Syd Mead designed the interior). It was meant to be claustrophobic, and cost $175,000, which Larry Paull said was way higher than any similar set he'd built before.

The Second Street Tunnel was used for the approach to Deckard's apartment (you have to have a futuristic car going through a tunnel in a sci-fi movie). The Yukon Hotel was filmed inside the Pan Am Building, also in downtown L.A.

L.A.'s beautiful Union Station (at 8, North Alameda Street), built in 1939 in a Spanish Revival style (where you feel like you're in a movie), stood in for the police HQ;[97] a lengthy crane shot descends into Bryant's office, constructed in the huge Union Station interior (part of the set was left in

---
[94] Seven sprinklers were mounted some 20 feet above the action for the rain.
[95] The climactic battle on the rooftops was also shot on the backlot at Warners, on a movable 22 foot high set, though it was planned to film on existing buildings in L.A. (FN, 189). As Ridley Scott told Paul Sammon: 'I was really paranoid that audiences would notice we were shooting on a backlot' (FN, 379).
[96] Used in numerous movies, including *The House On Haunted Hill, Rush Hour, Black Rain, The Karate Kid 3, Grand Canyon* and *Day of the Locust*.
[97] Union Station was also used in *Pearl Harbor, Charlie's Angels, Catch Me If You Can* and *The Replacement Killers*.

the station, and is used today as offices).

The White Dragon Noodle Bar, seen at the beginning of the movie, designed by Lawrence Paull and Syd Mead, came from a hamburger chain called White Castle.

Hannibal Chew's Eye Works starred longtime character actor James Hong as the aged, obsessive genetic engineer, who talks sweetly to his beloved eyeballs in Chinese. He sports a heated fur coat with an array of pipes attached to it, and wears an optical headset. The Eye Works scene was shot over 2 days in Vernon, California, in a 7°-below food refrigerator.[98]

Tyrell's office was constructed on a Ken Adam *James Bond* scale, with a huge amount of space dwarfing the characters. There were 28 ft columns, 80 x 80 ft floor space, and a gigantic window looking out onto the Babylonian pyramids. Designer Lawrence Paull said Tyrell's office used a *moderne* look combined with an 'Establishment Gothic' or neofascist look. Ridley Scott and Jordan Cronenweth used Scott's customary 'future noir' illumination, with harsh side-lighting (plus unmotivated reflected light on the walls – as Doug Trumbull pointed out, there wasn't a reason for it, but it looked great). The re-dressed office set stood in for Tyrell's bedroom.

The overweening emphasis on surface and style in *Blade Runner* was exemplified in the Tyrell office scene when Deckard says it's too light in the room: the windows are dimmed; not just a case of pulling the drapes, but a sequence with its own long shot and accompanying music to show the blinds sliding down the windows.

Sebastian's apartment was a strange, ghostly place, lit by Jordan Cronenweth with backlighting and sidelighting, in sepia, pink and white,[99] with whispers from the toys and automata added in post-production. Small actors and mime artists played Sebastian's toys. For Gothic strangeness and the authentic tingle down the back, *Blade Runner* was outdone by another film made at the same time: Ingmar Bergman's *Fanny and Alexander* (1982), which contained an unforgettable sequence set in

---

[98] James Hong recalled that his scenes were shot 'under extreme pressure', trying to squeeze 5 days into two days: it was 'among the most tense I've ever worked in my life' (FN, 135). Michael Deeley said he had cut four days down to two for these scenes in order to make up some days in the schedule (2008, 232).

[99] The reference here was to Mrs Havisham's Gothic house in Charles Dickens' classic *Great Expectations*, in particular the 1947 version by David Lean and Ronald Neame, one of the greatest British films. Hence Pris dressing in a veil.

the back of an antique shop, where the young boy, Alexander, wanders into a world of puppets that come alive.[100]

The filmmakers and fans often spoke of *Blade Runner* as an 'immersive' film, meaning, one supposes, that the look and feel of it encouraged immersion in the world of the movie. However, isn't all good cinema 'immersive'? Isn't all good art 'immersive'? It's another expression of fans of *BladeRunner* wanting to live in that world. A theme park ride or 3-D recreation of *Blade Runner* would certainly be popular among some punters. Geeks, Goths and gamers would line up around the block.

THE VISUAL EFFECTS IN *BLADE RUNNER*

The visual effects in *Blade Runner* were not by Industrial Light and Magic, but they were very much in the ILM mould (ILM, though, would provide the effects for *Minority Report*). With *Star Wars*, Industrial Light and Magic established itself as the premier fx house in the world, a position it still holds today. ILM's fx developed a particular in-house look and style, which influenced pretty much every other effects house. In the late 1970s and through the 1980s, it consisted of smoky, backlit motion control shots of miniatures comped into the frame with an optical printer (Doug Trumbull had set the precedent, followed by so many fx houses, for that kind of hazy, glowing imagery in *Close Encounters*, *Star Trek* and *BladeRunner*). It was effects work of optical layering and superimpositions, bluescreen, rotoscoping, models shot with motion control, travelling mattes, stop and go motion, beam splitters and front projection.

---

[100] *Fanny and Alexander* contains plentiful supplies of magic, fairy tales, ghosts and the supernatural. Fairy tales: *Bluebeard* (in the figure of the bishop and wife-murderer), *Hansel and Gretel* and *Babes in the Wood* (lost children). Magic: Ismael's talent for telepathy, hypnosis and killing the bishop; the statues and puppets that come alive (in the prologue, and in the antique shop). Ghosts: Alexander's father (and the bishop) coming back to haunt him, as in *Hamlet*; the bishop's two daughters.

The magic in *Fanny and Alexander* also relates to the perennial Bergmanesque theme of art and the artist: right from the beginning of *Fanny and Alexander* (in the prologue), Alexander is living partially in a magic world, when seemingly inanimate objects begin to move (such as one of the statues, of a white nude Venus, and a puppet of Death).

The models were shot in a dull, brown light, brown here connoting decay and death, a society in decline. It was the visual effects work, the superb matte paintings and miniatures, of the visual effects company EEG (Entertainment Effects Group), designed by Douglas Trumbull and Richard Yuricich, that added so much to *Blade Runner*.

The producers of *Blade Runner* clearly went for an expensive, impressive opening, with the extreme long shots of the L.A. wasteland evoking a kind of post-industrial sublime.[101] Note that the first shot of *Blade Runner* lasts for over 20 seconds: the producers wanted to milk the $2-3 million special effects sequence as much as possible.[102] It would be no good spending $3 million and having the shot on screen for only one second (the budget for 65 fx shots was c. $3.5 million. That's a tiny number of vfx shots by today's standards – but the visual effects here refers to the model and matte shots, and doesn't include the numerous shots with practical effects like smoke and rain, which more to the budget).

The opening shot of L.A. was filmed on the 'Hades' set,[103] a table-top model 13 by 18 feet (designed by Tom Cranham), using Plexiglas sheets, foam and etched brass model buildings, lit by 2000 points of light and 7 miles of fibre optics. Photofloods shone up from underneath the set. The plumes of flame were optically added later, onto card on top of the chimneys, taken from explosions that Doug Trumbull shot for *Zabriskie Point* (1970), and from gasoline explosions filmed in EEG's car lot (EEG was then based at Marina Del Rey).

Doug Trumbull had been attracted by *BladeRunner*'s subject matter, of androids being indistinguishable from humans, and liked the setting of the film – in a run-down urban environment, instead of the usual outer space and clean spaceships of sci-fi movies. Trumbull remarked in 2007 that although *BladeRunner* is perceived as a visual effects movie, it has far less visual effects in it in terms of the number of shots – compared to, say, *Close Encounters* or *Star Wars*. But it was the way those shots were integrated into the narrative that made it seem as if they were far more.

---

[101] The long shots of L.A. include real landmarks, such as the cylindrical Bonaventura Hotel.
[102] The Walkers scene in *The Empire Strikes Back* was, along with the Tyrell building approach in *Blade Runner*, cited more than any other visual effects sequence as the stand-out of the modern era.
[103] There were 3 stages at EEG used for *Blade Runner*: the big Hades stage and smoke room, Stage 2, where smaller models were shot, and Stage 3, where most of the smaller pieces, like clouds, video images and artwork were filmed (FN, 230).

BladeRunner benefitted a lot from *Close Encounters of the Third Kind*, because EEG now had all of the tools, cameras and working methods in place that had been developed on *Close Encounters* to be able to deliver the visual effects for *Blade Runner*.

EEG had developed its 'Icebox' motion control system for making multiple camera moves, and had used it on *Close Encounters of the Third Kind*. EEG employed a number of elements on *BladeRunner* that they had used on *Close Encounters*, including part of the mothership – seen in the circular roof of the police headquarters building.

The visual fx for *Close Encounters of the Third Kind* were shot on 65mm film, to minimize the grain and achieve a seamless integration with the live action 35mm footage.[104] The 35mm film was processed over a stop, explained DP Vilmos Zsigmond, so that it would match the grain of the 65mm film stock. Zsigmond said that one of the reasons the integration of fx, mattes, models and live action worked so well on *Close Encounters of the Third Kind* was because he and Trumbull helped each other out, and didn't fight.[105] That was important in *Blade Runner*, too.

For *Close Encounters*, the visual impact of the visually dense mothership was aided by Doug Trumbull's technique of shooting the model through smoke, diffusing the tiny lamps, creating areas of over-exposure on the large format film. Smoke was one of Trumbull's visual effects hallmarks, as well as Vilmos Zsigmond.[106] A number of passes were shot of the UFOs, as usual on visual effects work – some for a halo or ring light effect, others for beams of light in smoke.

The motion control system for *Close Encounters of the Third Kind* used an early digital recording system, so that camera moves performed on the set in Alabama could be recorded and played back in the visual effects photography studio in Los Angeles. This enabled Doug Trumbull and the EEG team to shoot moving camera shots, instead of having the camera locked, as was usual up that point in movies involving optical or post-

---

104 *Close Encounters of the Third Kind* was shot in standard 35mm anamorphic.
105 V. Zsigmond, in Schaefer, 1984, 321.
106 The mothership shots were achieved in a smoke-filled studio, sometimes taking hours to accomplish with the motion control camera crawling through a set-up. Dennis Muren, brought in to photograph the mothership, said some of the mothership shots would take a day and a half to perform, with the camera shooting a frame every few seconds. The smoke room was so dense with fog, moved around evenly by fans, sometimes the technicians couldn't see the camera when they went in every ten minutes to check everything was running OK.

production effects. So the camera could follow Lacombe walking onto the apron, below the UFOs, and pan with him.

Like *Blade Runner* and *E.T. The Extraterrestrial, Close Encounters of the Third Kind* is largely a nocturnal movie, with key scenes occurring at night: Roy Neary first seeing the UFOs, Neary coming back with Ronnie, Barry going AWOL, the UFOs abducting Barry in in his garden, and the whole final section at Devil's Tower. Designed as masses of lights (like L.A. in *Blade Runner*), the UFOs are never shown in daylight. They always remain mysterious and awesome. Trumbull said:

> putting a UFO on the screen is like photographing God – people have a very abstract, mind's-eye view of what they expect to see in a flying saucer. So the general look we went for was one of motion, velocity, luminosity and brilliance. We used very sophisticated fibre optics and light-scanning techniques to modulate, control and colour light on film to create the appearance of shape when in fact no shape existed.[107]

In *Blade Runner*, the 3 foot model of the Tyrell ziggurat, like the 6 foot skyscrapers, had to be well made, because, as with Doug Trumbull's other deliberately slow-paced special effects work, it would be on screen for a long time.[108] Trumbull spoke of wanting to create 'some crazy illusion that looks so great that you can really hang on it like a big master shot of an epic landscape' (FN, 79).

The computer-controlled camera technology, EEG's Icebox, made multiple passes of the models, building up the layers of detail. Using vaporized mineral oil to create smog in the 'Smoke Room' enhanced the sense of aerial perspective. The shot where Deckard goes out onto his balcony was what Trumbull called an 'enhanced matte shot', using a matte painting, live action, flying machines, and movement on the street below (FN, 256).

One complex shot, called FX Shot 19 – of Deckard and Gaff flying in the spinner over the city – contained 35 elements, included 20 miniature buildings, travelling mattes, 'RidleyVision' screens, Icebox camerawork, spotlights, strobes, and different-sized flying models; the city view was seen through the windscreen of the spinner: the shot also contained the live

---
[107] D. Trumbull in *Filmmakers' Newsletter*, 11, 2, 1977.
[108] Only one pyramid model was constructed – and that only had two sides.

actors and the many lights and screens inside the spinner. Marrying the practical props with the vfx was tricky, and some of the practical, on-set effects were difficult to pull off: flying the full-scale spinner down a street was a challenging shot, Terry Frazee said – orchestrating the prop on cables (on two cranes), the rain, the lighting, and hiding the cables.

In some shots, 'geisha billboards' were added, as were spotlights sweeping over the upper part of the frame (filmed in EEG's 'Smoke Room', then composited optically).[109] The 'blind' that Tyrell lowers was done by animation; the backgrounds and the upper half of the Tyrell room were matte paintings by Matthew Yuricich;[110] an fx shot of a spinner landing had to be dropped due to budgetary restrictions, so Ridley Scott and Jordan Cronenweth added one of his trademarks – rippling light reflected off water on the walls.

Doug Trumbull later moved into designing rides for theme parks; he founded Entertainment Design Workshop (one of his big early successes was the *Back to the Future* ride at Universal Studios. Other rides included IMAX ride-films for Universal Studios, and Circus Circus's Luxor Casino). Trumbull also had a go at directing, with 1983's *Brainstorm*. Not the greatest sci-fi film ever, but not a bad movie.

---

[109] These were shots with everything thrown in, including a kitchen sink – visual effects artists like to hide jokes in the back of scenes, so there's a kitchen sink in the back of one of the billboard skyscraper shots (similarly, there's a kitchen sink in the opening space battle in *Star Wars: Revenge of the Sith*). A model of the Millennium Falcon was stood on end to form a building in *Blade Runner*, as well as parts of the pyramid model.
[110] Matthew Yuricich is one of Hollywood's great matte artists, working on *Close Encounters, Logan's Run, Star Wars, Star Trek* and *Forbidden Planet*. Yuricich replaced most of the set above the heads of the actors with a matte painting (FN, 253). The matte paintings in *Close Encounters of the Third Kind*, for instance, contributed so much to the movie. There are many matte paintings in *Close Encounters* – the distant views over the towns; all of the extensions to the Alabama indoor set; the long shots of Devil's Tower, and so on. And *Blade Runner* contains quite a few matte shots.

THE CITY OF THE FUTURE

The future Los Angeles of *Blade Runner* was a mix of Fritz Lang's *Metropolis*, New York's skyscrapers, and the neon-rich landscapes of Hong Kong, Tokyo and Chinatowns around the world, a postmodern collage of architectural styles quoting from other films, from postcards, advertizing, as well as real cities.

Philip K. Dick's novel was set in San Francisco in 1992; *BladeRunner* was originally set in Manhattan (hence the constant rain); Ridley Scott wanted to feature the famous Chrysler Building in *BladeRunner*; Scott had used the title 'Gotham City' at one point; the modernism of New York City became the postmodernism of the City of Lost Angels. Los Angeles was chosen when so many locations in the city were used, such as the well-known Bradley Building.

Ridley Scott remarked that the city of *BladeRunner* could be seen as a combination of New York and Chicago, or of San Francisco and Los Angeles, a megalopolis of 100 million people. At one point the city was going to be called San Angeles, a giant city stretching between San Francisco and L.A. (that's a big city: they are 380 miles apart).

Ridley Scott admitted that his dystopian city in *Blade Runner* was 'overkill', but commented: 'I always get the impression of New York as being overkill' (FN, 75). Scott said the idea for the air traffic of the spinners came from his habit of landing by helicopter on top of the PanAm Building[111] in New York (the stylish way to arrive in Gotham City, the helicopter rides ceased when a helicopter crashed on top of the PanAm Building in the late 1970s).[112]

---

[111] A PanAm building can be seen in the cityscapes in *Blade Runner*.
[112] The accident may have inspired the famous scene in 1978's *Superman*.

SECONDARY CHARACTERS

William Sanderson's J.F. Sebastian was a prematurely aged 25 year-old, a loner and innocent, who made toys and dolls for rich clients, and to keep him company (the toys were mainly obtained from Benny Marvin, a toy collector in the San Fernando Valley). His character, being a misfit and ageing rapidly, mirrored that of the replicants.

Hampton Fancher created the idea of built-in obsolescence from the earliest drafts of the *Blade Runner* script; it was a way of Tyrell sustaining his business (FN, 174). Sanderson had appeared in *The Coal Miner's Daughter, The Executioner's Song, Raggedy Man, Lonesome Dove* and *The Client.*

Gaff was played by Edward James Olmos as a fastidious, multi-lingual guy who sports extravagant clothes (bow-ties, fedoras, waistcoats, silk suits), blue eyes, an Italian punk hair-do, a French-Spanish mustache, yellowy Asian skin, and a walking stick. He was a Mexican-Japanese mix; he spoke a mixture of Hungarian, Japanese, Spanish, French, Chinese, German and English (Olmos created his version of Cityspeak himself, and brought a lot of work to a relatively small part. He has appeared in *Wolfen, Hill Street Blues, Miami Vice, American Family,* and *Battlestar Galactica*).

Gaff's origami constructions comment ironically on the narrative. The first one he makes is a chicken, referring perhaps to Deckard's refusal of taking on the blade runner job. Apart from the unicorn, another origami Gaff makes is of a man with an erection: 'the stickman meant Gaff thought Deckard had a hard-on because of the way he went after a case', said Olmos (FN, 129). It's certainly an odd idea – in a deleted scene, Leon enters his hotel room and looks at the origami figure in disbelief.

INFLUENCES ON *BLADE RUNNER*

The French comic *Heavy Metal* (*Métal Hurlant*) and the artist Moebius (Jean Giraud, b. 1938) were among the visual influences on *BladeRunner*.[1] Mega-prolific Moebius designed Alejandro Jodorowski's abandoned 1976 adaption of Frank Herbert's *Dune*, the animated *The Orphan From Perdide* (1982), the alien in *The Abyss* (1989), worked on *Tron* (1982), *Little Nemo* (1992), *Les Maîtres du Temps* (1982), *Willow* (1988), *Masters of the Universe* (1986), and designed the spacesuits for *Alien*.

Among Moebius's comic output were *Jerry Cornelius* stories (from Michael Moorcock), *Arzach, The Long Tomorrow, The Horny Goof, Les Adventures de John Difool* (written by Alejandro Jodorowsky), *The Airtight Garage, The Onyx Overlord, The Fifth Essence* (later filmed by Columbia/ Gaumont/ Patrick Ledoux as *The Fifth Element*, 1997), *The Mysteries of the Incal, Is Man Good?, White Nightmare, Memory of the Future, Crystal Saga, Heavenly Venice, The Blind Citadel, Major's Holiday* and *The Goddess*.

Moebius was one of a few artists grappling with a 'concentrated city', a J.G. Ballardian 'metrocosm', the urban sprawl of Isaac Asimov, where a whole planet is a city (other comics dealing with the complex city included *Judge Dredd* and *Ranxerox*).

The metropolis was perhaps *the* site of cyberpunk fiction, urban conglomerates that swallowed up other cities (as in *Neuromancer* and *BladeRunner*), cities in crisis, urban dystopias. Phillippe Druillet and British artist Angus McKie also published in *Heavy Metal*, and created hi-tech visions of scale and monumentalism, enormous spaceships dwarfing cities.

Métal Hurlant was launched in 1975 by Bernard Farkas, Jean-Pierre Dionnet, Jean Giraud and Philippe Druillet. It published mainly French fantasy illustration, and spawned versions and translations in other territories, including a US version, *Heavy Metal*, in 1977. There was also an animated film, *Heavy Metal* (1981), based on the characters and art from the magazine. Fantasy and comicbooks are still hugely popular in France.

Artist Syd Mead was a key influence on the look of *BladeRunner*, and the most prominent artist attached to the project (Mead had previously

---

[1] Ridley Scott was a big fan of Moebius and *Heavy Metal*, and remarked that *BladeRunner* was an attempt at turning a comicbook into a movie.

worked on the first *Star Trek* movie).₂ Mead was responsible for the design of many elements, including the flying spinners.

Other influences on *Blade Runner* included William Hogarth's engravings, Jan Vermeer's lighting (a favourite with filmmakers), Jacob Riis's photos of New York City, and Edward Hopper's paintings (in particular *Nighthawks*). Hopper's clear, dream-like, hypnotic images of urban life have a 'cinematic' quality, and can be transferred onto the cinema screen.₃ Hopper's silent, empty paintings have influenced other films (such as *Dick Tracy*, Warren Beatty, 1990). 'I was constantly waving a reproduction of [*Nighthawks*] under the noses of the production team to illustrate the look and mood I was after in *Blade Runner*', Ridley Scott said.

U GOT THE LOOK

Like so much self-conscious cinema, of the European New Wave onwards, *Blade Runner* is full of images of eyes, screens and looking:[4]
  • the extreme close-up of the eye in the opening sequence[5] • the owl's eyes in Tyrell's HQ • the eyes grown in the genetic engineer's laboratory, Eye Works (sheep's eyes and plastic replicas were used) • Tyrell's eyes behind their thick spectacles (gouged later by Batty on a model of Joe Turkel's head) • Pris's eyes opening with a click on the Voigt-Kampff machine (stock footage from Oxford Scientific was used) • the eyes blown-up in the

---

[2] Mead's going rate at the time was $1,500 per day.
[3] The photograph in the Esper scene consciously evoked Vermeer and Hopper (FN, 258).
[4] Science fiction cinema is full of screens and technological ways of seeing, as Garrett Stewart pointed out: sci-fi cinema is filled with 'banks of monitors, outsized video intercoms, x-ray display panels, hologram tubes, backlit photoscopes, aerial scanners, telescopic mirrors, illuminated computer consoles, overhead projectors, slide screens, radar scopes, whole curved walls of transmitted imagery, the retinal registers of unseen electronic eyes'. (In E. Rabkin, 1985).
[5] A number of films have a close-up of an eye in their opening sequences: *White of the Eye, The Eyes of Laura Mars, Black Widow, Dream Lover, Incubus, Repulsion, Vertigo* and *Blade Runner*.

Voigt-Kampff test (with the replicant's eyes glowing red, like the owl's)6 • Deckard and Rachel talking to each other via video telephones.

The giant eye emphasizes the paranoia of being watched: it's a conscious allusion to Big Brother in George Orwell's *1984*. There are many screens in *Blade Runner:* of the giant billboards and neon signs on buildings (in the Leon-Deckard fight scene, a woman on one of the billboards was going to be seen reacting to the fight in a wide master shot); the 'RidleyVision' screens advertizing the Off-World colonies; the screens of the Voigt-Kampff and Esper machines; various computer screens; screens on the Trafficators; screens on the VidPhons; and the many photos. The 'Oriental' video commercials were shot at EEG; the women were filmed taking pills, or smoking, or flirting with the viewer.

The way *Blade Runner* is shot also emphasizes the gaze: many of the shots use long lenses, creating close-up images carved out of the detritus of the world (long focal lengths being one of the hallmarks of the smoke and back-light school of cinematography popularized by the TV-commercial-turned-film directors of the Seventies onwards).

The Esper machine sequence plays with looking and lying: reworking *Blow-Up* (1966), with Deckard controlling the virtual examination of Leon's photograph with voice commands like a movie director, the computer zooms in on parts of the photo, blowing them up with extraordinary detail, making them 3-D, as technically unbelievable in *Blade Runner* as enlarging the photo in *Blow-Up*.7

The Esper sequence makes cultural critics go gooey – it's all about looking, dissecting, analyzing, reframing. It's pure cinema (and it's very much an *editor's* scene, it's about montage as much as about looking: consider the way the scene is put together with a series of reaction shots of Deckard and reverse angles of Deckard at the machine, as well as frame

---

6 The Voigt-Kampff machine was 'a stroke of collective genius', Ridley Scott said: first Phil Dick had come up with a 'totally believable instrumentality and term', which Hampton Fancher 'brilliantly expanded and deepened', and finally Syd Mead had come up with 'a marvellous design for a working model of this imaginary thing. All of these accomplishments were quite extraordinary' (FN, 382).

7 Garrett Stewart, one of the best critics on the philosophy of photography and looking, says the Esper sequence is a lyrical exploration of reality and illusion: 'think of it this way: the photo is, in short, cinematized – edited, cut, motorized, even lent the illusion of three-dimensionality resulting from shifts of perspective as the camera roams the already fixed image plane.' (1999, 11)

There was originally going to be much more of the Esper supercomputer – it was going to appear on the streets, and inside cars (FN, 120).

grabs from the machine itself.

There are further lies to the Esper machine sequence: in the studio set, there was Rutger Hauer and a stand-in, and a stand-in for Zhora. As Hauer said, the Esper sequence

> shows how you can play with images and tell a story and, at the same time, completely bullshit someone. Which is just like making a motion picture, come to think of it. (FN, 146)

Using stand-ins has been part of movie-making since its beginnings in the late 19th century, though – not just for stunts or nude scenes, but in numerous other ways.[8]

For Scott Bukatman, a terrific commentator on vfx and cinema, the Esper scene 'with its fantasied control of the projected image, is a most hypnotic meditation on cinematic power' (1997, 47), and 'the most hypnotic demonstration of cinematic suture and control in contemporary cinema' (1993, 136). As Hampton Fancher and David Peoples recalled on their wonderful audio commentary for *Blade Runner*, it took a lot of narrative work to set up and get to the Esper scene (but it was worth it). It came about partly because of Harrison Ford's complaints that he didn't do much detecting.

Birds are another motif: Tyrell's owl; the eagle by Tyrell's bed; the herons behind the bed on a screen; Tyrell's owl; the owl on Tyrell's robe; statues of birds in Tyrell's office. Daryl Hannah was sometimes shot at slower speeds, to give her movements a quick, jerky quality, like a bird's, a technique used for her death scene (FN, 180).

Like other British film directors who spent years in advertizing (Hugh Hudson, Alan Parker, Adrian Lyne), Ridley Scott and Jordan Cronenweth employed complex lighting, much backlighting, tracking shots, and long lenses. Cronenweth and Scott seemed to have decided that nearly every shot in *Blade Runner* could be backlit, in keeping with the future noir look, often with spotlights. There was also a surprising amount of handheld camera, offering a looser feel to the otherwise highly stylized and formally precise film.

Two focal lengths were favoured in *BladeRunner*'s visuals: wide angle

---

[8] The Esper scene was partly re-shot, in London, by Filmfex and Lodge/ Cheesman.

shots, with elaborate, painterly deep focus compositions, and long lenses. After using one or two wide angle shots to establish a scene, the filmmakers shot much of *Blade Runner* using very long lenses, following people around apartments or along streets zoomed-in, in close-up, creating a claustrophic feel. One never knows exactly how, for example, Deckard's apartment is furnished – there is never an establishing shot depicting the whole main room, showing where the couch or piano is. Instead, Jordan Cronenweth covers the scenes in Deckard's apartment using either medium close-ups with a long lens, or low angle medium shots. Further, Deckard's apartment is dimly lit, with spotlights flashing into the windows regularly, like a lighthouse beam. (You simply have to accept all that unmotivated light, which moves through the scenes in *Blade Runner*: those spotlights outside Deckard's window, for example, are clearly only a few feet away from his windows, but he's meant to be on the 97th floor. Where do they come from? It doesn't matter – it looks cool. The mobile spotlights were Jordan Cronenweth's idea, not Ridley Scott's).

Rain and smoke suffused *Blade Runner* – smoke from cigarettes, from the streets, from the spinners, from the haze over L.A. As in Forties *film noirs*, many of the characters in *Blade Runner* smoke (opium in the Snake Pit, but usually French Boyard cigarettes). The spiralling smoke was inevitably picked out by stylized backlighting; cinematographer's Jordan Cronenweth's favourite shot was of Rachel smoking in Tyrell's office during the Voigt-Kampff test.

There was a great emphasis on costumes and fashion, and intricately decorated sets. Ridley Scott wanted *Blade Runner*'s world to look lived-in, everyday, shabby, it was not a 'hardware' film. *Blade Runner* was a triumph of art direction and lighting design, with post-punk fashion prominent (in the look of Pris and Batty especially).[9] 'In *Blade Runner* I would go so far to say that the design is the statement', confessed Scott.[10]

The costumes (by Michael Kaplan and Charles Knode, with hair by Shirley Padgett and make-up by Marvin Westmore and Bridget O'Neill) combined high fashion, post-punk chic, Asian contemporary, and plenty of

---

[9] Daryl Hannah said she got the idea for Pris's heavily made-up eyes from Klaus Kinski in the wonderful film *Nosferatu* (1979). The blonde fright wig Hannah had found when she was preparing for her screen test. Hannah was 21 at the time of filming, and had appeared in *Paper Dolls*, *The Fury* and *Hard Country*.
[10] Scott, *Cinefantasique*, 12, 5-6, 1982.

retro, 1940s, *film noir* look. The costumes both describe the characters and the world, but also pop out of the screen. The number of extras wearing goggles, for instance, is unusual, yet also fits in with the highly polluted environment the film is trying to evoke.

The hero would've sported a hat, to go with his updated trenchcoat, but that was one of the few stipulations that Harrison Ford had about his character: *no hat*, because he'd worn one for months on *Raiders of the Lost Ark*. But the trenchcoat, his one suit, and the shirts and ties all placed Deckard within a 1940s æsthetic (though updated to the early 1980s).

Rachel was given the *femme fatale* treatment, icy, cool, immaculate, with tight suits, tons of lip gloss and bright red lipstick,[11] and very flamboyant coats. Pris was decked out in a post-punk girlie outfit, with a micro skirt, stockings, a yellow zebra-stripe jacket, bleached blonde wig, and dark make-up around the eyes. She might have been the lead singer in a post-punk rock band, one of those Goth outfits playing industrial, doom-laden music such as The Cure, Bauhaus or The Cult.[12]

Roy Batty was given a high collar, updated version of the classic black leather jacket, one of the stereotypical outfits of rebellious youth ever since movies like *The Wild One* (1954), with Marlon Brando (Batty's the lead guitarist in *Blade Runner*'s post-punk band). The cropped, bleached hair placed him as a twin to Pris (they are the post-punk couple, contrasting with the retro, Forties look of the dark-haired couple, Deckard and Rachel). In some variants, Batty also sported face paint, and a map tattooed on his chest (which can be glimpsed only fleetingly). Undoubtedly the oddest wardrobe choice for Batty was having him strip down to tight cycling shorts.

Blade Runner's streets were inhabited by a mixture of ethnic groups and types: chanting Hare Krishnas, punks in spiky hair and shades, Chinese in large hats riding bicycles, people carrying umbrellas with fluorescent tubes, German chain-wielding midgets sporting goggles (they might have wandered in from a Werner Herzog movie),[13] cops with neo-fascistic uniforms and body armour, and so on. The filmmakers wanted a host of Asian extras to populate the streets: they were given coolie hats (made

---

[11] The Eighties was the decade of lip gloss, of course. Young remembered that Scott wanted *lots* of lip gloss on Rachel.
[12] It was Michael Kaplan's idea to have a scene of Pris applying her raccoon make-up.
[13] In particular, Werner Herzog's bizarre early movie *Even Dwarfs Started Small* (1971).

from baskets). The idea was to have everyone looking different – to reproduce the variety of a real city.

The headgear alone in *Blade Runner* is very odd – like the umbrellas, it's to provide protection against the acid rain. And the masks, too, to combat pollution (but you can see all those sorts of things in cities like L.A. today).

There were sushi and noodle bars; traffic signals (Trafficators) that robotically intoned 'don't walk' or 'move on' and were festooned with video screens; parking meters which threatened to kill law-breakers; giant Babylonian, Roman and Greek-style pillars; Chinese dragon neon signs; sleek cars beside overcrowded 'Megatrans' buses; and overhead, the spinners of the LAPD, the blimps advertizing Off-World vacations (with phrases such as 'Breathe Easy', 'All New' and 'Best Future'),[14] giant 'RidleyVision' video billboards, forests of neon signs, the ever-present acid rain, and the towering skyscrapers and apartments. As Paul Sammon wrote,

> it is to this bewitching visual surface which most viewers repeatedly return. Like its industrial counterparts in the worlds of high fashion and architecture, *Blade Runner* is a form of ultra-sophisticated "designer cinema", one whose astonishingly complex visual field has, despite a subsequent decade's worth of futuristic/ alternate world spectaculars like Tim Burton's *Batman* trilogy or the recent *Judge Dredd*, remained the high-water mark against which all other big-budget SF entertainments are measured. (FN, 3)

Blade Runner is a film in love with lights and lighting: from the opening sequence onwards, with its panorama of L.A. at dusk, with the plumes of fire and the thousands of lights of the city, *Blade Runner* bristles with lights. As with Douglas Trumbull's other visual effects work (on *Star Trek* and *Close Encounters*, for example), the models in *Blade Runner* contain thousands of tiny lamps (the Tyrell pyramid in particular houses many lights).

Throughout *Blade Runner* lamps dominate the *mise-en-scène*: they shine through the windows of Deckard's apartment (with its *film noir* blinds, also culled from Bernardo Bertolucci's *The Conformist*, a film that influenced directors like Francis Coppola, Paul Schrader and Martin

---

[14] EEG produced 15 TV commercials, directed by David Dryer, to be used in the film (FN, 241). Later movies, such as *Minority Report*, would develop the commercial angle even further.

Scorsese);[15] nightclub spotlights swirl above Sebastian's Bradley apartment block; the blimp advertizing Off-World vacations (a 4 foot model) is a Christmas tree of lights; the flying spinners have prominent headlamps, with disco lights on their roofs; their interiors are a forest of lamps.

Cinematographer Jordan Cronenweth said the lights were meant to be like prison search lights, invading people's privacy (H. Lightman, 1982). The lights also make noises – the ones outside Deckard's apartment make a whooshing sound as they rotate, like a lighthouse.[16] Ridley Scott said the shafts of light derived partly from the Thatcher Library and screening room in *Citizen Kane*.[17] There's no particular justification for the lights that shine into Deckard's apartment, like UFOs from *CE3K*, apart from the simple fact that they look good (there were explanations offered, such as the air traffic flying by). You'd think Deckard would get pissed off with 'em, and close the blinds (but drapes and curtains are never closed in movies, for practical as well as narrative and æsthetic reasons). Some of the influence for the huge amount of lamps on-screen and the OTT lighting fx likely comes from *Close Encounters of the Third Kind*: look at the extraordinary sequence where the UFOs buzz the Guilers' home and take away little Barry. I can't think of a movie before *CE3K* which has lighting and smoke used like that.

Blade Runner is founded on strong vertical and horizontal lines: the verticality of the skyscrapers, elevators, and shafts of light from above; the horizontality of the streets, the apartments, the window blinds, and the shafts of light entering the buildings.

Deckard's apartment is conceived as a cluttered, low-ceilinged space, often shot from a low, knee-high viewpoint, emphasizing the claustrophia

---

15 *The Conformist* was a key film for the 'New Hollywood' generation. Filmmakers such as Francis Coppola, Paul Schrader, Joel Schumacher, Sydney Pollack and Martin Scorsese cited it as an influence. Cinematographers such as John Bailey and Michael Chapman admired Vittorio Storaro's work on that film immensely. Bailey (DP on *American Gigolo, Ordinary People, Cat People* and *The Big Chill*, among others) said (in 1984) that he'd seen *The Conformist* probably 25 times. 'For me, it's a real treasure chest; it's almost a textbook on filmmaking'. So important was *The Conformist* to Bailey, he said 'I ask every director I work with to look at *The Conformist*; even if we decide it's flamboyant and totally wrong for us, there's such energy there and it's such a springboard for discussion, that it's always fruitful' (J. Bailey, in D. Schaefer, 1984, 55). For director Adrian Lyne, *The Conformist* 'is probably the best single film ever made. It's the perfect blend of visual and performance' (A. Lyne, in J. Gallagher, 1989, 167).
16 Many of the wonderful sounds in *Blade Runner* were created by Jim Shields.
17 *Citizen Kane* was a favourite movie of Ridley Scott's, as with so many filmmakers, and his company, Scott Free, produced a TV movie about the making of Orson Welles' masterpiece, *RKO 281* (1999). It's not surprising, then, just how much *Citizen Kane* looms behind *Blade Runner*.

(the most famous example of low ceilings as psychological oppression occurs in *Citizen Kane*). The design of the Tyrell Corporation building drew on Egyptian pyramids and Mayan and Aztec ziggurats; creating an atmosphere of wealth, power and grandeur, a 'op Egyptian extravaganza'.[18] The allusion to ziggurats and temples also evoked gods and sacrifice.

There is much on-screen advertizing in *Blade Runner*: logos for Coca-Cola, Atari, Budweiser, Trident, Michelob, Jovan, Shakey's, Jim Beam, and TDK are shown, for example. Sometimes the product placement is very prominent: in the climactic sequence, where Batty sits down and dies, he is framed against a giant TDK sign. Designer Lawrence Paull said the neon signs were not given to the film by the companies, but the companies paid for them to be made (by neon specialists American Neon). Some of the neons came from Francis Ford Coppola's expensive Las Vegas musical *One From the Heart* (1982), which probably uses more neon than any other movie. DP Jordan Cronenweth aimed to shoot by the available light coming from the neons.

VANGELIS

Vangelis Papathanassiou's music for *Blade Runner* contributed so much to its mood and impact. With the visuals so stylized and busy, it was a wise choice to have the music held back and simple. It was his music for *Blade Runner* and *Chariots of Fire* that made Vangelis's name, at least in the film world (although a single, 'Albedo 0.39', had attracted attention in 1976, and with Jon Anderson Vangelis produced the memorable 'State of Independence').[19] Undoubtedly, it's *Chariots of Fire* that has been quoted or spoofed in popular culture more than any of Vangelis's other works (*Bruce Almighty, Madagascar, How the Grinch Stole Christmas, National*

---

[18] G. Bruno, in A. Kuhn, 1990, 187.
[19] 'State of Independence' has also been quoted in pop culture, and was given an all-star treatment by Donna Summer.

Lampoon's Vacation, The Real Hustle, Late Night With Jimmy Fallon, etc).

Vangelis (born March 29, 1943, in Volos, Greece) made his base in London and Paris for much of his career (his Nemo Studio was in central London, near Marble Arch). His most well-known early incarnation was in the band Aphrodite's Child, with singer Demis Roussos (who can be heard warbling on the *Blade Runner* soundtrack).

Other soundtracks Vangelis produced included *The Bounty* (1984), *Mask* (1985), *Nosferatu a Venezia* (1987), *Francesco* (1989), the S/M fantasy *Bitter Moon* (Roman Polanski, 1992), *Missing* (Costa-Gavras), *1492: Conquest of Paradise* (Ridley Scott, 1992), and the ancient world epic *Alexander* (Oliver Stone, 2004). Vangelis also provided the title music for epic *Cosmos* TV series (Carl Sagan), and for Frederic Roussif's French films *Opera Sauvage* and *Apocalypse des Animaux*.

Vangelis Papathanassiou's solo efforts tended to be 'concept albums', in the prog rock manner, taking on notions such as 'Antartica', 'China', space travel ('Albedo 0.39'), or the painter El Greco. Essentially a studio recording artist, Vangelis tended to be reclusive, rarely performing live, giving interviews, or playing the PR game. For many years he lived in London, working out of his home studio, Nemo.

Due to contractual problems, and perhaps due to Vangelis himself (there were rumours that he had too much to do, or wasn't so keen on the music towards the end, or was reluctant to finish it), an 'official' soundtrack album of *Blade Runner* was delayed, and various bootlegs came out, even before the movie was released. The 'official' soundtrack was released on Atlantic in 1994, and included excerpts from the dialogue in the film. (Vangelis took longer to deliver the music than the producers hoped: he was contracted in December, 1981, and delivered the score in April, 1982. Vangelis is a composer who likes to do everything himself, and for a big movie soundtrack, that can take months instead of the usual weeks).

As well the soundtracks noted above, Vangelis's albums included *The Dragon* and *Hypothesis* (both 1971), *Earth* (1974), *Heaven and Hell* (1976), *Albedo 0.39* (1976), *Spiral* (1977), *Beauborg* and *China* (both 1978), *Short Stories* and *See You Later* (1980), *Private Collection* (1983), *Soil Activities* (1984), *Rhapsodies* (1985), *Opera Sauvage* (1987), *Direct* (1988), *City* (1989), *Page of Life* (1991), *Voices* (1996), *El Greco* (1998) and 'best ofs':

Best of Jon and Vangelis (1984), *Themes* (1989) and *Portraits* (1996).

Vangelis's solo and soundtrack music was marked by low drones, washes of string synthesizers, the patter of drum machines, chimes and bells, slow or half-time rhythms, echoey Moog and Arp siren calls, and simple musical patterns (sometimes two chords, sometimes one throughout, often major chords). Vocals were rare (instead, Vangelis used samples, or swathes of mellotron and choral samples).

Vangelis's music was about texture and atmosphere, rather than melodic or structural ingenuity, or *virtuoso* technique. It was dark, moody music, which took itself seriously, and tended towards the bombastic and operatic.

Vangelis was shown *BladeRunner* in an unfinished state, but was very impressed by it – 'thrilled' and 'terrified', he said. Vangelis is known for being cautious about accepting assignments to score a movie. Oliver Stone said he had to go back to Athens four times before Vangelis agreed to score *Alexander* (2004).

For *Blade Runner*, Vangelis used his customary washes of string synthesizers, tinkling pianos, and hi-pitched *glissandos*. For Sebastian's toy-filled apartment, Vangelis employed soft sounds;[20] for the threatening scenes of Batty and Leon, the prerequisite bassy synth drone was used; sad saxophones accompanied images of the lonely replicants and blade runners; for Deckard's dream, Vangelis used a plaintive piano;[21] the sound of echoey children's laughter is heard when Deckard contemplates Rachel's photograph of herself with her mother (which becomes animated, with the shadows moving);[22] Vangelis used one of Frédéric Chopin's lyrical *Nocturnes* (the 13th) as a basis for Rachel's piano music; towards the end, to accompany Batty, a synth sounding like a cat wailing was employed. Generally, Vangelis's music was held-back and wistfully melancholy,

---

[20] Andrew Hoy recalled that around this time Vangelis was fascinated by percussion, and mixing percussion instruments with synthesizers. 'Gongs and bells lay everywhere,' Hoy said, 'Vangelis used to collect them like a magpie' (FN, 273).

[21] There are a couple of moments where Vangelis's score merges with the diegetic sound of Deckard and also Rachel playing the piano, a nice musical moment. For Mary Ann Doane, the scene with the photographs condenses a number of critical terms, including 'representation', 'the woman', 'the artificial', 'the technological', 'history' and 'memory'.

The temp music which editors William Zabala and Terry Rawlings had put with the scene was by Maurice Ravel (his *Piano Concerto*). Vangelis, however, used one of Chopin's *Nocturnes* instead (FN, 162).

[22] The photograph was a freeze frame of some extras shot on the Burbank backlot; the shot shifted from a freeze frame to a regular running speed.

permeating the dark, weary, down-beat atmosphere of the film.

Other music in *Blade Runner* included Gail Laughton's New Age *Harps of the Ancient Temples*, jazz, and the plangent Japanese *biwa* and voice folk song played by the floating blimp. British light music singer Peter Skellern also appears, as well as the portly Greek vocalist Demis Roussos (both odd choices for a futuristic Hollywood thriller).

For Pauline Kael, Vangelis's music was overwhelming, which 'gives the picture so much *film noir* overload that he fights Scott's imagery; he chomps on it, stomps on it, and drowns it' (1986, 362).

BLADE RUNNER AND THE SUBLIME

Blade Runner is one of a number of science fiction films which emphasized the sublime: *2001: A Space Odyssey* is the obvious case, but also the films of Steven Spielberg (*Close Encounters of the Third Kind, Jurassic Park, A.I., E.T.*), *Star Trek, Solaris, Avatar* and *The Abyss*.

For a useful guide to the sublime in cinema, art critic Christopher Hussey defined seven aspects of the sublime (in art), derived from critic Edmund Burke: obscurity (physical and intellectual); power; privations (such as darkness, solitude, silence); vastness (vertical or horizontal); infinity; succession; and uniformity (the last two suggest limitless progression).[23]

These tenets of the sublime in art can be applied to cinema – to films such as *Blade Runner, 2001: A Space Odyssey, Citizen Kane* and *Apocalypse Now*, movies which consciously encourage notions such as obscurity, darkness, vastness and infinity.

---

23 C. Hussey: *The Picturesque*, Putnam's, New York, 1927.

THE REPLICANTS

Ridley Scott and Philip K. Dick disagreed about the nature of the replicants, so central to *Blade Runner*. For Dick they were 'deplorable', 'cruel', 'cold', 'heartless', and 'less-than-human'. They represent people who've forgotten how to be human, how to empathize: they are like Nazis. But Scott saw them as supermen who were 'smarter, stronger and had faster reflexes than humans'. Scott considered Dick's notion of the replicants as intellectual, and said he wasn't interested 'in making an esoteric film' (FN, 285).

The replicants are slaves, and work in the 'Off-World colonies', recalling the slave trade of Western nations. Another view is that *Blade Runner* portrays a conservative, reactionary politics (in keeping with the early 1980s Reagan era): Deckard's white alienated male is seen struggling in a multi-racial ghetto, confronting a variety of ethnic types (Egyptian, Chinese, Japanese). In that view, Deckard is in the minority, the white man surrounded by immigrants and other cultures.

For some critics, the replicants are at the centre of *Blade Runner*'s exploration of reality and dream, the imagined past and the real past, real and implanted memories. The replicants are an expression of a certain strand of postmodern theory, as espoused by Jean Baudrillard, who spoke of postmodernism as the era of simulcra and simulation. The replicants are pure simulcra, human doubles, down to their forged memory implants. These themes of reality/ fiction, real/ imaginary, are reflected in the tensions between the modernist and postmodern look of the movie, its 'retrofitting', the evocation of the future using elements of the past (director Ridley Scott said *BladeRunner* was 'a film set 40 years hence, made in the style of 40 years ago' [Warners press release]).

In this view, *Blade Runner* is a postmodern hybrid, using the past – 1940s *film noir* styles – to recreate the future. For Scott Bukatman, *Blade Runner*'s vision of the city is perhaps really modernist, 'a more deeply-historicised restatement of fundamental modernist ideas of the city' (1997, 60). Some of the 'retrofitting' is obvious – Rachel's hair and costume, for example, recalling the *femme fatales* of *film noir*, such as Lauren Bacall or Joan Crawford. Ridley Scott referred to Rita Hayworth, in the 1946 film

Gilda, in connection with Rachel, though Sean Young sure ain't Rita Hayworth ('Rachel was my homage to *Gilda* in a way' [FN, 383]). So Deckard's cop is a 2019 version of the Humphrey Bogart private detective, out of the stories of Raymond Chandler and Dashiel Hammett.

ROY BATTY AND THE REBEL ANGELS

> Fiery the Angels rose, & as they rose deep thunder roll'd
> Around their shores: indignant burning with the fires of Orc
>
> William Blake, 'America'

In the climactic fight, Roy Batty acts up a strange, playful and camp mixture of child and ruthless hunter; he strips down to cycling shorts,[24] howls like a wolf, lopes along around the interior like an animal, paints his face, pouts, returns to Pris's bloody body, and taunts Deckard in a British accent about fighting in a 'sporting' manner, about Deckard being man enough to fight. He also comes across as a Christ crucified and the god Pan.

Rutger Hauer said it was largely his idea that Batty should act like he was involved in a silly, wicked game ('more playful and strange than simply witnessing the last swan song of a machine', said Hauer [FN, 186]). Pauline Kael saw Hauer's performance as ridiculous, 'a shoo-in for this year's Klaus Kinski Scenery-Chewing Award', bringing

> the wrong kind of intensity to the role – an effete, self-aware irony so overscaled it's Wagnerian. His gaga performance is an unconscious burlesque that apparently passes for great acting with the director. (1986, 363-4)

Certainly, when one watches Rutger Hauer throughout the picture, he is very camp; for instance, look at the scene where he enters J.F. Sebastian's apartment and gasps 'what great toys you have!', then as the shot progresses, between cuts to and from Daryl Hannah's punkette Pris, Hauer

---
[24] Tom Shone called Rutger Hauer's replicant 'Nietzsche in cycling shorts'.

gives one of his Little Boy Hurt expressions as he talks about Leon's death. This childish frown also occurs just at the end of the celebrated shot of Hauer in the elevator, after murdering Tyrell.

Batty becomes superhuman, smashing his head through a bathroom wall, punching his hand through a wall, able to sense where Deckard is through walls and floors, able to lift up Deckard with one arm, and so on (Hauer thought the sticking-his-head-through-the-wall scene was over-the-top. It wouldn't be in a Chinese martial arts movie).

At one time in the script's genesis, Batty was to be dressed 'somewhere between a Comanche warrior and a transvestite' (S. Bukatman, 1997, 84). This section of *Blade Runner* takes on the narcissistic display of the male body found in many action films (consider Sylvester Stallone, Mel Gibson, Bruce Willis and Arnold Schwarzenegger, who often strip off).

Roy Batty in *BladeRunner* quotes William Blake and is portrayed as a Blakean rebel angel, a fallen Lucifer-type (he is depicted as a fallen angel after killing his creator, Tyrell, in the elevator outside the Tyrell ziggurat, when he looks up, shivers and the stars are seen for the only time in the film ['the expression of Rutger's face is so – well, I've never see anything like it on film before', commented Hampton Fancher [FN, 178]). The stars were shot with the track-zoom effect used in *Vertigo* (Alfred Hitchcock, 1958).

Tyrell calls Batty the prodigal son. In the climactic fight scene, Deckard and Batty are identified with each other (both are wounded in the hand, for example); there are also homoerotic overtones in this scene. The identification is complete when Roy rescues Rick, in a gesture of redemption and sacrifice (director Ridley Scott also said that Batty was being 'more human than human' here, more humane than Deckard, who wants to kill him, and he also wants someone to watch him die.)

Roy Batty introduces himself with lines from William Blake's poem 'America', a pæan to the American Revolution and the founding of modern America. David Peoples had put in a quote from Percy Bysshe Shelley's 'Ozymandias' in the scene where Batty kills Tyrell, and Ridley Scott suggested putting in some Blake too.

Batty's death soliloquy was cod lyrical, in keeping with the camp/sinister way Hauer played the character:

'I've seen things you people wouldn't believe. Attack ships on fire off the shoulder of Orion. I watched c-beams glitter in the dark near the Tannhauser Gate. All those moments will be lost in time. Like tears in rain. Time to die.'

David Peoples, not Rutger Hauer, as some claim, wrote the speech (FN, 195-6). Batty's character, like the others in *BladeRunner*, can be seen as a manifestation of the decline of modern America (Deckard and Tyrell are obvious examples of moral and social decay). The opening shots of *Blade Runner* depict Los Angeles as a 21st century Gomorrah or Hell, all pollution, decadence and darkness, with the fires of Hell raging intermittently from giant chimneys.

For writer Hampton Fancher, Batty saves Deckard's life partly because he appreciates Deckard's 'last, defiant, life-affirming gesture', as Deckard 'literally spits in the face of death' (FN, 194). For Thomas Byers, Batty's gesture is heavily ironic, one killer saving another, an act which questions Deckard's masculine identity. As Batty stalks Deckard he torments him with questions, such as 'aren't you the good man?'; after Batty's death, Gaff tells Deckard 'you've done a man's job'. Deckard's not sure whether he's as 'good' a man as Batty, or even if he's a 'real man' at all.[25] Ridley Scott thought maybe Batty wanted Deckard to witness his death, so he could tell others what had happened, and why the replicants should be treated like humans (FN, 193). Fancher said he never envisaged Deckard getting the better of Batty: it was always Batty who would win the fight.

Blade Runner questions human identity – this is a film in which the robots or cyborgs are more 'human' than the humans themselves. For critics such as Hal Foster, Mark Dery, Claudia Springer and Scott Bukatman, cyborgs in contemporary cinema are 'a last bastion of overdetermined human, masculinist definition, bodies armoured against the malleability and invisibility of the present' (S. Bukatman, 1993, 17).

Batty also recalls Christ, impaling his hand with a nail (in order, presumably, to prolong his life); the white dove, another Christian symbol, flutters up to a suddenly blue sky when Batty dies; however, Batty is not wholly a Christ-figure, having just murdered his 'father' and maker, Tyrell. In postmodern fashion, the Christian symbols and motifs are evoked but shorn of their power (the white dove and blue sky come out nowhere,

---

[25] T. Byers, "Commodity Futures", in A. Kuhn, 1990, 44.

narratively illogical, the imagery more reminiscent of a pop video).[26]

Although Batty is the Blakean 'dark angel', and Deckard the saviour, it is Batty who is associated with light, while Deckard is clad in dark clothes. However, Batty's blonde appearance in his black leather jacket recall a different kind of Superman, Friedrich Nietzsche's *Übermensch*, mistakenly taken up by the Nazis. The replicants, via Batty and Leon, evoke Adolf Hitler's vision of an Aryan Master Race (recall the replicants' strength, blondeness, racial 'purity' or pure origins, as machines). As 'positive monsters', then, the replicants ambiguously recall fascism (Ridley Scott conceived the replicants as 'supermen').

The blonde man in his black leather jacket is also a gay image; Nazis have often been portrayed as homosexual or sexually 'perverse' in Hollywood films. Batty, though, is given heterosexual aspects – exchanging furtive looks with Pris, and kissing her (a 'kinky' moment, by conventional standards, occurs when Batty kisses the dead Pris, pushing her tongue into her mouth).[27] But when Batty kisses Tyrell before killing him, it was not meant to be seen as homosexual or sexual, said Rutger Hauer; it wasn't a 'kiss of death', either, but just a farewell.

The shadow of Thirties Germany is also conjured up in the sleazy downtown bar, the Snake Pit (shot on the redressed Sebastian's apartment set), where Zhora works as a snake dancer: the camp (off-screen) voice of the master of ceremonies announcing the acts ('watch her take the pleasure from the serpent that once corrupted man') recalls Joel Grey in *Cabaret*, and also Peter Sellers mad scientist in *Dr Strangelove*. Another view (Kaja Silverman, 1991) is that, as a slave leader, Batty's 'hyperbolic whiteness' is a kind of blackness, which separates the issues of race and slavery.

---

[26] Hauer said the dove was his idea, and he hoped it wouldn't be only interpreted along Christian lines, because 'there's a lot of interesting connections to birds in mythologies and religions other than Christianity' (FN, 192-3). The dove was a last minute idea, and Scott wasn't sure if it would work – 'it's a bit on the nose, don't you think?' he told Hauer. Scott admitted that the bird he filmed next to the incinerator at Elstreee Studios didn't quite fit in (FN, 384).

[27] That was Hauer's idea, Daryl Hannah said (FN, 183).

TIME, MEMORY, REALITY

BladeRunner's David Dryer (visual fx) said there was a lot of *Metropolis* in *Blade Runner* (FN, 111). Aside from *Metropolis*, *The Big Sleep* and *The Maltese Falcon*, *Blade Runner* also alludes to Michelangelo Antonioni's *Blow Up*, in the Esper photographic sequence, where Deckard scans one of the replicant's photos.

    Blade Runner is thus part of a trend in Hollywood movies to raid the past, and particularly the history of cinema, then mix the elements together. Simultaneously *hommage* and parody, in which old films are used more than real history to recreate the future. In this respect, *Blade Runner* is a nostalgic film, lovingly evoking the history of cinema, exploring the viewer's nostalgia for cinema, the memory of Forties *film noir* (*Blade Runner* was shot on the Warners' lot where *The Maltese Falcon* and *The Big Sleep* had been filmed).

PHILIP K. DICK'S FICTION AND POSTMODERNISM

It's become a multiple cliché layered upon countless clichés in contemporary criticism to call *Blade Runner* and Philip K. Dick's fiction 'postmodern'. But they are. The argument is over on this one, but consider the following opposites:

modern	postmodern
industrial	post-industrial
reality	post-reality/ simulation
feminism	post-feminism
epistemology	ontology
depth	surface
centre	boundaries
inside	outside

subject	object
transcendence	immanence
time	space
order	flux / flow
mind	artificial intelligence
communities	networks
hermeneutics/ semiotics	acts/ performativity
body	machine/ cyborg
biology	biomechanics
sex/ reproduction	genetics/ replication

It's also commonplace to discuss *Blade Runner* and Phil Dick's cinema in terms of (yawn) cyberspace and cyberpunk (*Blade Runner* is lumped together regularly with movies such as *Tron, The Terminator, Aliens*, and other 1980s movies). What does cyberspace and cyberpunk mean? Well, cyberspace is a technological mirror, a place of infinite (digital) desire, reflecting back the virtual narcissism of the subject (Ovid by way of Julia Kristeva). The internet here is the ultimate inner space, which only individual imaginations can traverse, not groups, organizations, or institutions. A pleroma of connections always leading back to the self. E.M. Forster's 'Only connect', but connecting only with self. (The dream of total transparency, the fusion of self and technology, is a paradoxical one, because the technology is always there, always makes its presence felt. There is a desire to *become* the technology, but also to keep it always at a distance.)

This is all very much central to Philip K. Dick's speculative fiction, and to all of the films based on his stories. The ambiguity that Dick's fiction feels towards technology (and its manifestation in global consumerism) is fundamental.

> We are living in a system of technological temporality [asserts Paul Virilio], in which duration and material support have been supplanted as criteria by individual retinal and auditory instants...

It's a world in which the question of modernity and postmodernism has been replaced by *'reality* and *post-reality'* (1991a, 84). It's not Baudrillardian 'simulation', Virilio suggests, but 'substitution': 'new technologies are substituting a virtual reality for an actual reality' (1994b).

Cyberspace is also a 'nonspace' (*Neuromancer*, 63), a constructed space, and thus predictable, and therefore easier to understand than physical space.[28] It's noteworthy that the internet uses spatial metaphors: cyberspace, infoscape, chat rooms, surfing, navigation (*cp.* Arjun Appardurai's concept of 'scapes').[29] An electronic cartography, a geography of gigabytes.

Scott Bukatman (one of the best writers on *Blade Runner*) coined the phrase 'terminal space' to cover everything from virtual reality, interactive systems, computer games and flight simulators, to special effects movies, computer art and digital graphics on TV (1993, 107). What was true in 1993 (the year of Bukatman's key book *Terminal Identity*), is even more so now, with a 'cyberspace look' or 'cyber-style' occurring across many technological platforms: the internet, computer software, lifestyle magazines, fashion, TV ads, MTV and pop promos, CD cover design, children's TV, sci-fi in movies and TV, and so on.[30] For Bukatman, William Gibson's infoscape is a graphic but limited metaphor for the global economy, a theme park reduction of the circulation and organization of capital.[31]

Cyberspace is also the space of finance, capital and ATMs ('cyberspace is where your money is'). In cyberspace, crimes are difficult to detect: money can disappear into offshore accounts at the touch of a button.[32] And it's the realm of information and espionage war, being fought with computers, spy satellites and electronic espionage. And in cyberspace, replicants are virtually indistinguishable from humans.

---

[28] J. Bolter: *Turing's Man: Western Culture in the Computer Age*, University of North Carolina Press, Chapel Hill, 1984.
[29] A. Appadurai: "Global Ethnoscapes", in R. Fox, ed. *Recapturing Anthropology*, SAR Press, 1996.
[30] By the early 2000s, delivery systems were converging: interactive television, the internet, broadcasting, mobile phones, PCs, ISDNs, digital subscriber lines (DSL), satellites, wireless application protocol (WAP), broadband, and so on.
[31] S. Bukatman, in L. Cooke, 1995.
[32] Organised crime generates $750 billion a year, with drugs making $400-500bn, according to Z. Sardar (Z. Sardar & J. Ravetz, eds. *Cyberfutures*, Pluto, 1996). See also: "The Wired Scared Shitlist", *Wired*, 3, 1, Jan, 1995.

CYBORGS AND CYBERCULTURE

Cyborgs, robots and human 'hybrids'[33] have been a standard component of science fiction since the first great classic book of sci-fi and horror, Mary Shelley's *Frankenstein*. Since then, popular culture has been awash with cyborgs, androids and robots: the robot Maria in *Metropolis*, Gort in *The Day the Earth Stood Still*, *Forbidden Planet*'s Robbie, *2001*'s HAL, R2D2 and C3PO, the 'droids in *Star Wars* (partly based on the peasants in Akira Kurosawa's *The Hidden Fortress* [1958]), Lee Majors in *The Six Million Dollar Man*, Yul Brynner in *Westworld*, Arnold Schwarzenegger in the *Terminator* series, Judge Dredd, RoboCop, Tetsuo, Ash in *Alien*, NumberFive in *Short Circuit*, the Mark 13 cyborg in *Hardware*, *Max Headroom*, Data and the Borg in *Star Trek*, the military cyborgs in *Universal Soldier*, Max in *Dark Angel*, Haley Joel Osment's David in *A.I.*, television sci-fi (*Dr Who, Stargate SG-1, Farscape, Babylon 5, Blake's 7, Futurama, Total Recall 2070, The Bionic Woman, Quantum Leap*), and so on, not to mention children's toys (such as War Planet, Transformers, Digimon, Beast Wars, Warhammer), and the thousands of characters in comic books, cartoons, TV series, films and computer games which are turned into merchandising: *Teenage Mutant Ninja Turtles, The Mighty Morphin Power Rangers, Pokémon, The Mask, Tank Girl, X-Men, Men in Black* and *Judge Dredd*. And of course in Philip K. Dick's fiction: the replicants in *Blade Runner*, Arny's Quaid in *Total Recall*, etc.

For some commentators (David Bell, 2000), the cyborg is not limited to the characters in *The Terminator* or *Star Trek*, but texts can be cyborgian, or founded on a cyborgian consciousness (transgressing Cartesian epistemologies and Western philosophy's dualisms). They reaffirm bourgeois, dominant ideology, conventional notions of good/ evil, male/ female, human/ machine, self/ other (A. Balsamo, 1999).

Of course, contemporary Hollywood cinema doesn't get much further

---
[33] On cyborgs, cyberspace and cyberpunk, see: S. Bukatman, 1993; D. Haraway, 1985 and 1989; J. Prosser, *Second Skins: The Body Narratives of Transsexuality*, Columbia University Press, N.Y., 1998; E. Rabkin, 1987; S. Brewster, 2000; T. de Lauretis, *Technologies of Gender*, Macmillan, 1987; J. Rusher, 1995; B. Rux, 1997; P. Schelde, 1993; F. Botting, 1999; J. Telotte, 1996, in N. Ruddick, 1992, and "The Tremulous Public Body", *Journal of Popular Film & Television*, 19, 1, 1991; J. Bergstrom: "Androids and Androgyny", *Camera Obscura*, 15, 1986; R. Barringer, 1997; A. Balsamo, 1988; C. Berg, 1989; C. Springer, 1993; D. Larson: "Machine and Messiah", *Genders*, 18, 1993; G. Schwab, 1987; P. Warrick, 1980; C. Fuchs, 1993; F. Glass, 1989.

than the sensational image of humans interacting with cyborgs at the most extreme levels: sex, violence and death. Even movies enshrined by the critical academy, such as *Blade Runner*, don't go much beyond the titillating question: 'what's it like to fuck an android?'

The hospital scenes, featuring Deckard and Holden, which were dropped from *Blade Runner*, contain some absolutely vital information on this matter: Holden asks Deckard if he fucked the snake woman before killing her. The dialogue's in that locker room, macho fashion (*Blade Runner*'s a very macho movie), but it's a key point, about having sex with the androids. Holden tells Deckard (in the deleted scenes on the DVD releases) that Deckard shouldn't have a crisis of conscience about it – it's like fucking your washing machine, then switching it off (sex followed by death). Deckard doesn't really respond to Holden's taunts: if this scene comes *after* Deckard has made love with Rachel, the scene has a new dramatic inflection. The filmmakers left the scenes out, as they don't seem to add much to the film, but the exchange about having sex with Zhora is absolutely central to the theme of *BladeRunner*, not only the romantic sub-plot.

Associated with the cyborg or robot are the many monsters in the horror genre, what Slavoj Zizek calls 'return of the living dead': Leatherface in *The Texas Chainsaw Massacre* (with his trademark mask and chainsaw extension). Anti-heroes with knives for fingers (Freddy Krueger in *A Nightmare On Elm Street* and the youth in *Edward Scissorhands*). 'Jaws' in the *James Bond* films of the 1970s, with rows of metal teeth. *Hellraiser*'s Pinhead. Ghosts (*The Sixth Sense, What Lies Beneath, The Others*). Demons and the Devil (*The Exorcist, The Devil's Advocate, Spawn, Angel Heart*). Vampires (*Dracula, Buffy, Van Helsing, The Lost Boys, Interview With the Vampire*). Sub-humans or mutants (*The Fly, Basket Case*). Zombies (George Romero's movies). Werewolves (*An American Werewolf in London, Wolf, The Howling*). Devilish aliens (*Gremlins, Critters, Independence Day*, the *Alien* series). Poltergeists (*Poltergeist*). Killer dolls (*Magic, Child's Play*). Witches (*Salem's Lot, The Craft*, the *Blair Witch* films). And psychopaths and serial killers (the *Friday the 13th, Candyman, Scream* and *Hallowe'en* movies).

For critic Donna Haraway, the cyborg represents the possibility of new identities, moving beyond binaries, boundaries, universalisations. Transgression is a key theme in Haraway's thinking. New sutures, new borders. For Haraway, the technological revolution is as significant as industrial capitalism (1985). In "A Manifesto For Cyborgs", Haraway offered a chart of transitions 'from the comfortable old hierarchical dominations to the scary new networks I have called the informatics of domination'.

Here, simulation replaces representation, biotics replaces organisms, surface replaces depth, obsolescence replaces decadence, replication replaces reproduction, genetic engineering replaces sex, robotics replaces work, 'fields of difference' replaces the nature / culture binary, and 'cyborg citizens' replaces the public and private (we are all cyborgs claimed Haraway; Haraway has famously proclaimed herself a cyborg, a quintessential technological body [1985]).

In Harawayan cyborg culture, the boundaries of the 'self' are increasingly becoming blurred (many cultural theorists have concerned themselves with borders and marginality: Homi Bhabha, Paul Gilroy and Julia Kristeva). New terms are required: the 'trans-human' is halfway between the human and the 'post-human', a site of suture and marginality; the 'post-human' is an enhanced human (who may be 'post-biological'), with neurological, biological, psychological and technological enrichments.

The moment of the construction of the cyborg is a vital scene in the fantasy genre, whether it's in *Metropolis, Frankenstein* (VictorFrankenstein cries 'it's alive!'), *The Fifth Element, Ghost In the Shell* or in the title sequence of *The Six Million Dollar Man* ('we can rebuild him' – no one asks 'why bother?'). For Raymond Bellour, movies concentrate on this primal birth scene because this is what the cinematic apparatus is always doing, substituting a simulcra for reality.[34] The reanimation of the monster, the cyborg or the human is one of cinema's specialities. It's one of cinema's (and sci-fi's) primal scenes. Cinema is, physically, a continuous resurrection: people photographed eighty years ago at 16, 18 or 24 frames per second seem to come back to life. It's the flipside of Jean-Luc Godard's remark that cinema literally films death, that the people one films will die. Also, actors speak of enjoying playing death scenes, pantomiming the mysterious, perennially fascinating moment of ultimate transition.

---
[34] R. Bellour: "Ideal Hadaly", in C. Penley, 1991, 127.

DOUBLES

Doubles and *doppelgängers* is another motif in *Blade Runner*: Rick Deckard's rival is Roy Batty, but the two become doubles by the end; Deckard kills two replicants, and two save his life (Rachel and Batty); Rachel and Pris embody Western dualistic archetypes: one blonde, the other dark; one active, the other passive; one erotic, the other virginal. Rachel and Pris clearly correspond to the ancient Western mythic dualism of virgin/ whore.

There are two romantic couples as well: the bleached blonde robots, Batty and Pris, and the dark-haired, more 'human' couple, Rachel and Deckard (tho' they might both be robots too). Hollywood has long had a very simple way of differentiating characters, goodies and baddies, just by hair colour. As the film progresses, Deckard and Batty move towards each other; apart from hair colour, they have similarities of costume (the high collars, for example – *Blade Runner* is a film of many costumes having high collars, including Sebastian's faded New Agey jacket, and Rachel's 1940s *film noir* fur-lined coat). By the end, they are indistinguishable from each other, with Batty ironically turning out to be the nobler one, when he saves Deckard's life.

E.T.A. Hoffman's *The Sand-Man* (1816) is another literary reference point – it influenced films such as *Metropolis* (which in turn influenced *Star Wars* and *Blade Runner*). *The Sand-Man* features an automata, Olimpia, with obvious links with the robot in *Metropolis* and the replicants in *Blade Runner*. Also in *The Sand-Man* are themes which occur in *Blade Runner*: eyes (the Sand-Man putting out people's eyes, and the automata's eyes being taken out).

Apart from E.T.A. Hoffman, another obvious literary reference point is one of the grandmothers of all science fiction works, Mary Shelley's *Frankenstein*, with its images of creating life, playing God, subverting nature, and the monster as a shadow figure, an alter ego of the hero (compare Deckard and Batty, Tyrell and Batty).

BLADE RUNNER CRITICISM

When *Blade Runner* was first released, in 1982, some critics hated it, while many others were bemused by it: while acknowledging the impressive style of the film, the rest of it was seen as incoherent, insubstantial, and full of *film noir* private detective clichés. Brian Aldiss called it an 'overheated farrago of SF [sci-fi] crossed with private eye machismo and dragged down by pretentious sets'.[35] For Pat Berman, the movie was 'like science fiction pornography – all sensation and no heart'.[36]

The amount of academic and cult interest that *Blade Runner* has initiated since 1982 is substantial. There are collections of essays on *Blade Runner* (*Retrofitting Blade Runner,* edited by Judith Kerman); monographs on *Blade Runner* (such as Scott Bukatman's British Film Institute Modern Classics book); and very detailed explorations of the film, such as Paul M. Sammon's *Future Noir: The Making of Blade Runner*. Some prominent critics have studied *Blade Runner*: Kaja Silverman, Slavoj Zizek, Scott Bukatman, Andrew Ross, Vivian Sobchack and Guiliana Bruno.

There have been many articles and essays on *Blade Runner* and sections in books on *Blade Runner,* such as:

- on postmodernism in *Blade Runner* (for example, Guiliana Bruno's "Ramble City"),
- on the androids/ cyborg theme (such as Donna Haraway's *Simians, Cyborgs and Women* and J.P. Telotte's *Replications: A Robotic History of the Science Fiction Film*),
- or the design of the movie (such as D. Neumann's *Film Architecture: From Metropolis to Blade Runner* and Syd Mead in Danny Peary's *Omni's Screen Flights, Screen Fantasies*),
- or on the director's cut, and so on.

Chapters on *Blade Runner* appear in books such as L. Goldberg *et al*'s *Science Fiction Filmmaking in the 1980s,* Jim Collins *et al*'s *Film Theory Goes to the Movies,* Vivian Sobchack's *Screening Space: The American Science Fiction Film,* Linda Cook and Peter Wollen's *Visual Display,* and Annette Kuhn's *Alien Zone: Cultural Theory and Contemporary Science Fiction.*

---
35 B. Aldiss: *Trillion Year Spree,* Avon Books, 1988.
36 P. Berman: *State and Columbia Record,* Columbia, July 2, 1982.

Then there are pieces and chapters on:
- the visual effects in *Blade Runner* (such as Herb Lightman's articles, and in Christopher Finch's *Special Effects*),
- comic book tie-ins,
- novel sequels (K.W. Jeter's *Blade Runner 2: The Edge of Human* and *Replicant Night*),
- a fanzine (*Cityspeak*),
- a computer game (1997),
- and souvenir magazines (ed. Ira Friedman).

There are inevitably many internet sites and newsgroups dedicated to *Blade Runner*, including:
- Murray Chapman's *Blade Runner FAQ* page,
- Jon Van Oast's *2019: Off-World* page,
- Dan Hentschel's *Blade Runner* Homepage,
- Paul Brians' "Study Guide for Philip K. Dick: *Blade Runner*",
- Christian Rohrmeier's "Official *Blade Runner* On-line Magazine",
- BladeZone, an online fanzine,
- and Stephen Bowline and Michael Perkhofer's worldwide web page on Vangelis Papathanassiou.

Good websites for Philip K. Dick include philipkdick.com (the official site), and philipkdicksfans.com. The *Alien* series also had their own fan websites (such as *The Unofficial Alien 5 Website* and *The Alien 5 Discussion Forum*).[37]

The prospect of a sequel to *Blade Runner* was often discussed, mainly by fans (but Hollywood execs must have contemplated a sequel as the interest grew around the film in the late 1980s, and when the *Director's Cut* was released). A sequel to *Blade Runner* would be expensive, Ridley Scott acknowledged: for a start, you'd need to buy the title from the producers, which might be $2 million. And using Harrison Ford would mean $15-20 million (though it's unlikely that Ford would return).

Critics such as Paul Sammon rave about *Blade Runner*, saying it

> not only revealed an *adult* narrative and *complex* characters (subtle, dramatically wrenching ones at that), it also evidenced a *thematic* complexity every bit as intricate as its much discussed *visual* complexity. (1996, xvii)

---

[37] Also: alienexperience.com and avpoe.org/amr. And when the *Alien 5* movie eventually surfaced, it was a truly dreadful Alien versus Predator piece of junk.

In his 1999 book on Ridley Scott's cinema, Paul Sammon attested that *Blade Runner* is a

> haunting, hypnotic, harrowing achievement, one whose overwhelming visuals are strongly linked to its ideas – provocative, multi-textured ones, each subversively embedded in the understructure of what appears to be a mainstream Hollywood product. *Blade Runner* may be narratively flawed and (at times) precariously self-indulgent, but it also remains one of the truly lustrous jewels in Scott's creative crown, a cinematic milestone whose basic integrity, form of imagination and ideological sophistication forever altered the face of contemporary science fiction cinema. (1999, 73).

There is a truly amazing amount of critical material surrounding *Blade Runner*. 'In the world of blockbuster studies, *Blade Runner* nuts rank second only to *Alien* scholars in their devotion to the cause, although they are 50 percent more likely to use the word "hyper-reality"', as Tom Shone put it (119).

Sometimes it seems that the amount of critical attention that *Blade Runner* has generated is out of proportion with the film itself. It's a good movie, but is it really *that* good? Whatever, *Blade Runner* is certainly a movie that film critics and fans and PhD students love to discuss. *Blade Runner* is the modern *Citizen Kane*, a film that is widely taken to be one of the highpoints of contemporary cinema.

And the influence of *Blade Runner* in contemporary cinema is huge, too – most obviously in its look and design, but also in its themes and characters. And the impact of *Blade Runner* on pop music and MTV and fashion has been enormous, too. The long coats, the black leather jackets, the eye-liner, the rain and smoke – you might be at a Cure or Gary Numan gig.

Blade Runner is one of those films that have been quoted many times in pop music, within songs – like *2001: A Space Odyssey* or *The Wizard of Oz*. It's a movie that loved by musicians and composers – not least because of its marvellous soundtrack by Vangelis.

NEGATIVE CRITICISM OF *BLADE RUNNER*

Some negative criticism might include seeing *Blade Runner* as a flawed film, where the near-faultless camerawork, visual effects, lighting and set design are marred by the conventional hard-boiled cop story and *film noir* characters, the Hollywood romance, and some sexist stances.

The scene where the snake woman replicant, Zhora, is killed by Deckard is one such moment of grotesque violence: the near-naked character is dressed in see-through plastic fetish wear;[38] she is shot on L.A.'s streets, running away from Deckard, a woman being shot from behind, and a woman who's working in a lowly position in the entertainment industry ('[e]ven the most cynical forties *film noir* hero didn't do that', said actress Joanna Cassidy [FN, 157]). She crashes into a row of plate glass windows (and was also going to carry on and be hit by a bus).

Zhora's death occurs in Sam Peckinpah-like slow motion, accompanied by the quiet washes of Vangelis's synthesizers. The blood spatters inside the plastic coat. It still has a creepy exploitative aspect to it for me.[39]

Another serious flaw in *Blade Runner* is the climactic battle between Deckard and Batty, which on some viewings seems dragged out for far too long. Rutger Hauer's Batty is played far too camp to be fearsome, while Sean Young and Daryl Hannah often elicit only indifference. (Writers Hampton Fancher and David Peoples recalled the duel didn't seem big enough to climax the movie, but they were blown away when they saw how the filmmakers had done it).

The protagonists, as believable human (or cyborg) characters, fail to encourage empathy, and are swamped by the filmmakers' overpowering emphasis on the *mise-en-scène* and design. *Blade Runner* is not an emotionally engaging movie like, say, *Pelle the Conqueror* or *Fanny and Alexander*. The puzzle and detection aspects of the film (apparently added by David Peoples at Harrison Ford's behest) were also routine: Deckard searching apartments and finding snake scales and photos; Deckard interrogating Rachel (though using the new addition of the Voigt-Kampff machine).

---

[38] Joanna Cassidy's make-up of body paint and sequins took 3 hours to apply by 4 people, according to make-up artist Marvin Westmore (FN, 153).
[39] And I was unhappy about showing that part of the film to my students when we went through the movie scene-by-scene. It's kinda repulsive.

Other aspects came straight out of *film noir*: the hard-bitten, alienated, morally-dubious detective; the (futuristic, russet-hued) trenchcoat; hanging around in bars; drinking whisky; cigarettes; the jaded police captain; the *femme fatale*; the L.A. setting; the blinds; the fans; and the voiceover.

Quite a bit of *Blade Runner* was patched up in the editing suite – more than one might think. Or maybe it's because the mistakes or the gluing over the seams is more obvious than in some films. Sure, there are mistakes in every movie ever made, but in *Blade Runner* the film editing and the sound editing isn't quite slick enough to cover up the holes. There are a few scenes, for instance, where dialogue has been added in post-production – the scene where Deckard takes the snake scale to the Cambodian seller (Kimiko Hiroshige), for instance. There's hardly a shot of the woman speaking in close-up, always a giveaway that a scene has been rewritten and dubbed after it was shot. Other instances of awkward editing and crude post-production include the scene with the Egyptian animal trader, Abdul Ben-Hassan.[40] (Some of those errors were corrected in *The Final Cut*).

Twenty years later, films like *Blade Runner* would be made with thirty cameras running simultaneously, so some coverage or close-ups would be shot which could cover up mistakes (such as the tried and tested method of cutting to a meaningless close-up of some minor action with the hands to cover an ellipse in the action or an actor's flubbed line).

While there's plenty for critics following postmodernist, semiotic, psychoanalytic and other cultural theories to get their teeth into in *Blade Runner*, second wave feminists have much to complain about. *Blade Runner* is a very masculinist movie in many respects. It's a patriarchal culture, with all the key positions of authority being taken by men (cops, captains, replicant leaders, C.E.O.s). And the three most prominent women in the film are all robots. One is a dancer, one is a hooker, and one is a secretary.[41]

BladeRunner's not, in short, a movie with characters that second wave

---

[40] That came about partly because the producers wanted to clarify the information in the scene, and the scene was rewritten and looped, as editor Terry Rawlings explained (FN, 148). 'That didn't really work, though, did it?' Rawlings added.

[41] No mothers, carers, partners, wives or other types of women in *BladeRunner*, beyond the women in the bar, and the old woman who identifies the snake scale, as Mary Doane points out. But the concept of the maternal is still present (1999, 28). The 6th replicant, Mary, would have been a mother figure.

feminists can rave about (like the other Philip K. Dick adaptions). Third wave or postmodern feminists, though, can find much in *Blade Runner* to explore – the notions of identity, of cyborg status, of hyperspace, and so on.

FEMME FATALES AND 19TH CENTURY ART

The women in *Blade Runner*, Pris, Rachel and Zhora, recall the *femme fatales* in 19th century art, in painters such as Gustave Moreau, Edvard Munch, Félicien Rops, Odilon Redon, Jean Delville and Franz von Stuck. The *femme fatale* was one of the main types of women in 19th century European painting: there were other incarnations or versions of the same basic type: the woman as death, as a prostitute, as a dominatrix, a temptress, a queen, a warrior, an Amazon, and so on. Note that Zhora's stage name in 'Miss Salomé', Salomé being a key 19th century *femme fatale*, a version of the erotic, castrating woman.

The *femme fatale* type neatly melds sex and death, desire and fear, contact and loss, for the (male) artist. She appears in figures from myth and history such as Medusa, Salomé, Delilah, Jezebel, Judith, Lilith, Ninue (the lover of Merlin), Venus, Helen of Troy, La Belle Dame Sans Merci and Cleopatra. These female 'types' combined beauty with death, immense power and all manner of sadistic, masochistic and fetishistic fantasies. These are the women who will whip one to death, if one wishes, as in Leopold Sacher-Masoch's *Venus in Furs*. Easy to see how the punk blonde Pris corresponds with the powerful warrior or Amazon type, a teasing dominatrix for Deckard, who leaps on his shoulders and strangles him between her thighs. With her stockings, mini-skirt, thick make-up and bleached hair, Pris is a male fantasy, a prostitute, literally a 'love machine', with a penchant for kinky, fetishistic sex. The robot woman as sex machine is of course another common trope in science fiction.

Rachel can be seen as the 19th century flipside of the 'holy whore' figure of Cleopatra, Medusa, Venus and Salomé, the 'passive virgin' or 'good woman' type, repressed, dreamy, waiting. In Symbolist art she is the pale, drowned Ophelia in John Everett Millais' painting (1851-52, Tate Gallery, London), or the wistful madonnas of Pre-Raphaelite art (particularly in the work of Edward Burne-Jones, Millais, Holman Hunt and Dante Gabriel Rossetti), and in Gustave Moreau's softly dreaming images of *Sappho* (1872, Victoria & Albert Museum, London).

Zhora, the snake dancer, corresponds with the ancient associations between women and death, women and snakes. Painters such as Franz von Stuck produced famous depictions of *femme fatales* with snakes. Stuck's most popular image, which he painted 18 times, was *Vice* (1894, Cologne): in near-darkness, a muscley, nude woman reclines on her belly, the dark form of a snake curling around her. Her head turned to the viewer, wearing a lascivious smile, she holds her breast.

In Franz von Stuck's famous picture of the same theme (*Sin*, 1893, Neue Pinakothek, Munich), glowing female flesh again appears out of darkness. In *Sin*, female nudity is the focus of the image: the woman's breasts, belly and abdomen are glowing whitely, while her face and clothes are shrouded in shadow. So popular were Stuck's serpent-women, rows of seats were put in front of the picture for the visitors at the 1893 Munich Secession exhibition.

In *BladeRunner,* Jordan Cronenweth's baroque, shadowy lighting and design also looks decidedly 19th century: the browns and sepias of the Tyrell Corporation interiors, for example, recall the Egyptian and Babylonian architecture of Gustave Moreau's paintings (such as his densely layered, incredibly detailed image of *Salomé* in the Hammer Collection in Los Angeles). As yet, no movie has captured the intensity of detail in artists such as Moreau and Gustave Doré. If only!

❦

Watching *Blade Runner* again recently, I was struck by how much of the film is taken up by the romantic plot: indeed, it's not a subplot, but a dual plot with the narrative of Deckard hunting down the replicants. In short, *Blade Runner* is a very *romantic* movie: it's about a guy and his girl, after all (like a lot of Raymond Chandleresque detective fiction, too). It's Bogart and Bacall again (though, sorry to say, Sean Young ain't quite

Lauren Bacall). That was very much from Hampton Fancher's drafts of the script.

Because when Deckard isn't hunting down replicants, he's holed up with Rachel in his apartment. It's striking just how much of *Blade Runner* really is a romantic love story, with the narrative device of keeping the lovers apart this time being the slight problem that one of them isn't human. Or, if you buy into the theory that Deckard is also a replicant, you've got a love story between two robots. That's bizarre, certainly, but not in science fiction, or in science fiction cinema. There are many examples of machines, computers or robots wishing to become human (it's rarely the other way around – who'd want to be a robot?). The 1999 film *Bicentennial Man*, starring Robin Williams and directed by Chris Columbus, featured a robot hankering after humanity, including romantic love. And the 2001 film *A.I. Artificial Intelligence* also covered similar territory, with a child, played by Haley Joel Osment, wanting to become a real boy, as in *Pinocchio*.

THE INFLUENCE OF *BLADE RUNNER*

Probably the most influential aspect of *Blade Runner* was its *mis-en-scène*, copied in many subsequent films, such as *Judge Dredd* (1995), *Brazil* (Terry Gilliam, 1984), the *Batman* series, *Twelve Monkeys* (Terry Gilliam, 1995), *Cyborg* (Albert Pyun, 1989), *Total Recall* (Paul Verhoeven, 1990), *Akira* (Katsuhiro Otomo, 1988), *Strange Days* (Kathryn Bigelow, 1995), *Johnny Mnemonic* (Robert Longo, 1995), *The Salute of the Jugger* (David Peoples, 1990), the *Matrix* series, and *The Fifth Element* (Luc Besson, 1997).[42]

---

[42] Other flicks linked to Phil Dick's work include *A Nightmare On Elm Street, Mulholland Drive, Fight Club, Vanilla Sky, Donnie Darko, Videodrome, Existenz, Being John Malkovich, Adaptation, Eternal Sunshine of the Spotless Mind, Dark City, The Truman Show, Gattaca* and *Memento*.

BATMAN.

For my money, Warners' *Batman* films are among the most captivating and luscious of fantasy visions in contemporary cinema (the four movies, 1989-1997, not the recycled franchise from 2005's *Batman Begins* onwards). The depictions of Gotham City – futuristic, nightmarish, squalid, multi-level and multi-ethnic – are easily the equal of the highpoints of contemporary cinema's cities, whether in *Blade Runner*, the *Star Wars* saga, *A.I., Total Recall* or *The Fifth Element*.

Shot in Britain at Pinewood Studios, 1989's *Batman* was an epic of production design, for which Anton Furst rightly won the Oscar.[43] *Batman* was shot by Roger Pratt.[44] The backlot at Pinewood was transformed into a vision of Gotham City as a dark, shadowy recreation a *film noirish* 1940s New York, a slice of Art Deco American Gothic, brownstones, and fascist pomp.

Director Tim Burton didn't want to shoot on real New York locations, as *Superman* (1978) had done. He wanted something extreme and operatic, specially created for the characters, and to recreate the look of the comic books. Burton said he forbade the use of neon, which would be too reminiscent of *BladeRunner*, and persuaded the production designers to try for something that didn't follow *BladeRunner*'s highly influential style. The result was that *Batman*, with its combination of Roger Pratt's stunning cinematography, Anton Furst's designs, Bob Ringwood's outrageous (and very influential) costumes and Burton's vision, is probably the best-looking blockbuster of the 1980s and 1990s.[45]

BRAZIL.

Brazil (Terry Gilliam, 1985) is one of the most satisfying post-*Blade Runner* movies. The exaggerated dystopian vision of Universal's *Brazil* recalls *Blade Runner* (and *Mad Max*),[46] and clearly influenced later sci-fi and

---

[43] Anton Furst was assisted by protegé Nigel Phelps, who went on to design *Judge Dredd, Alien Resurrection, In Dreams* and *The Bone Collector*.

[44] Roger Pratt's previous credits included *Brazil*, a film which has affinities with *Batman* and *Blade Runner* – a nightmarish futuristic city, models, paranoia, and Pratt's later work included *The Fisher King* and *Twelve Monkeys*.

[45] However, Francis Coppola's *Bram Stoker's Dracula* would be a strong contender for the most beautifully crafted blockbuster, with outstanding lensing by Michael Balhaus, art direction by Andrew Precht, and production design by Thomas Saunders and Dante Ferretti.

[46] The influence of the *Mad Max* films is often under-estimated – and not only in their look, but in the big box office returns they generated (and the first *Mad Max* was very low budget, by Hollywood standards).

fantasy films like *Delicatessen, Alien: Resurrection, The Matrix* and *The Fifth Element.*

Although a film such as *Blade Runner* was regarded as the utter highpoint of (postmodern) production design in contemporary cinema, the vision of the city of the future which cultural critics continue to deify, *Brazil* was perhaps more inventive, more extraordinary, and more persuasive. The inventiveness of *Brazil* is overwhelming. And *Brazil*, like *BladeRunner*, hasn't aged at all (the breakneck pace of the editing certainly helps).

TWELVE MONKEYS.

Twelve Monkeys (Universal, 1995) was a sci-fi thriller written by David and Jan Peoples (Peoples had co-written *Blade Runner*). Although known as a movie directed by Terry Gilliam, *Twelve Monkeys* is much more significant for its witty, clever, intricate screenplay, the narrative is far more satisfying than *BladeRunner*. It features familiar 1990s sci-fi themes: time travel, paranoia, a post-apocalyptic vision (a deadly virus which wipes out most of humanity), paranoia, Big Brother, an individual against the world, and a romance. Chris Marker's 1962 film *La Jetée* was the starting-point for *Twelve Monkeys*.[47]

Two big Hollywood stars (Bruce Willis and Brad Pitt) appeared, with Madeleine Stowe as the romantic interest, Dr Railly, who tries to save the hero, James Cole.[48] *TwelveMonkeys* was impressive on many levels: it had a beautifully worked-out script, which tied together a wealth of motifs and tiny details, cleverly fusing foreshadowed events and pay-offs. And the screenplay of *Twelve Monkeys* pushed the narrative along at a cracking pace.

There was a deep-seated passion, anger (and sometimes despair) at the heart of *Twelve Monkeys*, a romantic, humanistic view of life,. What gave the film its emotional power was the intensity with which Cole pursued his quest. Here, the standard fusion of two plot strands of his quest – saving the world and heterosexual romance – were deftly, convincingly performed. In *Twelve Monkeys*, Cole's involvement with Railly

---

[47] *La Jetée* was a powerful photo essay, essentially a series of black-and-white still photographs accompanied by a voiceover and sound effects. *La Jetée* concerned a man being sent through time in a scientific experiment, in a post-apocalyptic world; the *mise-en-scène* was expertly evoked by shadows, *film noir* lighting and deft editing.

[48] Cole was a familiar Hollywood lead: the reluctant hero, violent but basically good, flawed but redeemed in the end.

was critical to the central plot of time travel to save the world from the virus. She was the only one who believed in him, and who helped him.

THE MATRIX.

Warner Brothers' big sci-fi adventure series of the late 1990s and early 2000s, the *Matrix* trilogy, clearly drew on *Blade Runner* and the fiction of Philip K. Dick (the paranoia, the Big Brother aspects, the altered realities, etc), and stole wholesale from *Ghost In the Shell*. Cultural theorists and fan boys get very gooey about the *Matrix* films, but for me, beyond some cool designs and fun action sequences (overseen by the wonderful Yuen Woo-Ping, the grand master of martial arts choreographers), I can't think of much to say about them.

THE FIFTH ELEMENT.

Films such as *The Fifth Element* (Columbia/ Gaumont, 1997) were practically *hommages* to *Blade Runner*: movies are full of tensions, and in *The Fifth Element* there were conflicts between director Luc Besson's French *cinéma du look* approach, with its emphasis on cool visual style, and the Hollywood blockbuster, with its big budget, visual effects, spectacle, action and mainstream star (Bruce Willis).

The Fifth Element built upon *Blade Runner*'s future city look, with a New York City crammed with yellow taxis and NYPD cars flying between the skyscrapers; Willis's Korben Dallas was a kind of Deckard character (rebellious, a loner and outsider – but basically good); who's divorced, childless (how few action heroes are lumbered with children!); gets 'phoned up and berrated by his possessive mother; and wins the girl at the end.

There was also a replicant/ cyborg plot, with the female superbeing character Leeloo (Milla Jovovich, at the time Monsieur Besson's partner) being rebuilt in a scientific laboratory (she's the missing 'fifth element'.) Other *Blade Runner* aspects of *The Fifth Element* included the casting of Brion James, who played Leon the replicant in *Blade Runner*, and having Dallas being served food from a kind of flying Chinese junk, recalling the advertizing blimps, noodle bars and Chinatown setting in *Blade Runner*.[49]

---

[49] Another connection between *Blade Runner* and *The Fifth Element*: it used Moebius as a designer, who had influenced the look of the Philip K. Dick film. (Moebius and Jean-Claude Mézières were comic book artists whom Besson had enjoyed as a youth).

However, *The Fifth Element* was a postmodern *mélange* of earlier sci-fi and fantasy films (*2001: A Space Odyssey* and *Blade Runner* included), which added nothing new to the genre. There were shape-changing alien baddies (courtesy of CGI and masks, and recalling the aliens in *Men In Black*, made the same year), a psychopathic villain, Zorg (Gary Oldman), hardware (such as an enormous *Rambo*-style gun that could deliver bullets, arrows, flames, freezing ice, nets, etc), big sets (the opera house interior, for example), amazing costumes, lightspeed space travel, a *Star Wars*-style space battle, a chase through the upper storeys of New York City (oddly, to the sound of North African pop, probably Cheb Mami or Cheb Khaled, a distinctly 'French', cosmopolitan choice), and a plot involving: ancient races (as in *Stargate* and the *Indiana Jones* films), Milla Jovovich as the reconstituted 'fifth element' needed to save the world, a search for the MacGuffin (the four 'stones' of the four elements), concessions to political correctness (Tiny List Jr's President was black, secondary characters such as Chris Tucker's Rudy Rhod and Tricky were black), and an attack by an alien planet. As in other disaster films of the mid-1990s (*Armageddon, Deep Impact, Asteroid*), Earth was again threatened by an asteroid hurtling towards it.

AKIRA.

But while Western films such as *Batman, Brazil* and *The Fifth Element* took up some of *Blade Runner*'s ideas and visuals, it was the Japanese animation industry that really explored them to the full. Three are worth mentioning here – three of the most extraordinary movies ever made.[50] (I would also include anything by Hayao Miyazaki).[51]

Akira (1988) was one of the biggest-selling of Japanese *animé* films overseas (that and *Legend of the Overfiend*). If you've seen an *animé*, it's probably *Akira*. *Akira* was the baby of Katsuhiro Otomo: he directed the movie, wrote the script, designed it, and it was based on his *manga* comic strip (published in *Young* magazine).[52]

While film critics have raved endlessly about the visualization of

---

[50] *Cowboy Bebop, Final Fantasy* and *Evangelion* would be others.
[51] But I have recently published a book about Miyazaki, I won't include his matchless movies here.
[52] Otomo's follow-up to *Akira, Steam-boy*, eventually appeared in 2004, after many delays.

futuristic cities in movies such as *Blade Runner*, *Akira* went far beyond them. *Akira* was set in a post-apocalyptic Tokyo (called Neo-Tokyo), a city rebuilding itself. The design work on *Akira* was staggering: the acreage of detail in every shot, the inventiveness of the locations, the combinations of modern and postmodern architecture, the staging of the action, the choice of camera angles, and the framing. This was filmmaking of a very high quality and power of imagination. If you haven't seen *Akira*, you *must* see it.

Like many sci-fi films of the 1980s, *Akira* explored a post-apocalyptic society, a social breakdown combined with draconian measures to keep the populace in check, with the military taking over from politicians in policing the city (a common theme in Japanimation). *Akira* pitted young motorbike gangs against the military-industrial complex, against scientists, committees and generals.

There was a strong messianic, religious strand to *Akira*: a project experimenting with telepathy and supernormal powers in children goes out of control. One of the biker gang members, Tetsuo, becomes super-powerful, in the traditional *anime* fashion (which means lots of superhero devastation); and, at the end of the film, in the apocalyptic climax, the real, long-awaited Akira arrives – glimpsed as a young boy enveloped in white light.

Nuclear holocaust haunts *Akira*, reflecting the time of its creation – the mid-1980s, when anxiety over an escalation of arms resulting in an atomic conflict was intense. There's also a disturbing undercurrent in *Akira*, because it's made in and set in modern Japan, the only country (thus far) that has been bombed by nuclear weapons. This gives the images at the end of *Akira*, of a colossal hemisphere of white light that expands outwards and eats up the city, an added *frisson* of despair and horror.

Akira doesn't disappoint as an action movie: lots of motorbike chases, fights between rival biker gangs, gun battles (though not too many), and extraordinary scenes of destruction as Tetsuo chews up Neo-Tokyo. And there's a genuine epic dimension in *Akira*, which's lacking in many action-adventure films ('big' doesn't mean 'epic'). *Akira* is certainly as big, loud, pacey (and silly) as the best action-adventure movies, but there's a genuine mythic grandeur to the film. It derives partly from *Akira* being animation: it can be much more extravagant, visually, than a live-action film, it can go places, use camera angles and compositions, that are impossible in live-action (even with digital embellishments).

GHOST IN THE SHELL.

One of the most impressive of all movies that developed science fiction cinema from *Blade Runner* is *Ghost In the Shell* (1995), a masterpiece of Japanese animation, directed by Mamoru Oshii and scripted by Oshii and Kazunori Ito, from the *manga* by Masamune Shirow. Certainly *Ghost In the Shell* is one of the best of its kind – and it's a sci-fi action-adventure movie that can hold its own with the best of them, whether in live action (*Total Recall, Minority Report, Westworld, Planet of the Apes*), or in Japanese animation (*Laputa: Castle In the Sky, Legend of the Overfiend, Akira,* etc).[53] On its own terms, which is how the best movies operate, *Ghost In the Shell* works like gangbusters. Although well-known in *anime* circles, it really deserves to be much better known.[54] Simply in terms of animation, it's a masterwork.[55]

Ghost In the Shell centred on the Major, Motoko Kusanagi (beautifully voiced by Atsuko Tanaka), a cyborg cop (and, yes, she just happens to have a pneumatic body, with big boobs and a tight ass, and has to take her clothes off from time to time – but only to do her work, you understand.[56] And, yes, the plot does explain what her body is, a robot's shell, but don't let that fool you – it's tits and ass. And there's stuff with thermoptic camouflage suits and other technofetishism to explain what is basically a nude woman kicking butt. Show *Ghost In the Shell* to your girlfriends, your sisters, your mothers, your daughters, and they'll look at the nude robot

---

[53] As well as the two *Ghost In the Shell* feature films, there is a *Ghost In the Shell* animated series (2002) – *Ghost In the Shell: Stand Alone Complex* (with a number of series within series, too). *Ghost In the Shell: Stand Alone Complex* is one of the most accomplished of all Japanese *anime* TV shows.
[54] According to producer Joel Silver, super-nerds the Wachowski brothers showed him *Ghost In the Shell* to indicate the kind of look they were going for. *The Matrix* (1999) turned out to be virtually a remake of both *Ghost In the Shell* and *Akira*, with some scenes seemingly lifted wholesale, and details right down to the use of green, or the computer read-outs against black. Director Mamoru Oshii wasn't so bothered – he acknowledged that everyone takes from everyone else's work, and the parts employed in *The Matrix* were well done.
[55] Computers and digital networks are a major thematic component as well as the primary theme of the *Ghost In the Shell* movies. It's all about humans and technology again – which may be Japanese *anime*'s chief theme (in some *anime*, for instance, the theme is given an ecological slant, as in the movies of Hayao Miyazaki).
[56] The poster for *Ghost In the Shell* features an image of the naked Kusanagi, with her breasts prominent.

Motoko Kusanagi and shake their heads and laugh – *Ghost In the Shell* is totally boys' stuff).

Yes, *Ghost In the Shell* teases and titillates the audience – 'fan service', as it's sometimes called, though the term 'entertainment' covers it all: the credit sequence, which's fabulous, involves the naked cyborg being prepared for action, dipped in baths of different kinds, and the first action scene has Kusanagi up on the roof of some skyscraper in Hong Kong (not Tokyo this time) just about to launch herself over the edge. And what does she do before becoming the Android Cop Supreme? Takes her clothes off! Nope, not even Arnold Schwarzenegger or Bruce Willis or Harrison Ford went this far. In Japanese *animé*, it's always best to take your clothes off before leaping into action.

Ghost In the Shell was stuffed with imaginative ideas, spectacular and intricately detailed visuals, and brilliant staging of action (the budget was 600 million Yen = $6 million). It was sci-fi, the usual futuristic city and technologically advanced society. Yet, incredibly, *Ghost In the Shell* managed to explore serious metaphysical issues, like the best science fiction – such as the relation between humanity and artificial intelligence, between bodies and robots, and between machines and global capitalism.

Ghost In the Shell was another of those movies – like *Solaris*, *A.I.* or *Blade Runner* – that explored what it means to be human. Can a machine or a computer have a soul? Can an android have a human soul implanted in it? Does self-awareness in a machine equate to identity in humans? Can machines have children, with variety and individuality, or merely copies of themselves? (This was one of the futuristic notions of *Ghost In the Shell* – the 'ghost' or soul in a metal shell. Many of those questions have been central to the fiction of Philip K. Dick, and the movies based on his work).

And in *Ghost In the Shell* those questions really were part of the fabric of the piece, and weren't pretentious or pompous at all. Partly because from the beginning, *Ghost In the Shell* announces that it's not going to be your usual shoot-em-up cyborg cop action-adventure movie. It's going to stop and *think*. Really think! Wow. A film that thinks!

Ghost In the Shell is highly successful in depicting computerization on screen. A difficult, complex and abstract thing, but *Ghost In the Shell* gets closer than most movies – especially in the fusion of computer read-outs, and those streams of green numbers, and the layers of coloured digital images sliding over each other. Because in this movie, as in the sequel, the 'check-mate' really occurs inside computer networks. So *Ghost In the Shell* is really *the* great cyber-thrillers, a movie in which the cyberspace/ cyborg/ hi-tech element really is fundamental to the plot and the theme (and the characters, who are all technologically augmented in some way or another).

There was also time in *Ghost In the Shell* for a few slower-paced montages, with dialogue and action replaced by mesmerizing (predominantly static) images set to music. The stand-out slow-paced montage was the canal sequence: highly unusual in an action movie, or a cop thriller, it comprised elaborate and beautiful images of downtown Hong Kong, focussing on the canal area (essentially a mood piece, it was dominated by Kenji Kawai's fabulous music).

And then there's the animation: *Ghost In the Shell* was mounted very much in the *Akira* style: moody images of a futuristic city coloured in blues and blacks, with many scenes taking place at night. Cars, buildings, props, weapons and bodies were sleek, professional, hi-tech. It's one of those cities of the future with soaring skyscrapers, multi-lane freeways and bridges, neons and signage everywhere, and dingy back streets and alleys (for the chases on foot).

The romance in *Ghost In the Shell* is between two cyborgs – Kusanagi and Batou (Batou is not a full android, but he's close). Or it's a romance between a guy with plenty of cyborgian embellishments and a robot. And that's weird – but no weirder than *BladeRunner* (it's sick, as Rutger Hauer put it – Deckard and Rachel – *yeeuuwww!*).

The sequel, *Ghost In the Shell 2: Innocence* (Mamoru Oshii, 2004), was similarly wonderful to look at, with some divinely accomplished animation (in particular the fusion of 2-D and 3-D elements). At the level of detail, *Ghost In the Shell 2* was sumptuous animation (the budget was high for a Japanese animated movie, at 1,000 million Yen (= $10 million). In the West, it would've cost a zillion times that). *Ghost In the Shell 2* was entered in the best movie category at the Cannes Film Festival.

So many aspects of *Ghost In the Shell 2* were superlative. There was so much going in *Ghost In the Shell 2*, so much that was astonishing visually (and musically – Kenji Kawai was back composing the music). For

Mamoru Oshii, the story in the *Ghost In the Shell* sequel wasn't complicated at all: 'it may look like a confusing movie as I have been told by many people, but to me, *it is a simple love story*' (my emphasis).[57]

LEGEND OF THE OVERFIEND.

Aside from *Akira*, the *Legend of the Overfiend* series (1987-1993) is one of the most remarkable examples of filmmaking in the contemporary era, which makes almost everything that Hollywood and Europe turns out look pitifully tame. *Legend of the Overfiend* is a mass of phallic, testosterone, hormone-driven Japanese *animé* fantasy.

Legend of the Overfiend is disarming and compelling because of the sheer intensity and rapidity of the imagery. The film barely lets up for a moment, careening from one gory superhero battle to the next. The comicbook style of Japanese *manga* is exaggerated to the point of total optical saturation: it's all bright colours, panoramic views of Osaka and Tokyo at night, giant full moons, human figures that soar through the air, demonic faces with livid red eyes, phallic tentacles hundreds of feet long plunging into flesh, and never-ending, violent corporeal transformations. For some, it's porn, sexist, violent, for others (myself included), it's visionary and boundlessly inventive filmmaking.

In *Akira*, *Ghost In the Shell*, and *Legend of the Overfiend* and similar Japanese animated films, the futuristic cityscapes of *Blade Runner* are expanded and energized. Above the city lights and skyscrapers in *Blade Runner* flying vehicles dreamily float along, accompanied by washes of Vangelis's melancholy synthesizers. In *Akira*, *Ghost In the Shell*, *Legend of the Overfiend* and other similar Japanese movies, mile-long tentacles hurtle through the air, storms rage, humans transform into gigantic demons, and whole sections of the cities are exploding or being crushed.

In the air above Los Angeles in *Blade Runner*, the worst that can happen is getting a bit of dust in your giant eye as you stare hypnotized through the spinner's windshield at distant flashing lights. In *Legend of the Overfiend*, if you're up in the air, you're going to be penetrated in every orifice and all over your body by speeding tentacles, or you'll be blown to pieces, or you might be fucked by some two hundred foot demon.

---

57 M. Oshii, in M. Koepke, "Fantastic Phantasms", *Hour*, 2004.

BLADE RUNNER TODAY

Today, *Blade Runner* can appear a little slow: made now, it would be much faster, with more action beats, and the action beats would be much louder, more violent, and much longer. Ironically, it would probably be a *longer* film, though: because despite editing being more rapid in contemporary cinema (i.e., shot lengths are shorter on average), Hollywood films are actually longer on average: instead of one hour fifty minutes or whatever *Blade Runner* is, it would probably be two hours twenty minutes, or even more (which's far too long, I reckon).[58]

The replicants mutineering on some spaceship (like a slave uprising) would undoubtedly be the action beat that would open *Blade Runner* if it was produced today: a long, complex visual effects scene costing 20 million, it would involve lots of gunplay and explosions and deaths, and would show the replicants in action as nasty critters. Having Leon shoot Holden in the Tyrell pyramid just isn't quite as juicy.

A scene introducing Deckard in a stylish and memorable fashion would be necessary, too: in the film he's standing in the street reading a newspaper, waiting for his food to be cooked. He could be anybody, and that static scene doesn't do much to describe his character.

A contemporary version of *Blade Runner* would surely introduce the character in action. An early draft of the script had Deckard showing up at a farm and wasting the farmer, who turns out to be a replicant. That's better, because it shows Deckard doing his job: in the film as is, Deckard doesn't get to show what sort of a blade runner he actually is until halfway through the movie, when he shoots and kills Zhora.

It's the stately pace of *Blade Runner* that would be altered today, that some newer viewers coming to the film might find just too s-l-o-w.[59]

In many circles, *Blade Runner* will be regarded as one of the great science fiction movies, as well as one of the great films of recent times. Maybe. But if it is a masterpiece, it is also flawed. *Blade Runner* is

---

[58] On shot lengths and changing fashions in Hollywood cinema, see David Bordwell's wonderful book *The Way Hollywood Tells It*.
[59] I've used *Blade Runner* with GCSE students in the U.K. (16 year-olds), back in 1992, when we looked at a bit of *Blade Runner* each week across 13 weeks. I just about got away with it: it was a slow movie for the classroom, but the spellbinding visuals kept them hooked. (I also used *Tess* (1979) – what was I thinking?! A girlie 19th century costume drama with a female lead in a room of restless working-class 16 year-olds!).

staggeringly good, but there are flaws: the plot creaks, there are clichés, the casting isn't quite spot on (Sean Young), and some of the performances are routine. *Blade Runner* isn't an out-and-out classic, like *Citizen Kane*, *The Seven Samurai* or *Contempt*.

Illustrations

• Some photos of locations used in *Blade Runner* taken by me in 2008.

• Some images from *Blade Runner*.
(Photos © The Blade Runner Partnership/ Warner Brothers).

• Some influences on *BladeRunner*, such as *Star Wars, film noir*, and future cities.
(Courtesy of MGM; Universal; Columbia; Warner Brothers; Lucasfilm; and 20th Century Fox).

• Some images from *Total Recall, A Scanner Darkly, Next, Paycheck, Screamers, Impostor,* and *Minority Report.*
(Courtesy of Universal; 20th Century Fox; DreamWorks; Dimension Films; Lion's Gate; Carolco; Warner Brothers; Paramount; Miramax; Sony/ Columbia; and Columbia/ TriStar).

The opening shot of *Blade Runner*.

Actually, no - it's Los Angeles at night from Griffith Park.

This and other *Blade Runner* locations on the following pages are from photos by the author.

This page and the following page,
the famous Bradbury Building in downtown L.A.

Union Station, in downtown L.A., used for the Bryant's office scenes in *Blade Runner*.

This page and the following pages:
the famous New York set on the Warners' Burbank backlot,
where much of *Blade Runner* (and countless other movies)
was filmed.

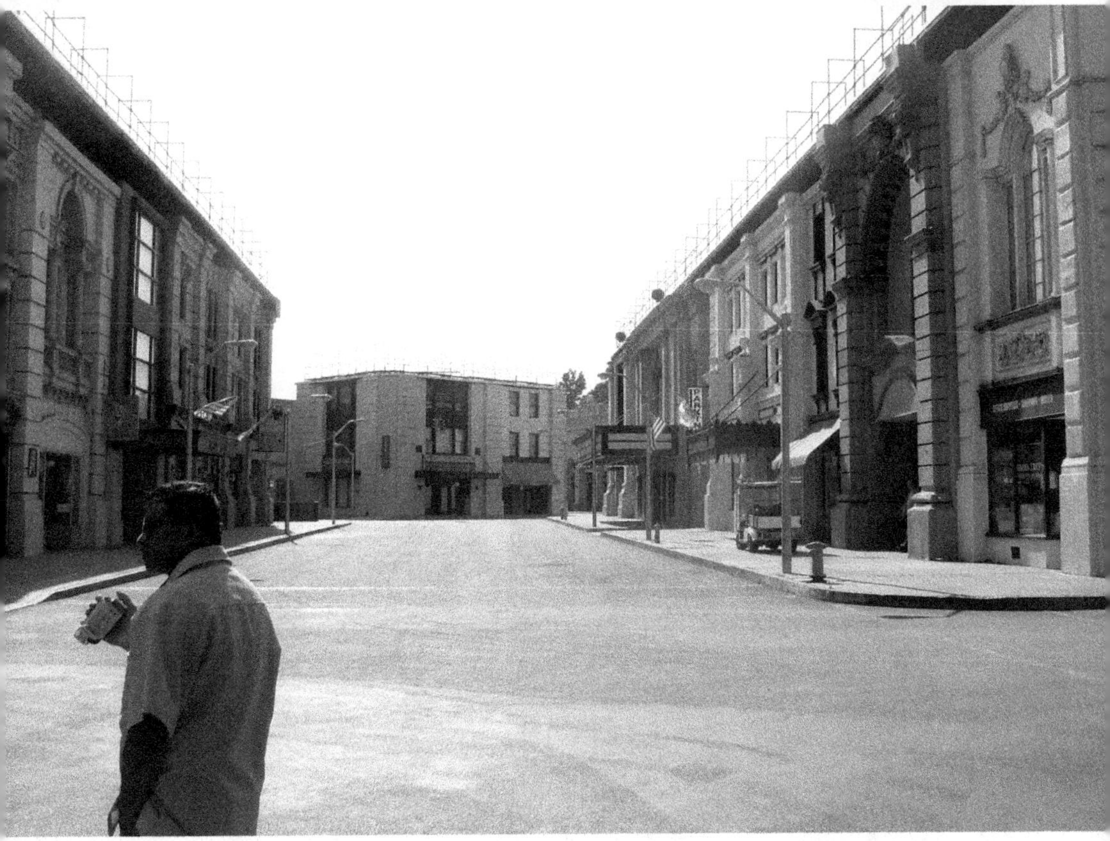

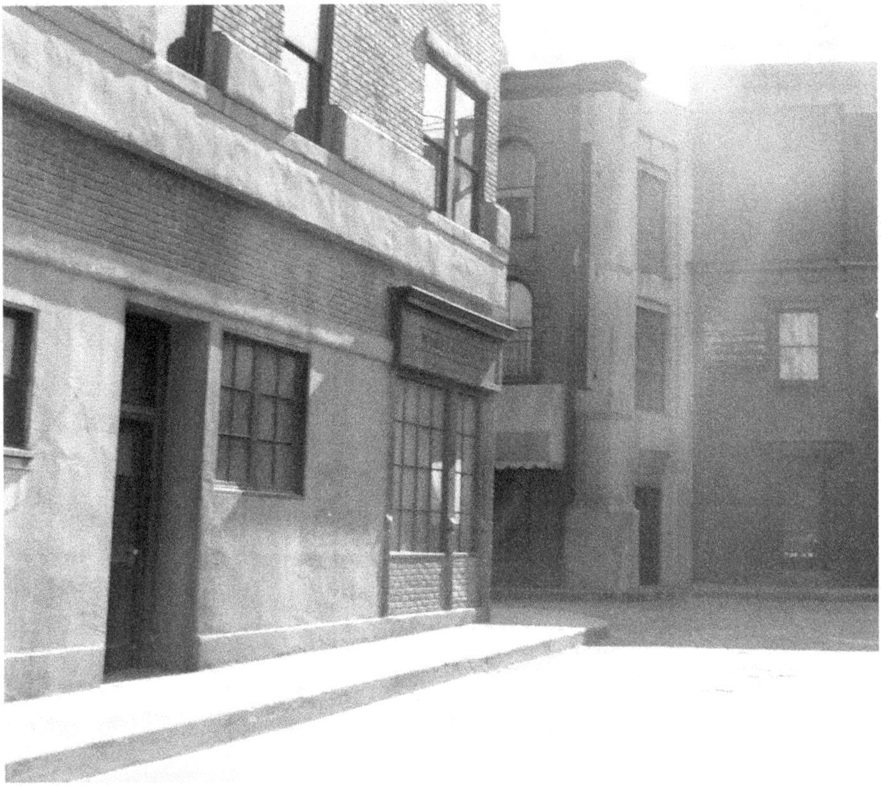

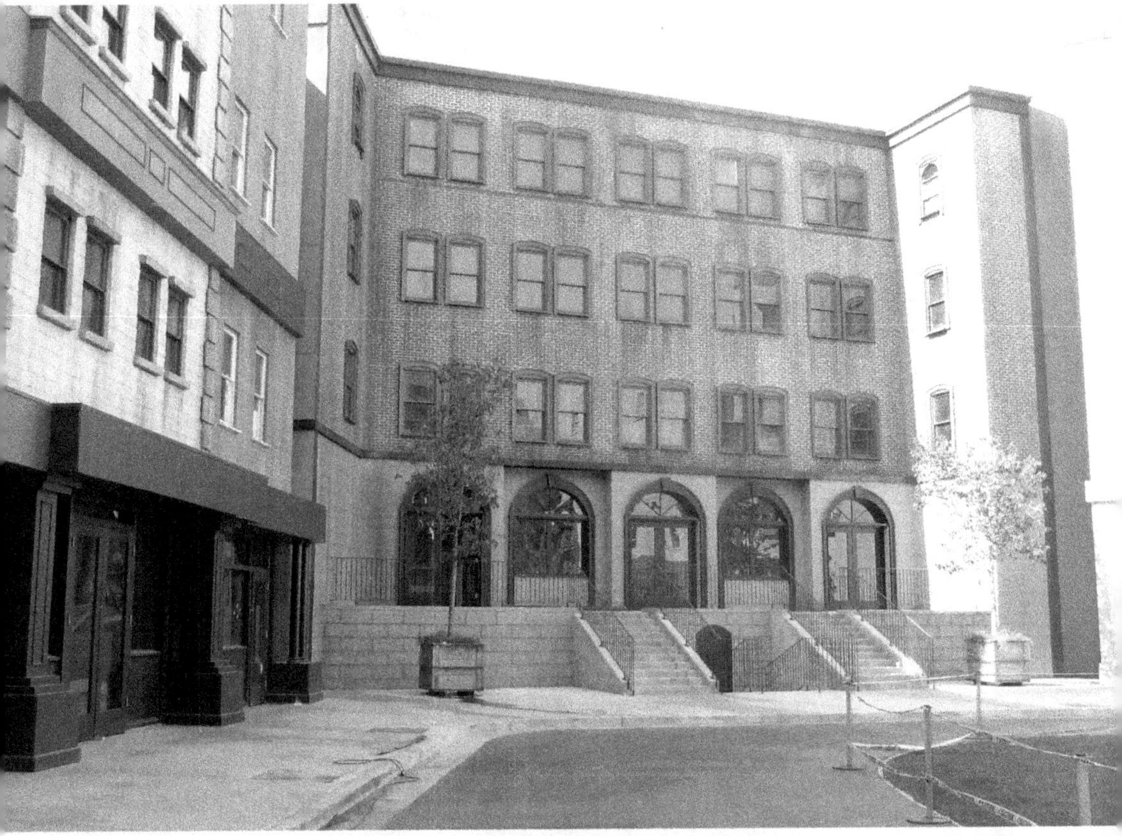

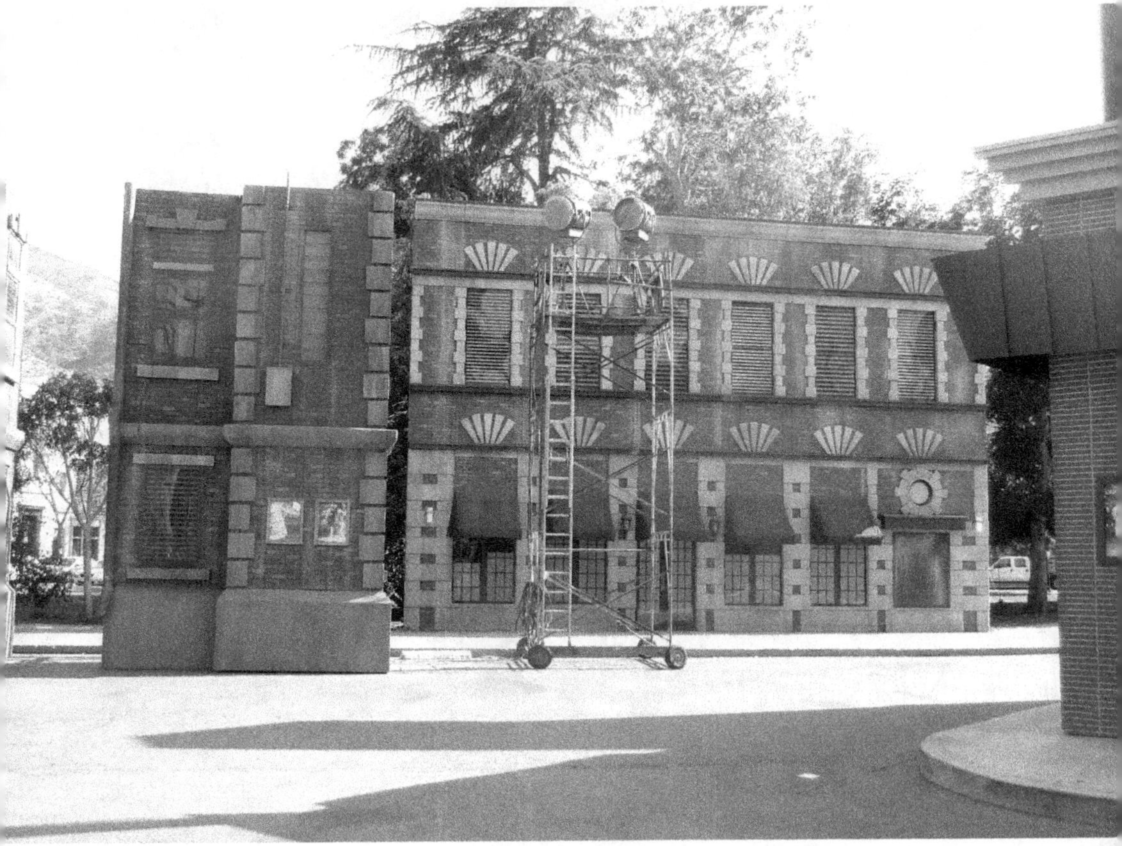

Cities of the future: *Blade Runner* took inspiration from cities such as
Los Angeles, New York City and San Francisco (above, photos by J.M. Robinson),
and from Hong Kong and Tokyo (below).

Chinatowns – in L.A. (below) and San Francisco (left and above).

Little Tokyo, in downtown L.A.

The great metropolis of New York City, in Fall, 2008.
Director Ridley Scott recalled that one of the inspirations for the city in *Blade Runner* was the experience of flying over New York in a helicopter, from the airport.

Midtown Manhattan, with its dense, busy street life that *Blade Runner* draws on

(© The Blade Runner Partnership/ Warner Bros.)

Blade Runner
(The Blade Runner Partnership/ Warner Brothers)

Some influences on *Blade Runner*:
Film noir classics: the sublime Rita Hayworth in *Gilda*, top left.
Bogie and Bacall in *The Big Sleep*, one of cinema's great couples, above right.
And Orson Welles' masterpiece, *Touch of Evil*, above.

Star Wars, below.
The director of *Blade Runner*, Ridley Scott, remarked of *Star Wars*: 'frankly, I couldn't believe it.' As *Star Wars* influenced *Blade Runner* (and *Alien*), so *Blade Runner* would in turn influence the later *Star Wars* films. The downtown area of Coruscant in 2002's *Attack of the Clones*, for example, with its neons and Asian look, resembles *Blade Runner* (as well as the cities in *Total Recall* and *The Fifth Element*).

(© Universal, Warner Brothers, Columbia, 20th Century Fox/ Lucasfilm)

The most influential city of the future in cinema,
in UFA's *Metropolis* (1927)

A hit movie for 20th Century Fox, which influenced *Blade Runner*: *Alien*.
(© 20th Century Fox, 1979)

2001: A Space Odyssey (© MGM, 1968)

RoboCop (© Orion/ MGM, 1987)

A signature image in *Total Recall*:
Arnold Schwarzenegger crossdressing, and an exploding head.
(© Carolco, 1990)

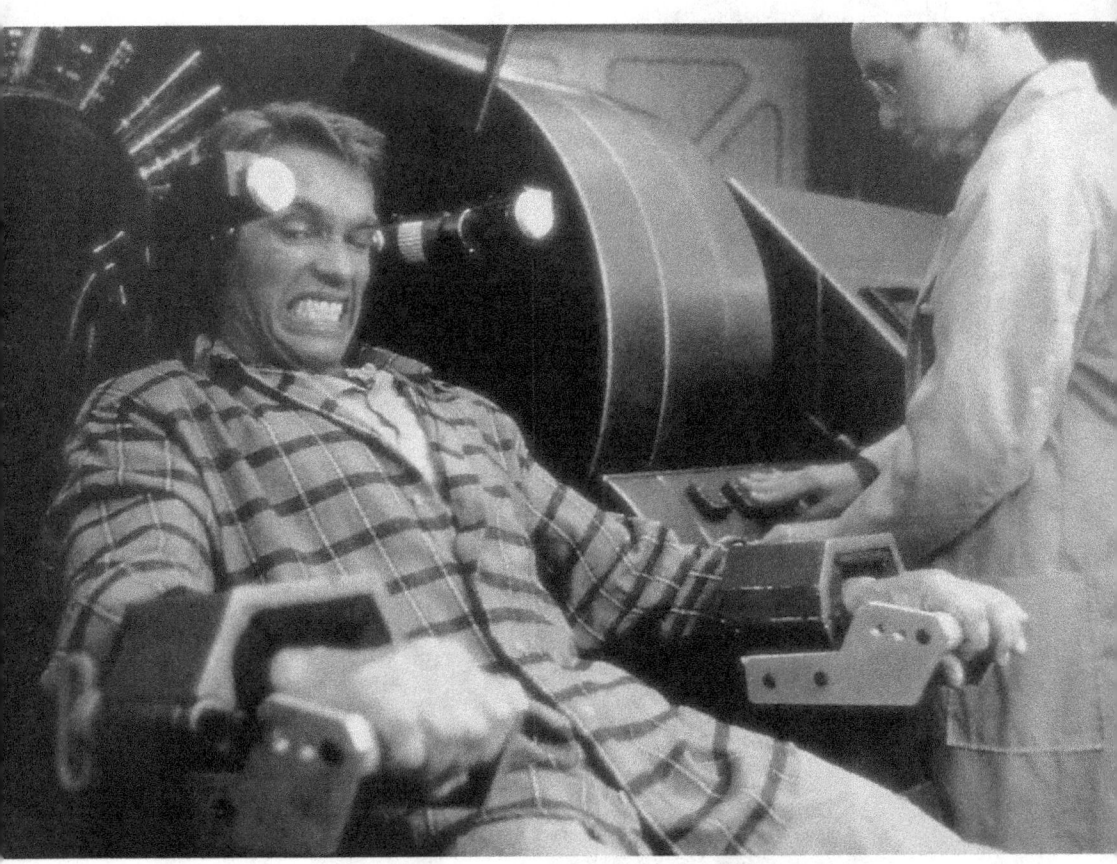

Total Recall (© Carolco, 1990)

Total Recall (© Carolco, 1990)

An influence on *Blade Runner*, especially in terms of visual fx, which were produced by the same company, EEG. *Close Encounters of the Third Kind* (Columbia, 1977)

Jurassic Park (© Universal, 1993)

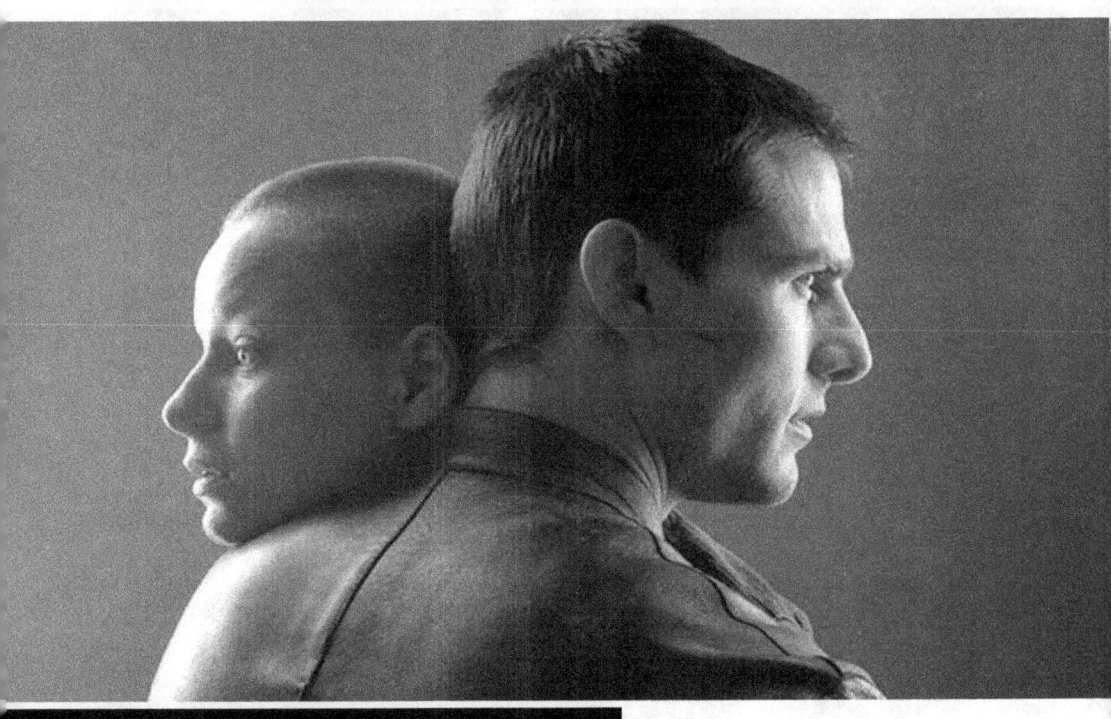

A nod to Ingmar Bergman's 1966 masterpiece *Persona* in *Minority Report*. Like many filmmakers, Steven Spielberg went thru an Ingmar Bergman period, seeing everything by the Swedish director. One of Bergman's favourite actors, Max von Sydow, stars in *Minority Report*.
(© 20th Century Fox/ DreamWorks, 2002)

(© Paramount, 2007)

Paycheck, above (© Paramount/ DreamWorks, 2003)
Impostor, below (© Dimension Films/ Miramax, 2002)

A Scanner Darkly (© Warner Independent)

Darn, why does the woman always turn out
to be a robot at the end of a Philip K. Dick movie?
Screamers (© Triumph Films/ Sony, 1995)

3
TOTAL RECALL

> He awoke – and wanted Mars. The valleys, he thought. What would it be like to trudge among them? ...*I will go*, he said to himself. *Before I die I'll see Mars.*
>
> Philip K. Dick, "We Can Remember It For You Wholesale" (MR, 267)

PAUL VERHOEVEN

Paul Verhoeven (born July 18, 1938, in Amsterdam) is a veteran of many movies, including, before his move to America: *What Zien Ik* (a.k.a. *Business Is Business/ Any Special Way*, 1971), *Turks Fruit* (*Turkish Delight*, 1973), *Keetje Tippel* (a.k.a *Cathy/ Katy Tippel/ A Girl Called Katy Tippel/ Hot Sweat*, 1975), *Soldaat van Oranje* (*Soldier of Orange*, 1977), *Spetters* (1980), the critically acclaimed *The Fourth Man* (1983) and *Flesh + Blood*

(1985), a mediæval action epic (and international co-production). With 1987's *RoboCop* (made for Rank/ Orion), Verhoeven went to Hollywood. He married Martine Tours in 1967, and has two children (Claudia and Helen).

Paul Verhoeven is not an 'ordinary' Hollywood director for hire. Because he's made some action films and sci-fi special effects extravangazas, he can be put in the same group as John McTiernan, Tony Scott, James Cameron, Michael Bay, Joel Schumacher, Andrew Davis, Peter Hyams, and fellow Europeans who came to Hollywood in the 1980s and after: Wolfgang Petersen, Renny Harlin, Jan de Bont and Roland Emmerich. However, Verhoeven is quite a different fish from the American action directors and his Continental cohorts; while most Hollywood directors, wherever they come from, are conservative, turning in standard, formulaic movies, Verhoeven is *much* stranger, and, importantly, politically subversive. There's no one quite like Paul Verhoeven.

The more expensive a film, the more pressure there is to turn in a product that will make its money back, that will have all the interesting edges smoothed off it, that will not do anything to disrupt its ability to maximize its potential audience. Paul Verhoeven's Hollywood pictures do all that, they deliver action, thrills, cliff-hangers, countdowns, chases, heroes, gore and violence, but there is also an exploration of the darker side, cynicism, pessimism, and, Verhoeven's particular penchant, the hypocrisy and lie of the Great American Dream.

Even when James Cameron, Renny Harlin, Michael Bay or Roland Emmerich are making films encompassing dystopias or corruption or cynicism, there is *always*, finally, by the end of the flick, an endorsement of the American way of life, a recourse to ideologically conservative values.

With Paul Verhoeven's cinema, it's different: by the end of his movies, the hypocrisies, lies and disillusionment underlying the American Dream are exposed: for example, many of the main characters in *Starship Troopers* die, and the audience has been cheering on a fascist state. *Basic Instinct* has no happy ending: Tramell and Curran may in bed talking about 'living happily ever after', fucking like minks (but maybe not raising rugrats), but there's still an ice pick under the bed. At the end of *Total Recall*, Quaid is maybe lobotomized, a vegetable, and the preceding hour and a half has been a dream. *Showgirls* ends with Nomi, after a lengthy dissection of the

American Dream in Las Vegas – having exploited all the other exploiters around her, put her rival in hospital (and her friend raped) – heading for Hollywood, another megalopolis of vice and corruption.

What distinguishes Paul Verhoeven from his contemporaries among action film directors – Cameron, Bay, McTiernan, Schumacher, Davis, Hyams – is that he is willing to push things further, to make his action extra violent, and to foreground his sly humour and subversive view of modern America.

Paul Verhoeven also makes his sex scenes more explicit and unashamedly sexy than any of his contemporaries in the blockbuster genre.[1] Action blockbuster directors have no problem with making violence graphic and gory, sometimes to a psychotic and repellent degree, but shy away from doing the same with lovemaking (and many won't even film nudity).[2] A Verhoeven blockbuster outing always has more layers than that of action and adventure and the single subtext allowed by a Hollywood studio of his contemporaries. A Verhoeven film routinely includes levels which criticize the ideology, the narrative and the form of the picture.

Like many of his contemporaries (including Ridley Scott and Steven Spielberg), Paul Verhoeven has tried many different genres – the Second World War epic (*Soldier of Orange*), the historical costume drama (*Keetje Tippel*), a contemporary Hitchcockian thriller (*The Fourth Man* and *Basic Instinct*), sci-fi blockbusters (*Starship Troopers* and *RoboCop*), horror (*The Hollow Man*), mediæval adventure (*Floris* and *Flesh + Blood*), and so on.

One of the reasons he went to America, Paul Verhoeven said, was so he could make those genres – thrillers, musicals and science fiction. In Holland, Verhoeven remarked, films tended to be about the middle-classes, intellectuals, doctors, lawyers (and Verhoeven also wanted to make high budget movies: the Dutch film industry, and European co-productions, can't really produce *Lawrence of Arabia*).

Paul Verhoeven was concerned not to go to America and make a 'state

---

[1] Sharon Stone wasn't willing to disrobe for *Total Recall*, though, Verhoeven remarked.
[2] Critics have drawn attention to the reserve or non-existence of love scenes in Ridley Scott's films, for instance: Scott says he regards sex scenes as redundant in a script. Maybe. But look at *Gladiator*: the violence is excessively brutal – far, far beyond what is necessary for the drama, the plot, the themes and the whole movie, and it goes *on* and *on*, in fight after fight (and seems even longer on DVD). But the romance between Maximus and Lucilla is as demure and restrained as a nun visiting a dying relative in hospital. (In *The Fall of the Roman Empire* Lucilla was played by Sophia Loren and Commodus by Christopher Plummer. Maximus is clearly drawn on Spartacus as played by Kirk Douglas).

of the nation' film straight away, a picture about contemporary America, which might have alienated the audience and the studios. Instead, Verhoeven explored present-day America via genre pieces (sci-fi in *RoboCop* and *Total Recall*, the *film noir* thriller in *Basic Instinct*). Sci-fi films weren't really about science fiction, Verhoeven said: *RoboCop*, for instance, was really 'about a man who has lost his identity' (R. van Scheers, 183). It was also about policing the State, and, being an action/ sci-fi thriller, was inevitably violent (it was re-edited 7 times before it was passed with an 'R' rating).[3]

Following *RoboCop*, the movie offers flowed in, and Paul Verhoeven considered making *Black Rain*. By 1993, Paul Verhoeven was no. 33 in *Premiere* magazine 'Power 100' list, above Robert Zemeckis, Harrison Ford, Jack Nicholson and Martin Scorsese. While many directors in Hollywood form their own production companies, shoot pop promos or commercials, executive produce other people's films, or become (like George Lucas, Steven Spielberg and Francis Coppola), new media moguls, with their own studios, Verhoeven was content just to make movies.

Total Recall was an even bigger success for Paul Verhoeven than *RoboCop*, beating all the other action movies in 1990 at the box office (*Back to the Future 3*, *Die Hard 2*, *Presumed Innocent*, *Teenage Mutant Ninja Turtles*, *The Hunt for Red October*, *Days of Thunder*, *Dick Tracy*, *Another 48 Hrs.*, *Rocky 5*, *Bird on a Wire* and *Arachnophobia*). However, at no. 5 in 1990, *Total Recall* was topped by *Home Alone*, *Ghost*, *Pretty Woman* and *Dances with Wolves*.

Paul Verhoeven is a director who likes to get involved with every aspect of movie-making, and is a big presence on set. Peter Weller, who starred in *RoboCop*, said that working with Verhoeven was not laidback:

> His is a very aggressive kind of movie-making; he's in your face; you feel it's not just a movie that you are making, you feel that this guy has a vision and it is going to happen his way or else he is going to die. (R. van Scheers, ix-x)

Spetters' star Renée Soutendijk remarked that Paul Verhoeven demanded 'unconditional loyalty. Every obstacle is seen as a personal

---

[3] Verhoeven had declined doing *RoboCop* at first: he thought it was a silly story, but his wife Martine convinced him to do it. She also persuaded Verhoeven to take on *Basic Instinct*, and to work with Arnold Schwarzenegger (PV, 28).

attack. If he senses mistrust, it drives him crazy' (ib., 134). Many commentators remarked on Verhoeven's energy, his single-mindedness, his obliviousness to danger when he's shooting. He wasn't a director to sit in his trailer, or direct by video or messengers, he loved being in the thick of things. He would do whatever was required to get the shot, even if it meant jumping into the sea next to an actor, or showing an actor how to drive a car at high speed (during *The Fourth Man*). Jan de Bont, who shot many of Verhoeven's films as cinematographer, and went on to direct himself (*Speed, Twister, The Haunting*), said that Verhoeven was obsessive about details and hard work, and expected everyone else working on the movie to be like that.

Like many European directors, such as Rainer Werner Fassbinder, Jean-Luc Godard and Wim Wenders, Paul Verhoeven became enamoured of American films: especially adventure epics, Errol Flynn, *Tarzan*, Westerns, and Alfred Hitchcock.[4] With his father, Verhoeven saw *The War of the Worlds* some ten times ('we both thought it was fantastic'). He said he saw *Vertigo* 20 times. Verhoeven agreed with Luis Buñuel that

> the films you see as a child, roughly between the ages of 8 and 16, determine your creative taste later on. You will even quote from them as a director without specifically or consciously searching for them. (R. van Scheers, 13)

At the Nederlandse Filmacademie in Amsterdam, Paul Verhoeven encountered the work of François Truffaut, Buñuel and Godard. His first films, made as a student, were highly influenced by the Surrealists, by Buñuel and Salvador Dali. He listed his ten favourite movies (in 1995) as *La Dolce Vita, Some Like It Hot, Lawrence of Arabia, Doctor Zhivago, Touch of Evil, Ivan the Terrible, North By Northwest, Ben-Hur, Metropolis* and *Gone With the Wind* (a typical set of 'classic' films, all of which feature regularly in many filmmakers' top tens).

Paul Verhoeven's penchant was for epic movies, 'made by directors with big reputations'. Verhoeven loved David Lean, and *Lawrence of Arabia* especially. Like Steven Spielberg, Verhoeven has tried to put a little of Lean's epic style on screen (there are obvious allusions to Columbia's 1962 desert epic in the battle scenes in *Starship Troopers*).

---

[4] Alfred Hitchcock, I still stubbornly maintain, is a British not an American filmmaker.

Lawrence of Arabia was a touchstone for many filmmakers of Paul Verhoeven's generation, including George Lucas, John Milius, James Cameron, Peter Guber and Martin Scorsese. There's more than a little *Vertigo* and *North By Northwest* in *Basic Instinct* (Alfred Hitchcock's work contains everything a film student needs to know about cinematic technique, Verhoeven avowed). There's quite a bit of *Touch of Evil* in there, too, as Verhoeven acknowledged – particularly Orson Welles's extraordinary camera movements, and the *film noir mise-en-scène*; Verhoeven said that *Touch of Evil* should be compulsory in film schools, 'because the way Welles leads the camera makes the film the most interesting production of the last forty years' (R. van Scheers, 241).

A scene of skeletons in *Metropolis* was quoted in *Total Recall*, while *Metropolis*'s Maria influenced the design of RoboCop (and *Metropolis* was a key film for *Blade Runner*, and for other films based on Philip K. Dick's fiction); *Ben-Hur*'s famous chariot race was referenced in *Spetters*; Peter Weller's walk in *RoboCop* recalled *Ivan the Terrible*; and *Flesh + Blood* took on Sam Peckinpah and *The Wild Bunch*.5

Akira Kurosawa was another Paul Verhoeven favourite. Verhoeven said he watched *Rashomon* or *The Seven Samurai* (or *Ivan the Terrible* or *Vertigo*) two or three times a year to remind himself that films could be art. The warrior ethics of Kurosawa's mediæval samurai and Kurosawa's total mastery of cinematic action can be seen in the movies of Francis Coppola, Hayao Miyazaki, John Woo, John Milius, Bernardo Bertolucci and George Lucas.

The nemesis of *Blade Runner*, Rutger Hauer, became something of an alter ego on screen for Paul Verhoeven, as with François Truffaut and Jean-Pierre Léaud. Hauer appeared as Floris in Verhoeven's TV series *Floris*, an artist in *Turks Fruit*, in *Keetje Tippel*, in *Soldaat van Oranje* and *Flesh + Blood*. For a long time Hauer was Verhoeven's favourite actor; Hauer made the move to Hollywood a year or two before Verhoeven, appearing in films such as *Blade Runner, Ladyhawke* and *The Hitcher*.

Paul Verhoeven returned to the sci-fi genre with *Starship Troopers* (1997), made by Sony/ Columbia, based on Robert Heinlein's 1959 novel. It was a special effects action-adventure movie, costing some 95 million

---

5 Verhoeven was a big fan of Peckinpah's movies, including his earlier, lesser-known films, such as *Ride the High Country*, a terrific Western (PV, 41).

bucks. The budget was Verhoeven's largest up to that time, and quite different from his films of the 1970s, which were made on one or two million guilders (with the director typically taking a 20,000 guilder fee).

Starship Troopers was a satire on contemporary America and on fascism. For Paul Verhoeven, it was a cheeky send-up of American right-wing politics, self-consciously subversive. However, many audiences (and critics) took *Starship Troopers* straight, assuming it to be an action-adventure movie about Earthlings travelling to distant planets to kill giant bugs.

There are numerous links between Ridley Scott, director of *Blade Runner*, and Paul Verhoeven. After *RoboCop*, Verhoeven had contemplated making *Black Rain*. Six directors had been involved with it since 1980, including Russell Mulcahy, David Cronenberg, Fred Schepisi, Lewis Teague and Richard Rush (Verhoeven got close to making it). The result, made by Ridley Scott, was a forgettable cop thriller set in the Far East.

Before directing *Showgirls*, Paul Verhoeven was due to helm a $120 million mediæval epic entitled *Crusade*, an Arnold Schwarzenegger vehicle. Cooked up by Verhoeven and Arny on the set of *Total Recall*, *Crusade* was to feature cinema's most famous cyborg as the slave Hagen in 1095, joining the First Crusade, led by Godfrey of Bouillon. 'I've always wanted to do a movie about the Crusades,' Verhoeven said, and his film would be in the style of Sergei Eisenstein's *Ivan the Terrible*.

Unfortunately, although the blockbuster project *Crusade* got near to shooting (22,000 costumes were made, contracts signed and locations selected),[6] Carolco dropped it, because it was producing another very expensive movie at the same time (*Cutthroat Island*, directed by Renny Harlin). The budget looked like it would reach $120 million.[7] The *Crusade* project eventually turned up in 2005, helmed by Ridley Scott. But, oh how woeful was *Kingdom of Heaven*!

Paul Verhoeven and Ridley Scott have produced movies in the same genres: *Kingdom of Heaven* has a counterpart in the mediæval warfare of

---
[6] Robert Duvall was going to do a cameo, and John Turturro would've played the evil brother.
[7] Verhoeven said, 'the more I know of the logistical difficulties, the high price of shooting in Europe, I don't see how I can do it for less. I'm talking about scenes where you take 10,000 people, move them through the mountains, then have battle scenes with that many people and 1,500 horses.'

Flesh + Blood, *Black Hawk Down* has links with Verhoeven's World War 2 films, they've both made costume dramas (*Katy Tippel*, *1492*), contemporary thrillers (*The Fourth Man*, *Black Rain*, *Hannibal*), and *Someone To Watch Over Me* is a kind of erotic thriller (though nowhere near as successful as *Basic Instinct*). And both Scott and Verhoeven have produced some of the key sci-fi flicks of the past decades: *Alien*, *Blade Runner*, *Total Recall*, *RoboCop* and *Starship Troopers*.

TOTAL RECALL

> He glanced up at Quail. 'You'll know you've been all right,' he said. 'You won't remember us, won't remember me or ever having been here. It'll be a real trip in your mind; we guarantee that. A full two weeks of recall; every last piddling detail. Remember this: if at any time you doubt that you really took an extensive trip to Mars you can return here and get a full refund. You see?'
>
> Philip K. Dick, *We Can Remember It For You Wholesale*[8]

Total Recall was based on Philip K. Dick's story "We Can Remember It For You Wholesale" (1966) about a man, Douglas Quail (it's Quaid in the film),[9] who undergoes a memory implant operation as a luxury vacation trip to Mars; the Rekal people find out he was an Interplan agent whose real memory had been buried under artificial memories; several plot twists later, it is not certain which Quaid is the 'real' one, which story is the true one, and so on.

The same Philip K. Dick themes explored in *Blade Runner* occur: the relation between 'reality' and 'artificiality', between 'reality' and 'illusion', between real life and dreams, real life and memories, etc. Conspiracy and paranoia abound. Alternate identities were of course fundamental to Dick's fiction (Quaid's alarmed to find he might once have been Hauser, Cohaagen's friend and key operative). One of the fascinating notions in

---
[8] In *Minority Report*, 270.
[9] According to John Brosnan, the name Quail was changed because of its similarity to Dan Quayle, the then Vice President (1991, 371). Or maybe it was because Arny didn't wanna play a guy called Quail.

Total Recall is the idea of taking a vacation away from yourself:

> Was this the answer? After all, an illusion, no matter how convincing, remained nothing more than an illusion. At least objectively. But subjectively – quite the opposite entirely. (MR, 269)

The 1990 film does ask serious questions – such as: what constitutes identity? How much of one's identity is one's memories and one's past? Is a person the sum of their experiences, their memories? And if memories – and dreams – can be manufactured and injected into someone, do they remain the same person? Similar issues were explored in *BladeRunner*, with the memories Tyrell implanted in the robots. 'More than the real thing, sir', as McClane puts it in Phil Dick's story (MR, 270).

Rekal's production of memories in the 1966 story will be even better than real memories, which can be vague and incomplete, as McClane tells Quail: the manufactured memories will be superior to real memories. Paul Verhoeven remarked:

> What interested me in *Total Recall* was its two different layers of reality: 1) the story about this man who finds out that he is a secret agent and people are chasing him and he is saving the entire planet at the end and 2) the fact that you could also see it as a story about a man that is dreaming all that up and ends up being lobotomized. And those two stories are indeed kind of interesting from a physical point of view. (PV, 102)

Paul Verhoeven said he wanted both the 'real life' and dream/ memory sequences to be 'true', the doubling effect expressing Werner Heisenberg's principle of uncertainty. 'The quintessence of the film is that Quaid likes the dream so much he does not want to wake up', remarked Verhoeven; but neither do the audience – they also want the dream to continue, and to partially forget that they're watching a dream (R. van Scheers, 223). Verhoeven asked scriptwriters Ronald Shusett and Gary Goldman to extend Doctor Edgemar's (Roy Brocksmith) monologue in the hotel room, the point at which it's announced that Quaid is dreaming (Edgemar takes over part of McClane's role in the short story).[10]

> A Brechtian theatre technique [Verhoeven said], with one of those teasing, omniscient narrators – but in 1990s fashion, geared towards America and so

---
[10] Apparently this idea was introduced by David Cronenberg.

hocus-pocus that they instantly forget that you did it. (ibid.)

Later, characters appearing within people's dreams or memories would be taken up in the *Matrix* movies, which used the cyberspace of the digital or computer world as its alternate reality (but far less elegantly than *Total Recall* – in the *Matrix* movies characters turn up and lecture the audience with philosophical garbage for hours. Soooo boring).

Total Recall, like Philip K. Dick's story, like all of Hollywood cinema's output, wants to have it both ways: that Quail did and did not go to Mars, that he is but is not a secret agent. Dick wrote:

> He'd have to hold two opposite premises in his mind simultaneously: that he went to Mars and that he didn't. That he's a genuine agent for Interplan and he's not, that it's spurious. (MR, 274)

It's what movies are, it's what the entertainment and leisure industries are, it's what the late capitalist world thrives on: living vicariously, living through others, living in virtual realities, living without costs and punishments, a world of imagination (the cultural imaginary), where nothing is real but everything is more real than real.

> Ironically, he had gotten exactly what he had asked Rekal, Incorporated for [wrote Dick in the story]. Adventure, peril, Interplan police at work, a secret and dangerous trip to Mars in which his life was at stake – everything he had wanted as a false memory.
> The advantage of it being a memory – and nothing more – could be appreciated. (MR, 283)

In *Total Recall*, the double or other looks exactly the same as the hero (even though Quaid has an implant, which aligns him with cyborgs). Later films that explored the issue of cloning and doubling in the action genre included *The 6th Day* (2000, which also starred Arnold Schwarzenegger).

*

Total Recall had a long and difficult journey to the screen. It was originally offered to Disney in the late 1970s by the writers of *Alien* (Dan O'Bannon and Ronald Shusett – *Total Recall* was essentially Shusett's pet project; he stayed with Paul Verhoeven throughout the shoot, determined to see his baby through to completion); Disney developed the project, and went into pre-production, but backed out when the movie was becoming too expensive.

Dino de Larentiis (DEG) then took it up in 1982, with Richard Dreyfuss starring and David Cronenberg directing. After that fell though, Bruce Beresford was due to direct in 1986, with Patrick Swayze in the lead (Jeff Bridges was also considered); after $6 million had been spent, a set built in Australia, and some 45 script rewrites, de Laurentiis's company DEG went bankrupt (in 1988), and the project seemed doomed. Yet Ronald Shusett persisted with it, despite so much money and time having been invested and not a frame shot. (Writing credits go to Shusett, Goldman, O'Bannon and Jon Povil).[11]

The venture was taken up by Arnold Schwarzenegger,[12] who persuaded Carolco's Mario Kassar and Andrew Vajna to buy it in 1988 for Paul Verhoeven (Arny had been impressed by *RoboCop*, and had invested in Carolco). Shusett and O'Bannon wrestled with a decent ending for a long time. Shusett said they 'tried every ending we could think of' (R. van Scheers, 212). The first act was great, most people agreed, but the narrative seemed to fall apart after that.

The shoot of *Total Recall*, in Mexico, at Churubuscu Studios in Mexico City,[13] was full of problems, and the film went over-budget.[14] There were 45 versions of the script by the time Paul Verhoeven came to the project. Having Arnold Schwarzenegger on board meant *Total Recall* would become an Arny vehicle, the character of Quaid would have to change from being a reluctant hero (in earlier scripts, Quaid was an accountant: now he became a construction worker, more in keeping with Arny's musclebound image).

Schwarzenegger plus Verhoeven made for a powerful combination of personalities; Bill Sandell said that Schwarzenegger was a big star who could get whatever he asked for, but in Verhoeven he found a director who

---

[11] Jon Povil was a producer who worked on *Star Trek*, *Sliders* and *The Outer Limits*, among others.
[12] On Arnold Schwarzenegger and *Total Recall*, see L. Mizejewski: "Total Recoil", *Post Script*, 12, 3, 1993; J. Goldberg: "Recalling Totalities", *Differences*, 4, 1, 1992; A. Liu: "The Last of Arnold Schwarzenegger", *Genders*, 18, 1993; Y. Tasker, 1993; J. Arroyo, 2000; S. Cohan, 1993; R. Miklitsch: *Total Recall*", *Camera Obscura*, 32, 1993; J. Schmertz: "On Reading the Politics of *Total Recall*", *Post Script*, 12, 3, 1993; A. Landsberg: "Prosthetic Memory: *Total Recall* and *BladeRunner*", in M. Featherstone, 1995; F. Glass: "Totally Recalling Arnold: Sex and Violence in the New Bad Future", *Film Quarterly*, 44, 1, Fall, 1990.
[13] The story was set in Chicago, and also went to New York.
[14] Filming in Mexico was supposed to be cheaper, because of the labour, but elements such as materials turned out to be costlier.

was his equal when it came to giant egos. Verhoeven said he couldn't have completed *Total Recall* without Schwarzenegger, because the shoot had been so difficult, and Schwarzenegger had backed him all the way. When it came to asking for re-shoots, for instance, or additional footage, if the money people were doubtful, a word from Schwarzenegger helped.

By the time of *Total Recall*, Arnold Schwarzenegger was a major Hollywood star – it was an extraordinary story, from Austrian bodybuilder to Hollywood action star to future governor of California. During the Eighties, Arny had become known as a laconic, unstoppable superhero – in the *Conan* movies, *The Terminator, Red Heat, Predator* and *Commando*. Not long after *Total Recall*, Schwarzenegger made moves to soften his gun-toting, ultra-violent image with comedies such as *Twins* and *Kindergarten Cop*. Schwarzenegger has never been better than in *Total Recall*, which was rejigged to fit his screen image, admittedly, but it still worked.

Apart from Arnold Schwarzenegger, *Total Recall* starred Ronny Cox as the corrupt Mars mine owner Cohaagen, Michael Ironside as his brutal aide Richter, Rachel Ticotin as Quaid's feisty love interest Melina, and Sharon Stone as Quaid's double-crossing wife Lori (a blonde *femme fatale* role Stone took up two years later in *Basic Instinct*).[15] Marshall Bell, Mel Johnson Jr, Michael Champion, Roy Brocksmith, Ray Baker, Rosemary Dunsmore, David Knell, Alexia Robinson and Debbie Lee Carrington also appeared. Paul Verhoeven regulars on *Total Recall* included Frank Uriosite (editor; Carlos Puente was the other editor), Jost Vocano (DP) and Jerry Goldsmith (music).[16] Casting was by Mike Fenton (who also cast *Blade Runner*), Valorie Massalas and Judy Taylor.

Steven Spielberg's version of a Philip K. Dick's short story – 2002's *Minority Report* – was practically a sequel to *Total Recall*. *Minority Report* had similar themes and settings, the similar plot devices of mistaken

---

[15] Verhoeven recalled that casting the two female leads was easy: they found Ticotin and Stone very early on in the casting process. Often that's not the case.

[16] It's an unusual and modernist soundtrack, sometimes experimental, far away from your average Hollywood score. Jerry Goldsmith was a veteran Hollywood composing, with a truly outstanding career. It included sci-fi, fantasy and horror movies, many of them classics – Goldsmith scored *Planet of the Apes, Logan's Run, Coma, Capricorn One, The Twilight Zone, Magic, Poltergeist, Gremlins, Legend, Innerspace, Outland, Star Trek, The Omen 2, Congo, Deep Rising, Small Soldiers, Hollow Man, The Mummy,* and *Alien* among others.

Jerry Goldsmith also composed movies such as *Chinatown, Patton, Tora! Tora! Tora!, Rambo, First Blood, The Russia House, Basic Instinct, First Knight, Chain Reaction, L.A. Confidential, The Shadow, Malice, Mulan* and *The Sum of All Fears*.

Terry Rawlings said he'd used a lot of Goldsmith's music when he was editing *Blade Runner* (FN, 272).

identity and being on the run from the authorities, and similar atmospheres of societal decadence and paranoia. Paul Verhoeven and Arnold Schwarzenegger confirmed that in their audio commentary on *Total Recall*, when they discussed the *Total Recall* sequel and how it would have concerned Arny and a bunch of the mutants from the first film, and their predictive powers.

There was also a spin-off TV series based on *Total Recall* (1999). For many years afterwards there were rumours of a sequel to *Total Recall* (as there are to any successful film in Hollywoodland).[17]

※

Paul Verhoeven directed *Total Recall* as an in-your-face special effects action epic, a $60 million Arnold Schwarzenegger vehicle, with visceral violence, a cacophonous soundtrack, and over-the-top visual effects (people's faces bulging and their eyes popping in Mars's atmosphere, and the wholly unbelievable but absolutely necessary upbeat ending – in this case, Mars being transformed into an Earth-like planet). The visual effects were by Rob Bottin,[18] Eric Brevig, Tim McGovern and Alex Funke (and 100s of others), and rightly won an Oscar.

One had to leave one's brain checked in at the counter before watching *Total Recall*, as with standard Hollywood action-adventure fare. The sheer exuberance of Paul Verhoeven's direction, his absolutely confident handling of action scenes, and the sly, subversive digs at contemporary Americana, pulled it off. One of the key reasons for the success of *Total Recall* is the strength of the script: for my money, it's the best screenplay of the Philip K. Dick adaptions.

The look of *Total Recall* was of concrete, glass and steel, a heavy, durable look, but also cruelly anonymous, something like fascist architecture of the 1930s. The Earth city was all angles and planes of white walls, concrete or iron. It was a classic movie view of the future (*Total Recall* was set in 2084, a nod to *1984*), with 'futuristic' cars and taxis (run by animatronic drivers, grotesque puppets like ventriloquist's dummies), and sleek trains. (Paul Verhoeven said that the look of *Total Recall* derived partly

---

[17] A remake of *Total Recall* was rumoured in 2011, with Colin Farrell to star.
[18] Rob Bottin made a huge contribution to *Total Recall*, Verhoeven acknowledged. Many of the memorable moments come from Bottin. Quaid hiding inside the fat lady, for instance, was Bottin's idea: 'a lot of things that you see in *Total Recall* are coming from him,' Verhoeven remarked (PV, 66).

from the decision to shoot in Mexico City, where locations such as the military academy employed the New Brutalist architecture of blocky concrete). It was a solid, workaday look far from the glittering neons and trashy streets of *Blade Runner* or the hi-tech Minimalism of *Minority Report*. (William Sandell, Jost Vocano, José Rodriguez Granada and James Tocci were responsible for the marvellous look of *Total Recall*, with hair by Peter Tothpal, make-up by Jeff Dawn, special make-up by Rob Bottin, and costumes by Erica Edell Philips, who worked with Verhoeven on *RoboCop*, and also designed the costumes for the Phil Dick adaption *Paycheck*).

Like most sci-fi films set in the future, *Total Recall* combined existing locations (such as city plazas and malls) with mattes and models. Venusville, with its mutant prostitutes, was modelled on Amsterdam's red lightdistrict.[19] Some of the sets consciously referenced earlier movies, such as *Metropolis* (a recurring point of reference for many sci-fi films). The arrival hall in the Mars city had tables and seating in front of giant wall-to-ceiling windows with a view of the Martian desert outside, recalling the restaurant at Mount Rushmore in *North By Northwest* (Paul Verhoeven was a massive Hitchcock fan, and some scenes, such as the hotel scene where Doctor Edgemar shows up, were consciously designed as Hitchcockian scenes).[20]

Paul Verhoeven's love of the grotesque was prominent – the prostitute with three breasts, for example, or the midget whore, in Venusville, and the dwarf-like guru, Kuato, growing out of his brother's belly (it was operated by 20 technicians; Ronald Shusett said he had the idea for Kuato after seeing Siamese twins). But it was Rob Bottin, Verhoeven said, who really brought Kuato to life – adding arms, putting him on the front of the body, etc (PV, 66). Kuato was a grotesque parody of the feminine mysteries of pregnancy, wombs and childbirth (the design of Kuato simultaneously evoked a helpless baby and a wise old man).

Unusual, though, that Paul Verhoeven and the writers didn't pick up on the bare-breasted secretary at Rekal, Incorporated in Philip K. Dick's short story: when Quail first goes to Rekal, she has breasts sprayed blue.[21] And

---

[19] The names Verhoeven employed in *Total Recall* also reveal Dutch and European origins (Richter, Hauser, Cohaagen, Brubaker).
[20] Paul Verhoeven said he studied Hitchcock's films 'intensively, even more than the works of Fellini, Lean or Buñuel' (PV, 41).
[21] *Minority Report*, 269.

later on, they're orange:

> 'Welcome back, Mr Quail,' she fluttered, her melon-shaped breasts – today painted an incandescent orange – bobbing with agitation. (ib., 288)

In the film, the secretary is painting her nails, much more pedestrian.

Like all movies of Philip Kindred Dick's fiction, hundreds of elements were added to the 1966 text: it's a fairly short short story. In the story, for example, Quail doesn't go to Mars (unless he really is an Interplan agent). *Total Recall* makes an enormous leap from the original story by taking the narrative to Mars (as well as adding millions to the budget). In doing so, the film adds numerous elements to the story – the whole battle for Mars, the alien structures, Melina and the rebels, and Quail saving the planet (there are aspects of that plot in the short story, though, when Quail has a childhood dream of saving Earth from aliens).

After the first act, of the 'confused man' (of Quaid signing up for the memory implant vacation, and the initial scenes of Quaid on the run), the narrative shifts to the Martian colonies, Quaid's involvement with the Martian resistance movement, led by the guru Kuato, and the other mutants, their battle against the dictator leader, Vilos Cohaagen, and his henchmen who hunt Quaid, the giant underground alien nuclear reactors, and so on. The dictatorial society on Mars isn't too much of a satire on modern America, or on other oppressive regimes, for Paul Verhoeven: Philip K. Dick's story was more about 'schizophrenia, double reality', Verhoeven maintained, and the dictator, Cohaagen, is played like a *James Bond* villain, and the political context is stereotypical, not satirical (PV, 75).

At the end of *Total Recall*, the aliens' nuclear power station turns Mars' atmosphere into breathable air when Quaid switches it on and the nuclear fuel rods melt the polar ice. An unbelievable sequence – it would take some 150 years to terraform Mars in this way, as Arthur C. Clarke pointed out. But this is a Hollywood blockbuster flick, which can't wait 150 years for a climax in a feature lasting one hour and forty minutes (Paul Verhoeven, trained as a physicist, put more hard science in *Total Recall* than there is in most Hollywood films, but understood the form, that *Total Recall* was bound by the rules of the game of moviemaking to break the rules of science). On the other hand, as Verhoeven pointed out, this part of the film was a dream or implant for Quaid, so it wouldn't be beyond the engineers at Rekal to create the memories of turning Mars into a liveable planet, after they'd already delivered an incredible adventure.

Other improbable scenes in *Total Recall* included Arny surviving an attack from 20 or so henchmen armed with machine guns sustaining only a few minor scratches – the standard unassailable Hollywood hero. Once again, the improbability can be explained within the film's terms by the whole thing being cooked up by Rekal's technicians.

Melina is helping Quaid waste the bad guys – it was nice to see the female sidekick getting to kick some ass, including a fight with Lori, before Arny kills her. This was the scene with the most famous line in the movie: 'consider that a divorce' (delivered in Arny's deadpan Austrian accent).

Two of the bravura visual effects sequences in *Total Recall* were Quaid meeting the underground leader Kuato, and the scene where Quaid tries to slip through immigration control on Mars underneath an enormous woman's skin (Priscilla Allen) which malfunctions and peels apart, revealing Quaid. He sets off a bomb and all hell breaks loose as the windows shatter, people are sucked outside, while Richter and his thugs try to gun down our hero. Part of the point of that scene, Paul Verhoeven explained, was to show that Mars didn't have an atmosphere to sustain human life, as well as to show how Quaid reached Mars in disguise.

Other action set-pieces in *Total Recall* included Quaid going nuts in the Rekal laboratory and murdering the technicians; chases in taxis, a mall, an escalator, and a subway train through the Earth city; Quaid killing four guys, including his co-worker, when they ambush him near the subway; another fight, in Quaid's apartment, with his wife Lori, and Richter's henchmen; another taxi chase, in the Mars dome; another chase; another gun fight – between Quaid and his pursuers in a partially-built concrete building (after Quaid has learnt more about his schizophrenic predicament from his 'real' self); a gun battle in amongst the large drums of the nuclear reactors (Quaid and Melina deploy a hologram of themselves as a decoy; silly, but fun); a girl-on-girl fight between Melina and Lori; a gun battle in the Venusville bar, between Richter and his henchmen and the mutants (high body count here); a fight between Quaid and Richter on an open service elevator (Richter's arms are ripped off and he falls to his death); a climactic confrontation between Quaid and Cohaagen in the nuclear reactor control room (Cohaagen tries to prevent Quaid setting off the reactor; an explosion creates a hole in the room, and Cohaagen suffers a movie villain's death: sucked out into the thin Mars atmosphere, where he dies, his face ballooning); and the climax, when the alien nuclear reactor heats up the icy core of Mars, turning the atmosphere into air (in this over-the-top, very expensive sequence, the film cuts from close-ups of Arny Schwarzenegger's and Rachel Ticotin's faces blowing up, their eyes popping grotesquely, to the windows of the Mars city exploding (stunt people flying everywhere), to the reactor rods entering the Martian rock, to plumes of smoke erupting from the mine pyramid, and finally to the boiling clouds turning the red Martian sky blue). Transforming the planet is literally 'saving the world', an epic ending.[22]

Total Recall was also a homage to some of the sci-fi movies Paul Verhoeven had loved as a child (Verhoeven was no different from the New Hollywood 'movie brats' like Joe Dante, John Carpenter, George Lucas and Steven Spielberg in this respect; European directors who came to Hollywood in the 1980s and 1990s – Renny Harlin, Roland Emmerich, Wolfgang Petersen and Verhoeven's cameraman, Jan de Bont – also paid homage to Hollywood's Classical studio era).

So in *Total Recall* there was *The War of the Worlds*,[23] *Invaders From Mars*, *Flight To Mars* and *Robinson Crusoe On Mars*, with Fritz Lang's *Metropolis* also providing inspiration.

Quaid gets to choose the dream woman for his implanted vacation: when he's at the Rekal facility he's offered different looks and body styles, opting for a woman who's both 'sleazy' and 'demure' (the virgin/ whore duality of Western culture). Creating the dream woman is a staple of sci-fi (including *Metropolis*).[24]

Following *Total Recall*, in the 1990s, there was a spate of films about Mars – *Mission to Mars* (Brian de Palma, 2000), and *Red Planet* (2000) – which reflected the discussions at NASA, in science magazines such as

---

22 Probably the most stupendous (and emotional) vision of the rejuvenation of the world at the end of a movie occurs in 1997's *Princess Mononoke*, directed by the inimitable Hayao Miyazaki.
23 When Spielberg revisited *The War of the Worlds*, a film he also loved as a youth, Mars was out of the picture: now the aliens came from far, far away.
24 1986's *Weird Science* is a jokey take on the dream woman gag.

Nature and in TV documentaries about manned missions to Mars (then thought to take three years), and discoveries of 'life' on Mars. Ray Bradbury's *The Martian Chronicles* (Michael Anderson, 1980) was made into a TV series. Mars was a recurring frontier destination in Philip K. Dick's fiction.

Some critics disliked *Total Recall* for its violence, but many sci-fi films are very violent – Vietnam grunts wasting aliens in *Aliens,* a woman being shot to death and crashing through glass windows in slow motion in *Blade Runner,* and even a whole planet being blown up in *Star Wars.* Dan O'Bannon said the violence went on for too long in *Total Recall,* as if the filmmakers lacked confidence, and thought that there wasn't enough going on without it (it also meant, O'Bannon thought, that they had to cut out more interesting stuff). But O'Bannon acknowledged that *Total Recall* was 'something rare. It's an actual science fiction movie', rather than being summat else like most sci-fi movies.[25]

Violence, of course, was one of Paul Verhoeven's specialities, as with the movies of Martin Scorsese, Oliver Stone, John McTiernan or Sam Peckinpah. A Paul Verhoeven flick usually meant some violence – especially if it was an action thriller. Violence was the norm in many of the top 25 films globally of each year from the 1980s onwards. 'One must recognize that violence does exercise a certain fascination on the human mind, and it's no good being too moralistic about it', said Verhoeven. Violence is part of a filmmaker's toolkit, for Verhoeven:

> I think it is really different from violence in real life. It doesn't mean anything. It is not true. Nobody is killed. Nobody is hurt. (PV, 69)

But there is a gleeful savagery about the action and violence in *Total Recall,* as if Paul Verhoeven instructed Vic Armstrong[26] and his stunt team to make the action especially brutal. There are moments, for instance, where Richter shoots a woman in the back (and not even with a 'good' reason, like the scene where Deckard kills Zhora in *Blade Runner*): in *Total Recall,*

---

[25] Quoted in J. Brosnan, 1991, 373.
[26] Veteran stunt co-ordinator Vic Armstrong (*James Bond, Indiana Jones, Starship Troopers, The Golden Compass, The Mummy, War of the Worlds, I Am Legend,* etc) headed up the second unit team, and delivered some marvellous fights and action scenes. A chief reason why *Total Recall* is a great action movie is because Armstrong is the stunt co-ordinator (he also doubled for Harrison Ford in *Blade Runner*).

Richter kills the whore with the three breasts just 'cos he's pissed off. But that's typical of Paul Verhoeven's films, and why some viewers find them too much, and other viewers enjoy them for the wild ride. You can say a lot of things about Verhoeven's movies, but they are never safe, never tame.

4
STEVEN SPIELBERG MEETS PHILIP K. DICK
MINORITY REPORT

> The greatest menace in the 20th century is the totalitarian state. It can take many forms: left-wing fascism, psychological movements, religious movements, drug rehabilitation places, powerful people, manipulative people; or it can be in a relationship with someone who is more powerful than you psychologically. Essentially, I'm pleading the case of those people who are not strong. If I were strong myself I would probably not feel this as such a menace.
>
> Philip K. Dick[27]

Steven Spielberg is the most high profile film director to be linked to the fiction of Philip K. Dick. Indeed, there's no filmmaker more successful than Spielberg, financially, in the history of cinema (he is worth about $3 billion according to Forbes). His films have entered popular culture in a way very

---
27 Quoted in C. Platt, 150.

few movies have, beginning with sharks in *Jaws*, UFOs and aliens in *Close Encounters of the Third Kind* and *E.T.*, action-adventures in the *Indiana Jones* series, World War Two in *Saving Private Ryan* and *Schindler's List*, and dinosaurs in the *Jurassic Park* series. And Spielberg is one of the very few contemporary filmmakers who is a household name.

Born on December 18, 1946 in Cincinnati, Steven Spielberg has directed 27 theatrically released features (plus TV movies), and has gone on to produce many TV shows and movies, and co-found the DreamWorks studio (in 1994). Spielberg has married twice (to actresses Amy Irving and Kate Capshaw), and has four children (Max, Sasha, Sawyer and Destry), and two adopted children (Theo and Mikaela).

Science fiction is a very big deal in the world of Steven Spielberg's cinema. *Close Encounters of the Third Kind*, *E.T.*, *Jurassic Park*, *The War of the Worlds*, *The Lost World*, *A.I.* and *Minority Report* are all sci-fi (as are many of the projects Spielberg has produced – *Taken*, *Deep Impact*, *Innerspace*, *Galaxy Quest*, *Batteries Not Included*, *SeaQuest* and *Back To the Future*).[28] So maybe it was inevitable that Spielberg would eventually take on an author like Philip K. Dick.

STEVEN SPIELBERG IN THE 1990s

Steven Spielberg's next film after *Saving Private Ryan* (1998) was due to be *Memoirs of a Geisha*, from Arthur Golden's novel.[29] Spielberg also planned to make *Minority Report* in Fall, 1999, in L.A., starring Tom Cruise – another 'popcorn movie', but also the 'most cynical film' he'll have made.[30] In the event, *Minority Report*, produced for Fox/ DreamWorks, started

---

[28] Horror is not far behind: *Jaws*, *Something Evil*, *Indiana Jones and the Temple of Doom* and *Ghost Train* (*Amazing Stories*), plus the *Jurassic Park* films (and Spielberg has produced plenty of horror: *Poltergeist*, *Arachnaphobia*, *The Haunting* and *What Lies Beneath*). Often fantasy is an umbrella term that covers all of the above films, which would take in *Hook*, *Always*, *Twilight Zone*, *Raiders of the Lost Ark* and *Indiana Jones and The Last Crusade* (and many of Spielberg's producer jobs).

[29] It eventually appeared in 2005, starring Zhang Ziyi and Gong Li, and helmed by Rob Marshall.

[30] Interview with S. Dubner, in *New York Times Magazine*, Feb 14, 1999.

shooting in Summer, 2001 (just before the strikes of actors and writers in Hollywood), for a Summer, 2002 release.

In the Nineties, Steven Spielberg started directing movies in batches: *Jurassic Park* closely followed by *Schindler's List* in 1993; *The Lost World*, *Saving Private Ryan* and *Amistad* appearing in 1997 and 1998; *A.I.*, *Minority Report* and *Catch Me If You Can* in 2001-02; and *War of the Worlds* and *Munich* in 2005-06.

While nothing seems to connect *Jurassic Park* with *Schindler's List* (as so many critics pointed out), *A.I. Artificial Intelligence* and *Minority Report* form an obvious pairing in Steven Spielberg's cinema, one following the other in terms of production: both were sci-fi, both were set in the future (and in America, on the East Coast), both attempted a believable vision of the future, both had male protagonists, and both originated in masters of modern sci-fi (Stanley Kubrick/ Brian Aldiss and Philip K. Dick).[31]

Another common theme in Steven Spielberg's works of the 1990s and after is science and technology and humankind's troubled relationship with it (*A.I.*, *Minority Report* and the *Jurassic Park* films), also a central theme in Philip K. Dick's fiction. Another is enormous social and political issues and events (*Amistad*, *Saving Private Ryan*, *Munich* and *Schindler's List*). Another common element in these pictures is the city: although known for his recreations of suburbia and Middle America, Spielberg's movies of the 1990s onwards increasingly looked to cities (and in particular US cities): Washington in *Amistad* and *Minority Report*, New York City in the *Jurassic Park* films, *A.I.* and *Catch Me If You Can*, San Diego in *The Lost World*, and the fictional Las Vegas-like Rouge City in *A.I.*

Steven Spielberg said that he had entered a dark period in the 1990s, from *Schindler's List* onwards, and his films became dark: *Amistad*, *Minority Report* and *Saving Private Ryan*, and even *The Lost World* was the dark side of *Jurassic Park*. And *A.I.*, which Spielberg said he made thinking about what audiences would enjoy, was also a dark picture. *Catch Me If You Can*, a Sixties caper movie, and *The Terminal*, a romantic comedy drama about a guy stranded in an airport, were both deliberately much lighter outings.

---

31 *Minority Report*, Spielberg's first crime thriller, also had affinities with the film that followed it, *Catch Me If You Can:* in both a man's on the run from the authorities (Gigolo Joe was fleeing the powers that be in *A.I.*); and there's a problematic relationship with a father figure.

THE SCRIPT

Scott Frank, Jon Cohen, Frank Darabont, John August, and others, wrote the script for *Minority Report* from Philip K. Dick's 1956 short story (which appeared in *Fantastic Universe* in January, 1956).[32] Rated 'PG-13' and released in the U.S.A. in mid-June, 2002, *Minority Report* ran for 144 minutes. It grossed $342m around the world.

Minority Report featured regular Steven Spielberg collaborators: Janusz Kaminski, Gerald Molen, Walter Parkes, Bonnie Curtis, Scott Farrar, ILM, Michael Lantieri, Gary Rydstrom, John Williams and Michael Kahn.

Ronald Shusett was executive producer of *Minority Report*, along with Gary Goldman.[33] Shusett had the finest sci-fi screen credentials of many on the film: he had been one of the original writers of the first *Alien* film (1979), and had been one of the driving forces behind *Total Recall* (1990) (Shusett had persisted with making *Total Recall* for years, even when several attempts to set up the project had failed).[34]

Minority Report starred Tom Cruise as John Anderton, a cop who works for the 'Pre-Crime' division in a futuristic Washington, in 2054. Anderton is part of a team that prevents crimes (in particular, murders) before they've been committed, with the aid of three 'pre-cogs', humanoid mutants.

Minority Report had a strong supporting cast, including: Tim Blake Nelson, Peter Stormare, Lois Smith, and Jason Antoon,[35] and included cameos from Cameron Diaz and Cameron Crowe (returning the favour of *Vanilla Sky*). In terms of casting, *Minority Report* is a busy film, like *Catch Me If You Can* and *A.I.*, with numerous minor roles. Since *Schindler's List*, Steven Spielberg's movies had been able to attract stronger actors in the supporting roles – actors who might take leading roles in other films.

The structure of *Minority Report* was a man on the run movie – i.e., a road movie (although most of the movie was set in Washington. Though the setting was D.C., Steven Spielberg & co. avoided including the

---
[32] Frank and Cohen got the screen credit; Frank's credits included *Get Shorty, Malice* and *Dead Again*. Cohen, according to Imdb.com, has no other movie credits apart from this film.
[33] Goldman, like Shusett, is something of a Philip K. Dick veteran: he co-wrote *Next, Total Recall* and was executive producer on *Minority Report*.
[34] Presumably, Shusett and Goldman had worked on earlier versions of the script.
[35] The virtual reality arcade, Cyber Parlor, was amusing, as was the non-stop banter of its owner, Rufus T. Riley (played with gusto by Jason Antoon).

landmarks of the capital: only in the stand-off between Burgess and Anderton was a landmark like the Washington Monument included, glimpsed in the background of the balcony scene). *Minority Report* followed the road movie structure of a character meeting a number of people along the journey: the eye doctor, the scientist, the virtual reality impresario, the prison warder, and so on.

The locations used for *Minority Report* included many Washington sites, such as the Reagan Trade Center for the exterior of the Pre-Crime building, the Gap store on Wisconsin Avenue, roads at Gloucester, Virginia, for the car scenes, a house on Ware Point Road, near Beulah, for Lara Anderton's place, and the climax was set in the Willard Intercontinental in DC.

Apart from studio shoots in Los Angeles, *Minority Report* also used L.A. spots such as the El Dorado Hotel, for Eddie's rundown apartment block, the shopping mall was the Hawthorne Plaza Mall, Hineman's garden was filmed at Descanso Gardens in La Cañada-Flintridge, and the Angelus Plaza was where Anderton encounters Leo Crow.

THE LOOK

Before going any further, you have to acknowledge that the influence of Japanese *animé* on *Minority Report* is immense – and you can see it across all of Hollywood's recent action and fantasy output, from the visuals to the staging to the characters and the scripts.

The look of *Minority Report* was all chrome, metal, shiny surfaces, cool greys, silvers, whites and blacks. Like previous futuristic films such as *Batman* and *The Event Horizon*, *Minority Report* studiously avoided the plethora of neons of *Blade Runner* (with which *Minority Report* would be inevitably compared, being another Philip K. Dick adaption). *Minority Report* did use *Blade Runner*'s giant hoardings and billboards, though (but they were animated holograms projected onto buildings and structures). (One of the sources for movies such as *BladeRunner* and *Minority Report* was the Far East and cities such as Tokyo and Hong Kong, as well as the grandfather of futuristic movies, *Metropolis*, and comicbooks too).

As with 2001's *A.I.*, *Minority Report* abounded in minimal sets and transparent materials – glass, plastic, mirrors, veils, rain and the pool of water the pre-cognitives inhabited. The office of the Pre-Crime department was dominated by multiple screens and computer interfaces: there was a giant glass screen and many smaller, clear screens on which images and data were projected (the open plan office, with its steel stairs and walkways and multiple levels, looked towards the striking airport set of *The Terminal*). The computer software consisted of small glass discs and glass screens. Instead of TV sets, everyone has giant wall screens (Anderton has a classy 3-D holographic system – the holographic version of surround sound – which can project lifesize images into the room, while the wall TV at Eddie's surgery plays old movies).

Steven Spielberg and DP Janusz Kaminski created a world of steely, desaturated colour, which they had developed on *Saving Private Ryan*; *Minority Report* was predominantly lit by blue and white lights, and graded towards the cool end of the spectrum. Warm colours were in short supply (the Lexus car was dark red, Anne Lively wore a red dress, and Anderton's memory of being in the swimming pool with his son was in bright, saturated colour, with his son in red swimwear. Red again identified a potential victim in Spielberg's cinema, as in *Schindler's List*). Spielberg and Kaminski also limited the no. of shots of the sky: *Minority Report* was primarily a movie of interiors (some squalid and claustrophobic, like the eye doctor's surgery, some sparse and glossy, like the Pre-Crime HQ, and some olde worlde, like Burgess's home), and the sky, when it was shown, was a blurred grey or white (as in *Saving Private Ryan*). Only at the end was there a full shot of the sun, in the helicopter shot above the lake and islands. Windows and light sources were allowed to bleach out (Spielberg admired Stanley Kubrick's use of 'hot' windows in films like *Barry Lyndon*).

At times, *Minority Report* had the loose, improvisatory feel of a young filmmaker's work (Steven Spielberg was 55 when he made *Minority Report*), with some shots blowing out, light flaring the lens, and the dark areas of other set-ups allowed to disappear to total black. (When Burgess slips up and Lara realizes that he could be behind it all, for example, Spielberg included a very bleached-out shot, the kind of footage that a producer or editor would automatically cut out. Spielberg allowed more of these self-conscious modernist moments in his later films).

*

British designer Alex McDowell, who had designed *The Crow, Lawnmower Man* and *Fight Club*,[36] contributed a look of metal, glass, plastic and hard surfaces, in whites, greys, pale blues and blacks (also favoured on *A.I.*, but here made even cooler by Janusz Kaminski's bleach bypass film processing). McDowell researched cutting edge architecture to develop the look for *Minority Report* (which meant entering postmodern space).

Alex McDowell's *mise-en-scène* absorbed a trend in contemporary design towards minimalism, lots of white spaces, glass, and empty areas. But there were also gentle curves in *Minority Report,* rather than the grids and angular geoemtric minimalism of the 1960s (in the art of Donald Judd, Frank Stella and Sol LeWitt), or a film like *THX 1138*. Again, the bubbles and S-bends coupled with whites, grey and light blues were part of design in the late 1990s (in companies such as Apple Macintosh and Gap).

Janusz Kaminski was all in favour of Alex McDowell's set designs, because the metal and glass made his lighting reflect and sparkle. Kaminski also liked a busy frame, and the large amounts of glass offered possibilities for layers or veils in front of the camera (the tenement set, though, Kaminski hated, because the cutaway ceilings meant there was nowhere to hide lights).

Steven Spielberg didn't want a futuristic look that would appear out-of-date soon after *Minority Report* was released. He didn't want costumes and sets and props that looked like *The Shape of Things to Come* or *Metropolis*. That's almost impossible, of course, and *Minority Report* is very much a film of its time (the early 2000s). Its design and look is locked into 2001-02.

---

[36] McDowell went on to design *Corpse Bride, Charlie and the Chocolate Factory, Watchmen, The Terminal* and *The Cat In the Hat*.

VISUAL EFFECTS

There were visual fx in abundance in *Minority Report*, but Steven Spielberg didn't dwell on spectacular vistas at length, as he had done in *Close Encounters of the Third Kind* with those endless views of the mothership.[37] The big, show-off images of downtown Washington in *Minority Report* were kept to one or two shots (the first occurred when Anderton is riding a car on the magnetic freeways in downtown D.C.). The visual fx were more integrated into the story rather than dwelt on for their own sake. At the same time, ILM, PDI, Asylum and other effects houses turned in a large number of shots for *Minority Report*, and probably an hour of the movie contained visual fx of some kind.

The visual fx in *Minority Report* (which included flowers, cars, freeways, spy machines, computers, screens, holograms, planes, phones, billboards, subway trains, and virtual reality orgies), certainly had the wow factor, but they were part of an attempt at creating a convincing futuristic America. As a vision of the future, *Minority Report* was stunning: Spielberg and his team (DP Kaminski, production designer Alex McDowell, art directors Ramsey Avery, Chris Gorak, Leslie McDonald and Seth Reed, costume designer Deborah L. Scott, make-up and hair artists Mark Anthony, Karen Asano-Myers, Terry Baliel and Michèle Burke, sound designer Gary Rydstrom, and visual effects supervisor Scott Farrar, plus the fx people)[38] succeeded in producing a coherent and credible version of what America might look and sound like some time in the future. Of course, some areas of Washington were impossibly clean and glamorous (apart from the 'sprawl').

The murders seen by the pre-cogs and projected into the computer screens at Pre-Crime were created by effects house Imaginary Forces. Steven Spielberg had been impressed by their work on the title sequence of *Seven* (1995), which had inspired similar credit sequences in other films. Spielberg's team handed over the material they'd shot for the murders to Imaginary Forces, who developed methods of making the footage look

---

[37] 'Unlike George Lucas, who indulges in effects like a hooker indulges in dark alleys, Spielberg weaves the visuals into his story, building the movie not around CGI, but around characterization and strong plot', commented David Litton at Hauntnut.com.

[38] Fx on *Minority Report* were by 3 Ring Circus Films, Asylum VFX, Black Box Digital, Digital Firepower, Imaginary Forces, Industrial Light & Magic, Kurtzman Nicotero & Berger EFX Group Inc., Pacific Data Images, Pixel Liberation Front, Reel Efx Inc. and Skywalker Sound

something like fragments of dreams or memories. One of the aspects Spielberg stipulated was a circular peripheral vision mask around the images (rather than a rectangular one).

The pre-cogs' visions were breathtakingly good in *Minority Report* – not only the manipulation of the images themselves (which were impressive enough), but also the way they were edited, how the images combined by Mike Kahn *et al* with the sound effects and music, and how the visions were cut into the rest of the film.

The 2002 film of *Minority Report* also adds many layers of design and visuals to Philip K. Dick's story. The operations room of Pre-Crime, for instance, is a slick world of floating glass screens, images piling upon each other, computer graphics, all cool greys, blues and blacks. In the story, the centre is cables, and words punched out on cards. Much more mechanical, rather than digital and virtual.

THE PITCH

Minority Report was a fast-paced thriller with a simple through-line: Anderton, on the run from the authorities, has to prove his innocence of a crime he is yet to commit.[39] It's the innocent man on the run theme that Alfred Hitchcock loved. Steven Spielberg's mastery of the action set-piece was fully in place in *Minority Report*: stand-outs being the prevention of an adulterous murder in the opening sequence; a car chase; another chase/ fight, this time with rocket power packs *à la James Bond* in an alley and apartments; and an infiltration of electronic spider bugs ('Spyders')[40] in an apartment block (spectacularly shot from overhead).

At times *Minority Report* came across as a hi-tech, 21st century *Indiana Jones* movie, though leaner and meaner (the not particularly

---

[39] 'Everybody runs' was one of the taglines of *Minority Report* – it was Anderton/ Cruise's line (and also described his psychological state of running from himself, of escaping in drugs). Agatha/ Morton's line was 'can you see?'
[40] The spider-robots are a steal from Japanese *animé*, such as in the TV show *Ghost In the Shell: Stand Alone Complex*

impressive fist fight between Anderton and Witwer above an automobile assembly line was pure *Indiana Jones*; it also resembled a scene from George Lucas's *Star Wars: Attack of the Clones*, which was released a month before *Minority Report*; the assembly line chase also had a feeble, let-down ending, with Anderton getting clean away).

Although *Minority Report* was a rollercoaster ride and action-adventure film, with plenty of speed, spectacle, gadgets[41] and stunts to satisfy action fans and multiplex audiences, it was also intended to be a thought-provoking piece of speculative science fiction (in the manner of other Philip K. Dick films – *Minority Report* is something like how *Blade Runner* would be if it were made today).

NARRATIVE AND SCRIPT

Parts of the plot of *Minority Report* were creaky (as so often with sci-fi films involving the theme of time). For instance, it wasn't particularly convincing that Anderton's wife Lara (Kathryn Morris) would suddenly turn into his saviour (after being estranged from him for six years), taking up a gun, infiltrating the prison complex on her own (improbably presided over by only one guard), and rescuing him (perhaps only Hineman could have believably done it, but she didn't have the motive). It stretched credibility that the Pre-Crime division could have piped images from the pre-cognitives' memories directly into the reception, which demonstrates to the gathering of D.C. politicos that Burgess is guilty. Colin Farrell wasn't old enough or convincing enough as a federal agent boss (an actor with more presence or weight would have been a better opponent for Anderton), but it was always a pleasure to see Max von Sydow in a major role (even if Lamar Burgess's character lacked depth, and was under-written). But von Sydow can do *anything*, and he's always wonderful.

---

[41] Other gadgets in *Minority Report* included animated newspapers and cereal boxes, billboards and ads which address the consumer by name, cars that run on magnetic tracks, voice-activated household appliances, wall-size holographic screens, virtual reality machines, and the super-computer which reads the pre-cogs' thoughts.

Samantha Morton's Agatha had little to do in another under-written role but hang onto Tom Cruise and pant and faint a lot (almost all the critics were wild about Morton's performance, however, and many thought she was the best thing in the film).[42] Morton did a lot with a little. Towards the end, though, Agatha does have a speech (Janusz Kaminski deliberately lit Morton in the movie so she would look angelic, and particularly so in this scene, where she paints a picture of the Andertons' lost son's future life for them). Morton provided some great physical acting as the floppy, boneless pre-cog who's overwhelmed by the world outside the temple.

It shouldn't have taken too much effort for the screenwriters to add some embellishments for the characters, to give them some more levels, which would have enriched the narrative. In a Raymond Chandler detective yarn, even minor characters are fleshed out, but in *Minority Report* they remain fairly one-dimensional.

Further holes in the film included the whole Pre-Crime programme relying on just one person (Agatha). And five or six of the Pre-Crime squad, equipped with hi-tech gear (and no doubt trained by Anderton himself) are unable to capture their chief. Like the one-dimensional characterizations, it shouldn't stretch a scriptwriter too much to come up with solutions to these plot holes.

You can see the different drafts in the script of *Minority Report*: the religious aspects, for instance, probably came from one writer, while the car factory chase[43] and fight might have been added at a studio executive's insistence. *Minority Report* suffered from some lazy screenwriting. Ideas such as the pre-cogs being worshipped by people in America was interesting, but they weren't developed at all. It was the same with *Blade Runner*, a movie which film critics and cultural theorists have gone nuts about. All of those elements which critics have discussed *ad infinitum* in *Blade Runner* – the racial, ethnic, feminist and cyborg aspects of the replicants, for instance – are not essential to the plot, which is basically: the replicants are robots which Deckard has to hunt down and destroy.

Other weaknesses in *Minority Report* included Steven Spielberg's lack of

---

[42] Agatha, thin, wasted, physically feeble, resembles a drug addict and, more sinisterly, a concentration camp inmate (in the 2nd half of *Minority Report* she's dressed in ill-fitting stripey trousers). Who thought that Gap would be producing a range of concentration camp clothes?

[43] Apparently, this sequence was a survivor of the Shusett-Goldman script.

interest in talky scenes. There was too much dialogue – pages of it – in a couple of scenes which would have benefitted from some pruning: the scene where Anderton confronts Dr Iris Hineman (Lois Smith), the aged, eccentric inventor of the Pre-Crime scheme and the pre-cogs, and the eye surgery scene (Spielberg has acknowledged that he finds such scenes difficult). The encounter between Anderton and Hineman took place entirely in a conservatory filled with genetically modified plantlife. (A similar greenhouse scene had appeared in *Amistad*). In the *film noir* tradition, one of the best greenhouse scenes occurs in *The Big Sleep* (1946), where Bogie sweats and drinks while talking to the patriarchal Sternwood.

Here, Dr Hineman was a sci-fi version of the wise old crone of fairy tales, imparting wisdom by the ton to the hero (every inventor or scientist in movies seems to be eccentric). Steven Spielberg and his team invented all manner of bits of actorly business to make the conversation interesting (the actors move there, over here, pick up this, contemplate that, tend wounds, make tea, get bitten by plants, and so on). It was the kind of essentially static scene that Orson Welles could have made riveting (like the famous discovering-the-shoe scene in *Touch of Evil*), but in Steven Spielberg's hands, it became too long and far too talky. (Spielberg and his team added some odd elements to the Hineman scene, not usually found in his cinema: for instance, the elderly Hineman kisses Anderton, for no apparent reason, and to underline a point about survival, allows a plant to wriggle in her palm and scratch her).

Similarly, in the scene where Anderton goes to sleazy eye surgeon Dr Eddie to have his eyes removed (cue nods to *A Clockwork Orange*), Peter Stormare rambles on for ages. He and the writers do add some quirky aspects to his role, though, as he explains about being a burns doctor in Baltimore who liked to set his victims on fire (it's a gruesome monologue which almost slips past the viewer, because there's so much going on visually, as Eddie prepares to remove Anderton's eyes). And Steven Spielberg and Michael Kahn are back on form visually in that scene, skillfully manipulating image (and sound) to suggest the disorientating effects of anaesthetic and blindness, as well as the slow creep-along of time. For a director like Spielberg, even temporary blindness would be terrifying. Spielberg adds one of his anxieties – about how one would go about getting food (it's a resurgence of the schoolboy Spielberg, who liked to scare cinema-goers by pouring fake vomit on them from a balcony, a much-recounted prank in the Steven Spielberg Legend).

If critics had one major gripe with *Minority Report*, it was the ending, and Steven Spielberg's and the writers' sentimental additions. The picture didn't end the same way as Philip K. Dick's story; Spielberg, Frank and Cohen opted for a more upbeat climax, involving a *film noir* hero-villain stand-off between Anderton and Burgess at a party to celebrate the Pre-Crime scheme going national.

Following the villain's demise, Anderton is improbably reunited with his wife Lara, who is now pregnant (the husband-wife reunion is not as significant as Lara expecting a baby, which will maybe assuage the loss of their son. It's improbable because they seem to have been separated for years since their son disappeared, and Lara isn't particularly friendly towards Anderton. It's Hollywood hokum, but the script laid the foundation for the reunion by having no other love interest for Anderton (or for Lara) – he's not going to fall for Agatha, for instance, and by having Lara explain (to Witwer) that she left Anderton because of their son).

Minority Report closed with an image of rustic, Henry David Thoreau bliss: Agatha and the pre-cognitive twins were shown quietly reading books (no computers or electronics in sight, God forbid!), wearing sweaters and casual clothes, now with long hair, in a log cabin on a wild island, surrounded by water and other islands, and a glowing sunset. The return of the American Sublime, out of the Hudson River School painters.

John Anderton narrates the climax of the film, via the telephone link to Burgess, as the film cross-cuts between the reception in downtown Washington, the Pre-Crime office, the pre-cogs in the temple, and the images from the pre-cogs' vision. Anderton also winds up the movie in the *dénouement*, which includes a description of the abandoned Pre-Crime scheme, Anderton reunited with his wife, and the idyllic scene of the pre-cogs.

❦

Steven Spielberg, Frank and Cohen increased the sentimentality in Philip K. Dick's original story: typical additions by the writers were the emotional scenes between Anderton senior and his young son. Early on the filmmakers established John Anderton's yearning for his son and estranged wife Lara when Anderton returns to his apartment at night and plays back holographic tapes he'd made years ago, when the family was still intact. And just before Anderton slips underwater at the swimming pool he kisses his son (it's the last time he sees him).

It was pure Steven Spielberg that the key relationship in Anderton's life was not with his alienated spouse, but with his lost son. Most other Hollywood adaptions of the same material would have made Anderton and Lara the core relationship. The importance of the relationships between parents and offspring was emphasized in the subplot involving Agatha and her murdered mother, and Burgess as a kind of surrogate father (and Colin Farrell's Witwer also talks about not having children). Spielberg, Cohen and Frank gave similar relationships to his next Tom Cruise film, *The War of the Worlds* (with Cruise's Ray unable to protect his children). But guess what folks, they're all re-united at the end! Hooray for Hollywood! When has Steven Spielberg ever killed off his heroes? Only in *Saving Private Ryan*, but that was the typical Hollywood heroic sacrifice (*The Sugarland Express* and *A.I.* are different stories).

THEMES

Eyes in *Minority Report* control security, legal status, and consumer preferences, as well as identity. Retinal scanning is everywhere in this post-Orwellian future: the authorities know where every citizen is at every moment (a dramatic extension of discussions in the 1990s and 2000s about new technologies such as identity cards, cel phones and G.P.S.). Thus, to obtain a new identity, Anderton doesn't don a wig, beard or shades, as in old *Mission: Impossible* episodes or 1960s spy series, but undergoes a Frankensteinian operation to replace his eyes with those of a corpse (the concept was foreshadowed in the dialogue in an earlier scene, describing how a criminal got away with a crime).

Steven Spielberg said that the increase in surveillance and the invasion of privacy was one of the outcomes of the think-tank on the future which he'd convened to help plan the film. At the time that *Minority Report* was in pre-production (2000 through 2001), in many Western countries CCTV cameras were common in public spaces, such as banks, hotels, airports, theatres, and trains, along with speed cameras, crime and other surveillance technology. Police cars and officers carried cameras (with the possibility of a lucrative sideline for the police by selling footage to sensationalist tabloid TV shows). 'Reality TV' was a concurrent manifestation of the increasing proliferation of cameras and voyeurism ('ordinary people' or celebrities living together in houses, jungles or desert islands, while being filmed continuously). Post-9/11 America was even more severe on surveillance and security. All of this Philip K. Dick had predicted and explored in his stories.

The religious elements of Philip K. Dick's fiction survived in 20th Century Fox's film: the pre-cogs were worshipped as saints or mystics by parts of the populace (the chief pre-cog is called Agatha, a saint's name); the pre-cogs' room is called the Temple; the cops think of themselves as priests (clergy) rather than policemen (because they interfere with destiny); the church organ the moralizing prison guard Gideon (Tim Blake Nelson) plays to the inmates; and Burgess and Hineman playing God, controlling human destiny and altering nature.[44] (Most of the religious motifs were added to Philip K. Dick's original story, and were part of the unmade *Total Recall* sequel written by Shusett and Goldman).

Among the visual rhymes in *Minority Report* were bodies lying in water (the pre-cogs in the temple; Anderton in the swimming pool, and the bath; Anne Lively drowning); and two actors holding each other, with their heads together (Anderton and Agatha, Anderton and Hineman). Holding one's breath under water was another recurring motif (with an ironic twist, because Anne Lively is killed by drowning).

Clocks and watches and countdowns were another recurring element: primarily, the countdowns to when the murders would be committed, a time-honoured method of controlling suspense and release in movie narratives (but also employed in the scenes where characters hold their breath under water, or Anderton spending twelve hours under bandages).

---

[44] *Minority Report* links notions such as predestination, prophecy, free will, fate, coincidence and chance with personal, social and national security. It has a strong thematic centre.

There are two sets of parents and children in *Minority Report*: Anderton and his lost son Sean, and Agatha and her dead mother Anne Lively (a third set includes the symbolic parents, Hineman and Burgess: Hineman remarks that she and Burgess are like the parents of Pre-Crime – and, by extension, of Anderton).

John Anderton manipulates the images coming from the pre-cogs on giant computer screens, like a classical conductor (accompanied by Franz Schubert's *Unfinished Symphony*, a rare instance of classical music in a Steven Spielberg movie. Peter Tchaikovsky, Johann Sebastian Bach and Joseph Haydn also feature in the soundtrack of *Minority Report*, as well as Henry Mancini and Duke Ellington.[45] Spielberg has included much more classical music in his later pictures). The images are rapidly re-arranged by Anderton on the screens, until he can decode them and discover the crime's location, before dispatching the Pre-Crime squad to the Georgetown location.

John Williams regarded *Minority Report* as a combination of a *film noir* and a futuristic thriller. Williams opted for a score that evoked the hard-boiled detective films of the 1940s and 1950s, rather than something postmodern and electronic. In searching for the emotional core of the piece, Williams latched onto John Anderton's relationship with his dead son (which was also Steven Spielberg's chief identification).

※

Critics seized on the over-abundance of product placement in *Minority Report* (some 15 major brands were included: Gap, Bulgari, Reebok, Nokia, Lexus, American Express, Aquafina, Ben & Jerry's, Burger King, Century 21, Fox, Guinness, Lexus, Pepsi, Revo and *USA Today*), though supporters claimed it was justified because of the media-saturated, consumer-driven world the filmmakers were trying to depict (i.e., an extension of American society of 2002). Many of the brand names appeared on electronic billboards and adverts, addressing the consumer, and tailoring their pitch based on previous buying habits. One scene, where Anderton goes to buy clothes for Agatha, was set in a Gap store. Anderton wore a Bulgari digital watch, and drove a custom-built Lexus sports car. Communication devices

---

[45] *Minority Report* also employed the low drones and rumbles which were fashionable in contemporary Hollywood movies (especially playing underneath the pre-cogs' visions. The 'temple' scenes had a low throb in them).

advertized Nokia.

The budget for *Minority Report* was $102 million. Some reckoned that the product placement in the movie might have accounted for up to $25m of the budget. (*Cast Away*, starring Tom Hanks, and made around the same time, was also criticized for its over-use of product placement – Federal Express).

The reviews of *Minority Report* were generally favourable, and some strongly praised the movie, which critics said combined an action-adventure with a thoughtful science fiction film. *Minority Report*, for the enthusiastic critics, made good the disappointments of the previous year's Stanley Kubrick project *A.I.* (I don't agree here – *A.I.* is a stupendous movie, though it's flawed; but *Apocalypse Now* is flawed and yet a masterpiece).[46]

Tom Cruise (another connection with Stanley Kubrick and Ridley Scott) played John Anderton in his usual intense and serious fashion, throwing himself wholeheartedly into the role, as well as combining plenty of the action dynamics of the *Mission: Impossible* franchise. Steven Spielberg had made a cameo appearance in the Tom Cruise vehicle *Vanilla Sky* (2001), a film with some similarities with *Minority Report* (including Cruise wearing disfiguring make-up).[47]

Tom Cruise's films, since the mid-1990s, had tended to be Tom Cruise vehicles, with the star assuming a name above the title stature – which extended to the publicity, advertizing and global image, as well as the narrative and presentation. By the time of *Minority Report*, Cruise had become one of the biggest box office draws in the Hollywood star system, alongside Tom Hanks and Julia Roberts.[48] Steven Spielberg has tended to avoid star vehicles (though he has directed some – such as as *Hook* and *Indiana Jones and the Last Crusade*), preferring to cast known actors, but not superstars like Cruise. By agreeing to work with Tom Cruise, the

---

[46] Andrew O'Heir opined: 'if he will never be Kubrick, [Spielberg] has become fully Kubrickian – a master genre stylist with a surprisingly cold heart. If you really want to be cynical, you might call this the best Paul Verhoeven film since *Starship Troopers*.

[47] *Vanilla Sky* was very expensive, but oddly unengaging and pointless. You emerge from it thinking: 'Eh? What was that all about?'.

[48] Tom Cruise was known for his boyish looks, toothy grin, high profile girlfriends (Nicole Kidman, Penelope Cruz, Katie Holmes), and A-list celebrity status. Cruise was a bigger star than actors such as Richard Dreyfuss, Roy Scheider, or Liam Neeson (at the time they made films for Spielberg). Cruise brought an action star aspect to the Spielberg protagonist, which had been there in the *Indiana Jones* films, obviously, with Harrison Ford, but to a lesser degree in the Spielberg movies of the Nineties (Cruise would be the up-to-date equivalent of Harrison Ford: an action star with an intelligent edge, who could also play serious dramatic roles).

Spielberg film becomes a star vehicle as well as 'a Steven Spielberg film'.[49]

The cinematic allusions in *Minority Report* were many, and took in *Blade Runner*, *A Clockwork Orange* and *Dark Passage* (in the eye surgery scene), *Blow Up* (in the decoding of the pre-cogs' visions of murder), and the Forties *film noirs* of Raymond Chandler and Dashiell Hammett (such as *The Maltese Falcon* and *The Big Sleep*), which had also been referenced in *Blade Runner*.[50] Although it was full of action, Steven Spielberg regarded the film as a thriller and a mystery, with lots of clues left for the audience to guess who was behind the framing of Anderton. Spielberg likened *Minority Report* to the *film noirs* of John Huston, in which many of the really interesting characters were glimpsed along the journey, but weren't necessarily the main characters (although *Minority Report* doesn't quite have the class or nuance or toughness of *The Maltese Falcon*).

Minority Report crossed genres: it was a futuristic *film noir*, but also an action-adventure movie; a thought-provoking science fiction film, but also a thriller and mystery; and a star vehicle for Tom Cruise (he was in most every scene, one of the prerequisites for a star vehicle movie).

*

There was plenty of story and theme packed into *Minority Report*: aside from the central man on the run plot, there was:

(1) the pre-cognitives and the Pre-Crime project (and the links to politics);

(2) the moral and social implications of the Pre-Crime scheme;

(3) Anderton's nostalgic longing for his wife and son;

(4) the abduction of his son, and his guilt;

(5) Anderton's relationship with Agatha;

(6) Agatha's relationship with Anne Lively's death (her mother);

(7) the creepy relationship between Agatha and her keeper, Wally (Daniel London; Wally still lives with his mother);

(8) the pre-cogs being idolized by society (and the religious aspects of pre-cognition);

---

[49] *Minority Report* was the first of a series of collaborations between Spielberg and Cruise. Spielberg said he had wanted to work with Tom Cruise for years, and they had of course collaborated for months on *Rain Main* (before the director left to work on the second *Indiana Jones* sequel).

[50] Another reference to detective fiction were the names of pre-cognitives: Arthur, Agatha and Dashiell (as in Arthur Conan Doyle, inventor of Sherlock Holmes, Agatha Christie, and Dashiell Hammett).

(9) Anderton's rivalry with Witwer;

(10) Anderton's relationship with surrogate father Burgess;

(11) Anderton's drug addiction;

(12) the theme of eyes, vision and voyeurism;

(13) the invasion of privacy;

(14) the view of society in the future, including futuristic law, government, transport, housing, prison, etc.

*

Both *Catch Me If You Can* and *Minority Report* are about white American males on the run from the authorities, but the difference in the two historical periods is marked. *Catch Me If You Can* is pre-CCTV, pre-miniature video cameras, pre-internet, while *Minority Report* is a world entirely driven by surveillance in all areas of life.[51]

Probably the most prominent motif in *Minority Report* was everything to do with vision, eyes, voyeurism, and surveillance invading every aspect of social life. *Minority Report* contained more images of eyes and looking, of people watching other people, than any of Steven Spielberg's other films (and his films are packed with eyes and looks - shark's eyes, E.T.'s eyes, and dinosaurs' eyes).

There were retinal scanners used to I.D. citizens in stores, subway trains, shopping malls and entrances (and later, to track Anderton across the city), gruesome eye operations, Anderton chasing his eyes rolling down a slope, a drug dealer with empty eye sockets (who recalls Tiresias and the Cyclops), closed circuit TV in every public space, computer screens and video screens,[52] video billboards and adverts,[53] cameras, holograms, Anderton and Agatha escaping the Pre-Crime cops by hiding momentarily (behind balloons, and an umbrella), and the 'spyders' (the whole spyder flophouse scene is based on the machines infiltrating the building to scan people's

---

[51] Like *Minority Report*, *The Terminal* was also a film of surveillance and CCTV. Frank, the airport security boss, standing at the bank of TV monitors manipulating a joystick to direct the camera recalled Anderton in *Minority Report* in the Pre-Crime control room (as well as a film editor). Closed circuit TV had been a key element in the narratives of the *Jurassic Park* movies, as well as *Minority Report*.

[52] Eddie's shabby rooms are dominated by a wall screen over the bed, which replays old crime shows (when Anderton enters the apartment the first thing he sees it someone being shot on the giant screen).

[53] These were projected everywhere in the city - including underpasses and the sides of buildings in the sprawl, places where you wouldn't imagine many of the target audience for the adverts lived.

eyes).54 Yet again, out of Japanese *anime*.

The name of Eddie's assistant nurse, Van Eyck, is another reference to sight – the Early Netherlandish painter Jan van Eyck being famous for playing with the viewer's perceptions (also cited in *BladeRunner*). Anderton has to go blind willingly in order to escape his predicament (there are references to sight and blindness in the dialogue, such as when Anderton scores drugs from the blind dealer). Agatha repeatedly says 'can you see?'. *Minority Report* is a film which explores different forms of seeing.

Computer and video screens were employed in numerous ways, including the playback of the pre-cogs predicting a murder, Lamar's faking of pre-cog visions, CCTV footage of Anderton, Anderton's home video holograms, Anderton decoding Burgess's faked pre-cog vision, and the climax (Burgess is thus also a kind of filmmaker, putting together the fake vision).

Yet another layer of vision and recording devices was added to the narrative of *Minority Report* by making John Anderton's wife a photographer (and an old-fashioned snapper, not a digital, one: it's 2054, but she's still using chemicals in a traditional darkroom). And note how Anderton is also a cameraman, taking holograms of his wife and child (Lara teases him, telling him to put down the camera. Steven Spielberg himself is known for going about filming with video cameras).

The 'movieness' of *Minority Report* is everywhere apparent. As if he were fresh out of film school (although he didn't go to one), and not a veteran of 19 features, Steven Spielberg and Janusz Kaminski chose all manner of weird camera angles (justified by Kaminski because *Minority Report* is a *film noir*). Sometimes, as a scene plays, you think it's not possible for Spielberg and Kaminski to think up a new angle, but they do (for example, in the crime of passion opener, a shot behind a pair of spectacles on a table, or a p.o.v. shot of Agatha underwater looking upwards with her hand passing in front of the camera, or the amazing – and so simple – two-shot of Anderton and Agatha holding onto each other and facing in opposite directions – a *hommage* to Ingmar Bergman's *Persona*).

---

54 In the flophouse scene, people are interrupted by the army of electronic spiders in the midst of their lives – fucking, arguing, defecating – for a brief retinal scan, then they go back to their business.

Many of the underwater scenes were covered with point-of-view shots, a recurring fascination of Steven Spielberg's. For an urban thriller, *Minority Report* contained plenty of scenes involving characters immersed in water.55

Drug addiction, which hadn't really featured in a big way in a Steven Spielberg picture before, was a key element of *Minority Report*. In *film noirs* of the 1940s (under the Production Code), it was alcoholism. In the 2054 of 2002's *Minority Report*, Anderton is addicted to a psychoactive drug called Neuroin (and the drug is also linked to the mutation of the pre-cognitives, another way of tying together Anderton and Agatha).

A.I. and *Minority Report* saw a return to modern America for Steven Spielberg. For quite some time, prior to *A.I.* in 2001, he had made films about other places and other times. *Schindler's List* and *Saving Private Ryan* had been set 50-odd years in the past, in war-torn Europe; *Jurassic Park* was set in the present-day, but mainly in Costa Rica; *Hook* was set in a fantastical Edwardian era, and an intentionally unrealistic present-day; *Amistad* explored 19th century Africa and America, and the third *Indiana Jones* film took place in many locations, but in the 1930s. The beginning and ending of *The Lost World*, however, was set in present-day America.

With *A.I.* and *Minority Report*, though, Steven Spielberg returned to contemporary U.S.A.: *A.I.* contained scenes set in a ruined New York City, while *Minority Report* was based entirely in Washington and its environs. Both New York and Washington (whether futuristic or not) were unusual Spielberg settings: the typical Spielberg environment, if it was American, was a small town or suburbia (as in *E.T., Poltergeist, Close Encounters of the Third Kind, Sugarland Express, Jaws, The Twilight Zone, The Color Purple, Always*, or the Spielberg-produced films such as *Back to the Future*,

---

55 Water, often as a fearsome, dangerous presence, is a recurring motif in Steven Spielberg's cinema. The ocean dominates *Jaws* even more than the shark; it's there in *1941* (Japanese submarines approach the U.S.A., and ferris wheels roll into it); in *Raiders* Indy swims across a large chunk of the Mediterranean (and in the opening teaser he dives into a wide river); in *Indiana Jones and the Temple of Doom* there's the river raft sequence, and the climactic battle on the rope bridge; the ocean recurs in *Indiana Jones and The Last Crusade* (which opens with the older Indy brawling on a cargo vessel in a storm), and a fight in a Venice canal; *Always* opens with fishermen on a lake; *Empire of the Sun* opens and closes with water scenes, and Jim crawls through pools; in *Hook* Banning flies over the sea to Neverland, and water surrounds Hook's ship; the *Jurassic Park* films feature the Pacific in many scenes (with a major water sequence climaxing *Jurassic Park 3*), and key scenes occur in streams and rivers; the English Channel is the setting for the carnage at the beginning of *Saving Private Ryan*; in *A.I.* David dives into the sea in Manhattan, and into a swimming pool (and later, the super-robots' craft navigates layers of frozen ocean); Elliott washes E.T. in the bath (in the *Special Edition*), and the alien's found lying beside a stream; and a major action scene occurs in *The War of the Worlds* when a ferry's attacked by aliens.

Gremlins, The Goonies, Casper, Small Soldiers, American Beauty, Galaxy Quest and *Twister*).

MINORITY REPORT: THE BOOK AND THE FILM

The 1956 short story by Philip K. Dick differs greatly from the 2002 film. It has been common in adapting Dick's fiction for the cinema to use his stories as starting-points, rather than texts to be faithfully translated to the screen (Dick's eccentric titles are usually altered, but not in the case of *Minority Report*).

The film of *Minority Report* inevitably fleshes out the story, and adds a good deal to it. Some of the alterations are cosmetic (in the story, the pre-cogs sit on chairs, in the film they inhabit a circular, luminescent pool, with flickering screens in the ceiling). But many of the changes from written word to moving image are considerable. The whole plot about Kaplan and Fleming being involved in the army is gone, and the International Veterans' League, and the Military Intelligence agents (as is the Chinese war). Now, the movie is set in Washington, D.C., not New York City, and the background is not military, but governmental. John Anderton is older in the book, and wonders if he's getting 'bald and fat and old'. In the film, he's Hollywood hunk Tom Cruise, a very different characterization. In the book, Anderton thinks he's being ousted by Witwer (and he is, very rapidly). In the film, the rivalry between Anderton and Witwer is not so much between an older guy approaching retirement and a young buck, but between equals.

A significant addition to the film of *Minority Report* is having Anderton alone; in the movie, his wife Lara has left him, and he has a son (Sean), whom he lost during a swimming session six years ago.[56] The film turns Anderton into a lonely widow, a man who's lost his family and watches holographic tapes he made of them in his solitary, drug-aided evenings. That gives Anderton a different back-story from the book, making

---
[56] The key event in Anderton's back story is not his wife leaving him 6 years ago, but his son's disappearance and possible death.

the movie more deeply emotional, much more about loss and desire (and with children as the focus of that loss, in the true Spielbergian manner, rather than just the loss of a lover or wife).

In the book, Anderton smokes; in the film, he's addicted to drugs, and wanders out into the dark, dangerous realms of the District of Columbia (the 'sprawl') to score drugs from menacing, blind pushers (with a distinctly Homeric or mythical atmosphere).

The movie adds sections where Anderton needs to undergo a disguise, and visits Peter Stormare's crazy eye doctor Solomon Eddie and his eccentric assistant, Greta van Eyck (Caroline Lagerfelt). There are sequences where Anderton wanders about in his new disfiguring disguise, which are also additions to the story.

The action beats – the chase atop the speeding magnetic cars, the car factory, the jet-pack alley chase, the spyders scanning the flophouse, the shopping mall chase – are all additions to the story. They all have the look and feel of early 2000s action cinema, rather than Philip K. Dick's science fiction of the 1950s.

The opening sequence, too, is a complete addition to Philip K. Dick's short story: in the text, John Anderton receives the card informing him he will kill Kaplan in the first scene (when Witwer comes to visit). The film adds two action scenes which demonstrate how the whole Pre-Crime organization works: the viewer sees the operations room, the screens, the surveillance software, the name being carved onto a wooden ball, the elaborate machinery, the pre-cogs in their pool, and Anderton at the centre of the operation, working out where the murder will occur (that sequence in itself is very elaborate and dense, with Cruise's Anderton orchestrating imagery on multiple screens to the sound of classical music).[57]

The prologue doesn't bear directly on the plot in terms of the people (Howard and Sarah Marks) involved in the potential crime: they do not feature at all in the rest of the film (and aren't referred to, either). So in

---

[57] Steven Spielberg is very good at beginnings and endings in his films. From *Jaws* onwards, Spielberg's movies have had terrific openings: the burst into light of *Close Encounters of the Third Kind* and the discovery of the planes in the desert; the exploration of the forest in *E.T.* and abandonment of the alien; the menacing teasers of the *Jurassic Park* films; the war is hell first reel of *Saving Private Ryan;* the bloody slave insurrection in *Amistad*; and most famously, the celebrated prologues of the *Indiana Jones* adventures. Even a film like *Hook*, which opens with a children's school play of *Peter Pan*, has more charm for some critics than the rest of the movie. In the George Lucas School of Filmmaking, the first 5 minutes and final 20 minutes are the most important sections of a film.

that sense, the prologue is there to introduce some of the major characters (principally, John Anderton), and to show who he is, where he works and what he does. It also serves to lead audiences into the world of the movie, the futuristic setting, and so on. The adultery theme is ancient drama – a man catching his wife in bed with a lover – it's a cliché times a million. All sorts of crimes of passion or sudden violence could have been used, but sexual desire and adultery feeds into Anderton's back-story (that his wife Lara has left).[58]

※

In the story, Anderton does return to the Pre-Crime building, to find out exactly what the pre-cogs previsualized about him, but he doesn't kidnap one of them and go on the run. The abduction of Agatha is a complete addition to the story (it adds to the jeopardy having Anderton haul Agatha about, as well extending the role of the pre-cogs in the drama. And it gives Anderton someone to play against, rather than talk to himself or narrate his own predicament. With Agatha in tow, *Minority Report* becomes another buddy movie).

In Philip K. Dick's 1956 short story, John Anderton finds out from the Pre-Crime system that he's going to murder a retired army general, Kaplan, who's secretly head of a military organization. The army also monitors the Pre-Crime set-up. The film ditches that, and introduces the murder of Anne Lively (who turns out to be Agatha's mother). Now it's Anderton's boss, Lamar Burgess (Max von Sydow) who's behind it all, framing Anderton. In the film, Anderton is still going to kill someone he's never met, but it's Leo Crow, whom Burgess links with the person who abducted Anderton's child Sean (Burgess knows how much Sean meant to Anderton, and uses that as a way of getting to him).

There hasn't been a murder in the six years the Pre-Crime scheme has been running. The establishment of the Pre-Crime system six years ago is tied in emotionally with Anderton (with the loss of his son), a classic screenwriting technique of making the hero's motives personal and emotional.

---

[58] The movie also added a layer of voyeurism to the adultery scene, with Marks (Arye Cross) spying on his wife after he's left for work, and watching her lover appear, whom he's already seen across the road. Later, he sits beside the marital bed in a hopeless, ineffectual state as they begin to make love right next to him. It's a mite silly, really – you have to admit that depicting adult sexual relationships is not one of Steven Spielberg's strong points.

In the story, John Anderton suspects that his wife Lisa is involved in the framing, until he finds out otherwise, and teams up with her against Kaplan's heavy, Fleming. In the film, his wife (now Lara not Lisa – perhaps a nod to the David Lean epic *Doctor Zhivago*?) fulfils a rather unbelievable narrative function (including springing Anderton from prison). That whole prison sequence is another lengthy addition to the short story.

The closing scene of the three pre-cognitives in the house on the island, surrounded by lakes and other islands, is an idyllic evocation of the American frontier and wilderness which recalls Henry David Thoreau at Walden pool, or Mark Twain's *Tom Sawyer* (Anderton reminisces to his wife how his son Sean was scared by *Tom Sawyer*). It's a sentimental evocation of the American sublime, a back-to-the-land fantasy which doesn't fool any of us for a minute.

5

A SCANNER DARKLY

by Thomas A. Christie

Philip Kindred Dick (1928-1982) is one of the most important figures in twentieth-century science fiction, and arguably one of the most significant American authors of the postwar period.[59] He has become best-known for his probing and psychologically challenging novels which include *The Man in the High Castle* (1962), *The Three Stigmata of Palmer Eldritch* (1965), *Ubik* (1969) and *Flow My Tears, The Policeman Said* (1974), as well as a great many short stories. A multiple literary award-winner in his lifetime, it is difficult to overstate Dick's intricate skill and momentous impact on both

---

[59] A summarised account of Dick's many novels and other works can be found in: John Clute and Peter Nicholls, *The Encyclopedia of Science Fiction*, rev. ed. (New York: St Martin's Press, 1995), pp.328-330.

Also well worth consulting is 'The Men in Their High Castles: Dick and Other Visionaries', a chapter which appears in the following invaluable reference work: Brian Aldiss, with David Wingrove, *Trillion Year Spree* (London: Paladin, 1988) [1986], pp.390-426.

literary science fiction and indeed American fiction in general, and this influence has been seen to continue even since the time of his death.

An extremely prolific writer, adaptations of many of his novels and works of short prose fiction have been popular in film, television, radio and on stage. There have been a number of significant cinematic adaptations of his work, most notable among them being Ridley Scott's *Blade Runner* (1982) (based on the novel *Do Androids Dream of Electric Sheep?* (1968)), Paul Verhoeven's *Total Recall* (1990) (from the short story *We Can Remember It For You Wholesale* (1966)), Christian Duguay's *Screamers* (1995), Steven Spielberg's *Minority Report* (2002) and John Woo's *Paycheck* (2003). It is no small testament to Dick's skill as a writer that with each passing year, his damning indictments of modern society, authoritarianism and human nature seem ever more prescient, and indeed his intensely keen foresight and the uncomfortable potency of his finely-drawn psychological awareness would be of special relevance to Linklater's adaptation of one of Dick's best-known novels, *A Scanner Darkly* (1977) in 2006.

Richard Stuart Linklater (1960-) is one of the most interesting, original and exciting independent filmmakers active in America today. He has become known as the high priest of slacker culture, a persuasive and distinctive proponent of complex philosophical issues, a socio-political filmic polymath, and one of the most expressive articulators of the Generation X ethos. But in truth, his body of work presents a far wider remit than even these fashionable appellations would suggest, and the intricate range of themes with which he has engaged over the past two decades has proven to be both extensive and comprehensive. Renowned for finely-observed character studies such as *Dazed and Confused* (1993), *BeforeSunrise* (1995) and *Before Sunset* (2004), his influential and surreal masterpiece *Slacker* (1991), and mainstream comedies such as *School of Rock* (2003), Linklater is a filmmaker who always finds something extraordinary in the ordinary, and who is never blind to the beauty of the smallest details of everyday life, no matter how mundane or commonplace they may seem at face value.

A Scanner Darkly was a significant film for Linklater in a number of ways. Noteworthy was his return to the pioneering new digitally interpolated rotoscoping technique, Rotoshop, which had been developed by Bob Sabiston and employed to such striking effect in Linklater's earlier film *Waking Life* (2001). Here, however, it was to be used less obtrusively, with even greater refinement, and for very different reasons.[60] But Linklater's choice to adapt a novel by the late Philip K. Dick was also a significant one. His interest in the writer's work had been apparent from *Waking Life*, where the 'Pinball Playing Man' (portrayed by the director himself) discusses one of Dick's many essays at the film's conclusion, and indeed Dick's persistent exploration of the themes of human perceptions of reality and his deep suspicion of the role and motivation of central government in the modern age seemed tailor-made for Linklater's leading edge filmmaking.[61]

Linklater's film remains true to the spirit and content of Dick's original novel. Some years in the future, the world is awash with a highly addictive (and gravely damaging) narcotic drug known as Substance D, covertly developed from a small blue flower and smuggled to all points of the globe. Trafficking of the narcotic has become endemic, and the American government is struggling to track the supply and demand of the illegal substance within their country, gradually establishing a highly sophisticated monitoring system to trace the communication and movement of citizens in order to pin down the source of the drugs.

In Anaheim, California, Bob Arctor (Keanu Reeves) is an anti-narcotics agent in the employ of the government who is responsible for stymieing the flow of Substance D in the immediate area. For some time he has been working undercover in a ramshackle house in the locality which he shares with a number of drug addicts including the addled Ernie Luckman (Woody Harrelson) and the conceited, thoroughly inscrutable James Barris (Robert Downey Jr). Other regular visitors to this curious hideout are Charles Freck (Rory Cochrane), who is heavily addicted to Substance D and now suffers disturbing symptoms of long-term exposure to the drug, and Donna Hawthorne (Winona Ryder), a cocaine addict who is also the group's supplier of Substance D. However, it soon becomes clear that Arctor himself

---

[60] Linklater discusses Sabiston's processing technique, and many other aspects of the production, in Marc Savlov's interview 'Securing the Substance' which appears in the 7 July 2006 issue of *The Austin Chronicle*.

[61] Linklater has an interesting dialogue with Rob Nelson in the 30 May 2006 edition of *The Village Voice*, where he explains his selection of subject matter in choosing *A Scanner Darkly* for adaptation, as well as relating it to his other major film project being released that year, *Fast Food Nation* (2006).

has become addicted to the drug during the course of his covert operations, which greatly complicates matters. His initial plan had been to manipulate Donna into revealing her source of Substance D, thus allowing the police to shut down the operation at its foundation. Instead, he finds himself romantically attracted to her, and becomes drawn ever deeper into the murky, drug-soaked world that he has been assigned to infiltrate.

Back at police headquarters, Arctor is known only as Agent Fred, his visual identity masked by a scramble suit – a full-body technological gadget which constantly obscures an individual's features, voice and gender in order to ensure that no two operatives are ever able to identify each other (thus avoiding the potential for corruption within the department). Fred regularly reports to his immediate superior, Agent Hank (voice of Mark Turner), who has been monitoring the situation within Arctor's house via a comprehensive system of concealed video cameras. By a process of elimination, Hank has now determined that Fred is in fact one of the house's occupants, but is unable to establish which one he might specifically be. He thus orders Fred to intensify his scrutiny of the situation, specifically with regard to heightening observation of Arctor himself, whom Hank believes may be the key to the whole investigation.

Now faced with the intricate task of supervising a surveillance operation of his own undercover identity, Fred/ Arctor finds that his addiction is further encumbering his ability to perceive the difference between his two discrete selves. As the inhabitants of Arctor's house become ever more paranoid, suspecting that their movements are being monitored by the state, Arctor himself becomes increasingly immersed in his clandestine role, slowly losing his ability to recall his other identity as Agent Fred and suffering acute hallucinations. Meanwhile, Barris quietly becomes distrustful of Arctor, suspecting that his romantic relationship with Donna is merely a front for a covert professional association between the pair. Barris thus deduces that Arctor and Donna are both members of a terrorist cell, which fuels his already-rampant anxieties.

Barris approaches the police about his suspicions, and ironically ends up airing his wild notions to Agents Fred and Hank. However, Fred is unmoved by Barris's detailed betrayal of Arctor, as he now has no way of differentiating between his 'real' and undercover identities. Hank has Barris remanded in custody 'for his own protection', but his testimony is of little benefit as Hank has already deduced Fred's true identity and thus already knows that he has no connection to either terror organisations or the source of the drugs supply. Police psychologists have also become conscious of Fred's impaired mental functionality due to his heavy abuse of Substance D, deducing that conflict has been agitated between the right and left hemispheres of his brain. Hank informs Fred that he will be reprimanded on account of breaking the law.

Hank then reveals that he is fully aware that Arctor is also Fred (and vice-versa), which comes as a total shock to him. This heightens Fred/ Arctor's state of confusion still further, and – exhausted and crushed by the ramifications of his drug use – he has no choice but to comply with Hank's insistence that he attend a facility operated by New Path, a mysterious corporation which manages rehabilitation clinics throughout the country.

What Fred/ Arctor remains entirely unaware of is that Hank's alter-ego is none other than Donna. Far from being the drug runner that Arctor had originally suspected, Donna is actually working to enforce a government agenda – to plant an operative within New Path in order to ascertain the corporation's true motives. Therefore both of Fred/ Arctor's separate identities have been manipulated by Donna and her superiors to achieve this end, with the consent of neither of his two selves.

At New Path, Fred/ Arctor reacts badly to his sudden withdrawal from Substance D, and suffers extensive neurological damage. After a long period of mental and physical rehabilitation, he is given a new name – Bruce – and shipped out to one of the corporation's secluded farming facilities. Now suffering profound mental defects, he is put to work tending the vast cornfields. Eventually, he discovers that beneath the rows of corn, thousands of tiny blue flowers are being cultivated – the organic source of Substance D. Although mentally incapable of determining the true nature of the flowers, he is subconsciously compelled to pick one from the ground and conceal it in his boot, determining to pass it on to his friends the next time that he returns to the New Path clinic. (It is left to the audience's judgment as to who these 'friends' may be.)

A Scanner Darkly is an extremely faithful adaptation of the Philip K. Dick novel, accurately translating not only its content but also its oppressively claustrophobic, paranoid approach to its subject matter. Apart from updating the film for an indistinct near-future setting (Dick's novel having been set in 1994), only a small number of variations are in evidence between the book and Linklater's screenplay, such as the explicit revelation that Hank is in fact Donna (Hank's identity is only suggested in the novel, but never fully revealed), and the elimination of novel character Jerry Fabin from the events of the film. Linklater utilises Sabiston's rotoscoping effect very successfully in heightening the edgy disorientation of the narrative, and this is particularly effective in the realisation of the constantly shifting scramble suits, with their dizzying visual characteristics. Highly efficient too is the skilful contrast between Fred's continuously changing exterior aspect and the unnervingly confined Arctor speaking from within the suit's interior, growing ever more psychologically disturbed as the film continues. Bob Sabiston's software is applied in a very different way to its previous employment in *Waking Life*; although Fred/ Arctor's drug-influenced perceptions could conceivably suggest that the same kind of dream-state environment is evident in *A Scanner Darkly*, the effect is much more restrained throughout the film. Even the cockroach transformation sequence, where Arctor's observational acuity grows ever more unreliable, appears much more low-key than the vibrant conceptual buoyancy and shifting visual styles of *Waking Life*, and the moody, oppressive effect suggested here seems much more inclined to unnerve and disorientate the audience than to suggest the wild and exciting subconscious possibilities suggested by Linklater's earlier film.

The casting of star Keanu Reeves was also an inspired choice. Well known to audiences from a high-profile career reaching back to the mid-eighties, Reeves was at the time enjoying considerable acclaim for his role as Thomas 'Neo' Anderson in Larry and Andy Wachowski's *The Matrix* trilogy (comprising *The Matrix* (1999), *The Matrix Reloaded* (2003) and *The Matrix Revolutions* (2003)). Although *The Matrix* series had featured a similarly Descartes-inspired exploration of a fractured reality, its apocalyptic far-future backdrop seemed a world away from the foreboding imminence of Dick's grim, despondent realism, and Reeves brilliantly subverts the kind of cool heroism displayed by Neo to create the perplexed dejection and idiosyncratic mumbling mode of speech of Agent Fred/ Bob Arctor. The shuffling, confused Arctor has a perfect foil in the rangy physicality of Robert Downey Jr, whose surreal verbal articulacy in the role of James Barris contrasts sharply with his eccentric, spasmodic mode of speech. Downey Jr excels in expressing Barris's quick (if oddly oblique) wit, along with his devious, paranoid scheming, and his uniquely mannered portrayal reminds the audience of the reason why his acting skills had gained him a nomination for an Academy Award in 1993 for his leading role in *Chaplin* (1992). He gives a particularly well-observed performance following a malfunction with the accelerator pedal of Arctor's car, an unfortunate accident which Barris uses to gradually manoeuvre the other men (and possibly even himself) into believing is part of an intricately planned state-controlled plot to have them all murdered.

Past Oscar nominations could also claimed by two of Downey Jr's co-stars, Woody Harrelson (for Best Leading Actor in *The People Versus Larry Flynt* (1996)) in 1997, and also Winona Ryder, who was nominated for Best Supporting Actress in 1994 (for *The Age of Innocence* (1993)) and Best Actress in a Leading Role in 1995 (for *Little Women* (1994)). This tightly-knit quartet of actors creates a fascinating collective character study, the qualities of each contrasting effectively with the other as the film progresses. Ernie Luckman, for instance, has all the traits of a spaced-out surfer dude who has strayed into dark and uncertain territory, yet when the thin surface of his easygoing disposition is scratched he can be seen to match Arctor and Barris step for step when it comes to agitated paranoia. Donna Hawthorne, on the other hand, is a much more evenly collected character, encouraging Arctor's affections whilst steadfastly refusing his physical advances. Her intractable and continuous rebuff of Arctor on a physical level raises Barris's suspicions as much as it inspires a vague, unrealised infatuation towards her from Luckman. Ryder impeccably carries off Donna's duality of purpose, demonstrating her character's deft ability to flawlessly manipulate the proceedings around her, and even managing to out-scheme the arch-conspirator Barris. Completing the central ensemble is Rory Cochrane, whose frenetic, twitchy performance as Charles Freck – constantly in motion and haunted by vivid hallucinations which have tangibly aggravating physical symptoms – seems to form a kind of extreme flipside of the affably stupefied Ron Slater from *Dazed and Confused*.

Cochrane brings great pathos to the slow-motion disintegration of Freck, heavily addicted to Substance D and even more thoroughly disorientated than the inhabitants of Arctor's house, yet he still manages to bring just enough dark humour to the role to take the edge from Freck's hopelessly bleak situation.[62]

The critics were generally supportive of *A Scanner Darkly* following its release, though there were a few dissenting voices nonetheless. While some reviewers praised the film for the great care taken to respect Dick's original text,[63] others considered it to be too faithful to the deliberate, idea-driven novel, divesting the film of momentum.[64] Some commended the thoughtful use of Bob Sabiston's digital rotoscoping technique,[65] while others questioned why Linklater had felt the need to employ the process at all.[66] However, a majority of commentators found aspects of the film worthy of approval, including its relentless sense of disquieting claustrophobia,[67] willingness to engage with potent political issues,[68] speculative and theoreticalvigour,[69] and the fact that it never shies away from engaging with the difficult range of concepts evident in Dick's novel.[70]

A Scanner Darkly was conferred the Austin Film Award at the 2007 Austin Film Critics Association Awards, and also won the Best Animation Award at the Online Film Critics Society Awards in the same year. It was additionally nominated for Best Animation at the Golden Trailer Awards in 2006, and was also nominated for two of the most prestigious prizes in science fiction, the Saturn Award for Best Animated Film from the Academy of Science Fiction, Fantasy and Horror Films (2007), and the Hugo Award for Best Dramatic Presentation (2007).

With *A Scanner Darkly*, Linklater had created quite possibly the most faithful cinematic evocation of Philip K. Dick's style and thematic concerns

---

62 Cochrane talks about the role of Charles Freck, as well as his experience of working with Richard Linklater, in an interview with Cassie Carpenter in the 21 July 2006 edition of *The Chicago Sun-Times*.
63 Philip French, '*A Scanner Darkly*', in *The Observer*, 20 August 2006.
64 Justin Chang, '*A Scanner Darkly*', in *Variety*, 25 May 2006.
65 Marjorie Baumgarten, '*A Scanner Darkly*', in *The Austin Chronicle*, 7 July 2006.
66 Duane Byrge, 'Animation wasted in static *Scanner Darkly*', in *The Chicago Sun-Times*, 7 July 2006.
67 Michael Wilmington, '*A Scanner Darkly*', in *The Chicago Tribune*, 7 July 2006.
68 Peter Travers, '*A Scanner Darkly*', in *Rolling Stone*, 23 June 2006.
69 Keith Phipps, '*A Scanner Darkly*', in *The Onion A.V. Club*, 5 July 2006. <http://www.avclub.com/content/node/50156/>
70 J. Hoberman, 'Brain Candy: Richard Linklater's literate Dick adaptation is a brain-bending D-light', in *The Village Voice*, 5 July 2006.

since Ridley Scott's atmospheric *BladeRunner* almost a quarter of a century earlier. Praised by many admirers of science fiction for its fidelity to the source text, while still augmenting the dialogue and technology evident in the film to reflect cultural and scientific advances made since the time of Dick's novel, Linklater's film offers further exploration of the nature of existence in the modern world – namely the importance of self-expression in the face of growing surveillance of public life. In terms of free speech, it is interesting to compare the treatment of Alex Jones's outspoken protester character – unceremoniously silenced and bundled off by the oppressive authorities – with Jones's unfettered cameo appearance in *Waking Life*, where he has the ability to freely broadcast his views just as the audience are at liberty to draw their own conclusions about the statements that he makes. Thus, like Dick's novel before it, Linklater's defence of freedom of expression within the film is of paramount importance to the core of its narrative, and *A Scanner Darkly*'s preoccupation with Orwellian scrutiny of the masses, the culture of suspicion, and corporate interference with the direction of society is, in the grand tradition of the very best of the science fiction genre a cautionary tale with bold allegorical resonance.[71]

The discussion contained in this chapter can also be found, in a modified form, in *The Cinema of Richard Linklater* by Thomas A. Christie, which is also available from Crescent Moon Publishing.

---

[71] For an interesting discussion of Linklater's interest in the works of Philip K. Dick, his interview with Mike Russell of the *CulturePulp* website is both valuable and very detailed. The site also contains an illustrated summary of the interview in a cartoon style, as well as both a truncated and unexpurgated transcript of Linklater's detailed conversation with Russell, and is not to be missed: Mike Russell, 'The *CulturePulp* Q&A: Richard Linklater', in *CulturePulp*, 54, 16 July 2006.
<http://homepage.mac.com/merussell/iblog/B835531044/C1592678312/E20060701140745/index.html>
    See also: Mike Russell, 'The Richard Linklater Interview', in *CulturePulp*, 54, 16 July 2006.
    <http://homepage.mac.com/merussell/iblog/B835531044/C1162162177/E20060717001411/index.html>

6

OTHER PHILIP K. DICK MOVIES

PAYCHECK

Paycheck (Paramount/ DreamWorks, 2003) was a Philip K. Dick story made over as a John Woo action thriller. All of the usual elements of a John Woo actioner were there: the elaborate gun battles, car and motorbike chases, lots of explosions, plenty of slow motion, multiple cameras – hell, Woo even squeezed in his customary lyrical shots of flying birds (and Christian motifs). But *Paycheck* wasn't a patch on John Woo classics such as *Hard-Boiled* and *The Killer* (and Ben Affleck was no Chow Yun-Fat, either).

And *Paycheck*, written by Dean Geogaris, although it tried hard, wasn't a particularly distinctive entry in the Philip K. Dick sub-genre of science fiction cinema. As John Woo explained, the filmmakers jettisoned a large amount of the sci-fi, to concentrate on the dramatic and thriller aspects

(*Paycheck* became consciously more of an Alfred Hitchcock thriller than a sci-fi movie, Woo commented, with Affleck modelling himself on Cary Grant).

It's his themes and idiosyncratic worldview that help to mark Philip K. Dick out as a really fascinating writer. No one else sees contemporary America or contemporary history quite like Dick. Unfortunately, most of those Dickian elements were missing from *Paycheck*.

Oh, *Paycheck* was fun, over-the-top, ridiculously heightened and noisy, like the typical John Woo movie (and like your average Hollywood actioner). But it also came across, ultimately, as not a lot more engaging than an average episode of a US TV fantasy drama show like *Stargate* or *Enterprise*.

There was the future vision machine with its intricate controls and blue smoky visual fx, the prowling camerawork, the gun fights, the FBI agents, the TV and computer screens, the slick one-liners – all of the usual elements of American television shows. But it was all too predictable, too obvious, too uninspired. (The hero, Michael Jennings did get to save the world, though – by averting the war that the machine predicts).

Paycheck was set in the hi-tech *milieu* of new technology; it was based in Seattle, but it could have been any US city. A world of laboratories and research centres, big business, briefcases and gadgets. (If the concrete look of *Paycheck* looks familiar – the production designer was William Sandell, who created the design for *Total Recall*).

Like *Total Recall* and *Next*, *Paycheck* was another movie for writers and editors: like those Phil Dick adaptions, *Paycheck* explored alternate narratives, using the dual focus of memory wipes and seeing into the future. The memory wipes and recalls evoked *Total Recall*, of course, with our hero strapped to a chair with a brain scanning device attached to his head. And the plot device of seeing into the future threw out all the usual possibilities of alternate realities, which writers and film editors enjoy exploring. These narrative devices enable the filmmakers to rewrite the film as it goes along. They can show a scene then have its meaning or outcome reworked, keeping the audience guessing.

John Woo was famous for mounting extravagant, heightened action films, marked by gunplay, car chases, and themes of loyalty, brotherhood,

Christianity, and masculinity. As in the typical Woo movie, the villains came across (at least initially) as charismatic and affable: Jimmy and his sidekick Mr Wolf were charming, and Jimmy has known Michael for a long time (the first time they meet they hug and share cigars like old buddies).

John Woo's style of filmmaking – violence, guns, squibs, multi-cameras, slow motion, stunts, montage – comes from Sam Peckinpah and Akira Kurosawa (with Sergei Eisenstein and montage as a distant ancestor). It's a world of cops and gangsters, lonely men and brotherhoods, an identification between the hero and the villain, and an exploration of religion and morality.

John Woo's early successes were produced by Tsui Hark[72] – *A Better Tomorrow* and *Bullet In the Head*. As well as the *Better Tomorrow* films, Woo was also known for *The Killer* and *Hard-Boiled*, two masterpieces of the action genre.[73] Woo was among the many Asian filmmakers who moved to Hollywood: his American movies included: *Hard Target, Broken Arrow, Face-Off, The Windtalkers, 1949, Red Cliff, Blackjack, All the Invisible Children* and a *Mission: Impossible* sequel.[74] Woo, like Hong Kong and Chinese action cinema in general, had plenty of imitators: soon it became *de rigeur* for action films to feature extended gun battles shot with multiple cameras running at different speeds, producing elaborate montages of slow motion. Woo's influence on 1990s Hollywood has been substantial: it occurs in the *Die Hard* and *Lethal Weapon* series, in the 1990s *James Bonds*, in the work of Quentin Tarantino, Abel Ferrara and Robert Rodriguez, and in films such as *The Matrix, Demolition Man* and *Mission: Impossible* (Woo directed the sequel, the most lucrative movie of 2000).

John Woo seems to have found it difficult, like so many non-American directors coming to Hollywood, to make a film in the Tinseltown system, about contemporary America. Paul Verhoeven said he deliberately went for sci-fi genre movies (*RoboCop* and *Total Recall*) and another genre outing (the psychothriller *Basic Instinct*) before trying to tackle a portrayal of

---

[72] In my opinion, the best action director working today.
[73] John Woo had already made some twenty films prior to *Hard-Boiled* (including *Princess Chueng Ping, Hand of Death, Last Hurrah For Chivalry, From Rags to Riches, Laughing Times, Sunset Warrior, Run, Tiger, Run, A Better Tomorrow, The Killer* and *Bullet in the Head*).
[74] Rather than being a hardened cynic, as his high-power, kinetic, violent films might suggest, John Woo came across in interviews as a romantic, someone shy, a Christian, who came to America for personal and family reasons as much as for professional or career reasons. Woo spoke lovingly of his family, and how he had been unhappy in the intensely competitive world of Hong Kong cinema.

contemporary America society head-on (in *Showgirls*. However, one could say that *RoboCop* was very much about the contemporary concerns of policing the State, of laws, of the freedom to bear arms, of proto-fascist regimes. Unfortunately, the audience didn't see a satire on Reaganite politics, as intended, but RoboCop as an avenger and pop icon).

SCREAMERS

The Canadian *Screamers* (Christian Duguay, 1995) starred Peter Weller as the chief of a mining colony on a remote planet (Sirius 6B) quarrying a radioactive superfuel (berynium) in the year 2078. It was based on a Philip K. Dick story ("Second Variety", 1953), with a script co-written by Dan O'Bannon and Miguel Tejada-Flores. Franco Battista and Tom Berry produced for Triumph Films/ Sony.

Screamers was essentially a sci-fi thriller/ chase movie with some *Alien* horror added, boiling down to Peter Weller's Hendricksson leading a motley crew of survivors across a war-ravaged wasteland, armed with giant guns, blasting 'screamers' in the dirt (quite a bit of *Screamers* involves characters traversing empty Canadian landscapes or abandoned factories).

As the film begins, the outpost has been abandoned by Earth during trade wars between the New Economic Bloc (NEB) and the Alliance. The enemy have manufactured 'screamers', robots with buzzsaws that plough through dirt and cut people to ribbons; the 'screamers' are mutating into bionic creatures, including replicating humans.

The 1953 story was set on Earth (in France, actually), with a distinctly Cold War scenario of the United Nations vs. Russia. The 1995 movie exported the conflict to a distant planet, but the Cold War aspects and the post-atomic elements remained (*Screamers* emphasized radioactivity and living through a nuclear war, for instance).

The *mise-en-scène* of *Screamers* is the familiar one of a post-war, post-nuclear world, with Sirius 6B resembling a rocky, dusty desert, populated by a ragtag of survivors in bunkers, and a landscape of rusting machines and vehicles. It's a world of quarries, power stations, rusting metal, pipes, walkways, etc (it's handy, isn't it, that so many sci-fi and futuristic movies just happen to be set in quarries, warehouses, and abandoned power stations?). It's the world of *Mad Max, Stalker, The Terminator,* etc, all over again. The mining colony setting is also familiar stuff, as in *Total Recall* (some critics related *Screamers* to *Alien*).

Screamers explored familiar Philip K. Dick territory – the blurring of reality and artificiality, as the 'screamers' evolved into androids that seemed 'more than human' (similar themes are found in *Blade Runner* and *Total Recall*). As the screamers emulate humans, the film explores similar themes to *Blade Runner*, but only on a minor level – the issues of machines growing smarter, technology getting out of control, and human simulation are very secondary.[75]

Screamers does have a similar ending to *Blade Runner*, though: the hero and heroine, Jessica (Jennifer Rubin, who's been replaced by a robot) hope to escape in a small craft away from the chaos and their former lives. It's a guy falling for a robot, yet again (complete with goodbye kiss), and *Screamers*' ending consciously evokes *Blade Runner*.[76]

Screamers is a minor film in the cinema of Philip K. Dick, it has to be said, but it's an enjoyable piece of sci-fi pulp.[77] It doesn't take on the grander, philosophical themes of movies such as *Blade Runner* or *Minority Report* or *Total Recall* (and it's also mounted on a much smaller scale). But not so small it doesn't take in tons of visual effects, including models, matte paintings, animation, explosions, numerous stunts and practical effects. By Hollywood mega-budget standards, *Screamers* would be classed as 'low budget', but it clearly isn't. You've got spaceships, planets, cities, hardware, all the usual paraphernalia of a sci-fi movie (the budget was around $20 million).

It's also minor because the characters and issues are pretty run-of-the-mill and unengaging. Peter Weller (best known in sci-fi circles as

---

75 Cigarettes and smoking is a running gag – characters smoke red roll-ups to counter-act radiation! Of course! Smoking cigarettes as a cure.
76 In the book, Tasso (as she's called) is a whore (and a young one, too), and Klaus and Rudi pay her a visit (actually, that's how they survive – the rest of their Russian chums are wasted by the claws (the robots) in the bunker while they're at Tasso's cellar). But Tasso becoming one of the claws wasn't added by the film – that's in the story.
77 Minor, but it did lead to a sequel, *Screamers 2: The Hunting* (2009).

RoboCop) is always good, but his character is bland and uninvolving. Somehow, Weller makes Hendricksson interesting, but he doesn't have much to work with. The action, the pace, and the technical aspects are all satisfactory, but nothing special.

The performances,[78] as in all Philip K. Dick films, are adequate at best. For some reason, adaptions of Dick's fiction just don't have really interesting characters. The movies are great on the look, on the action, on the hardware, but not on relationships and characters. So *Screamers*, like *Blade Runner, Minority Report* and others, is unengaging on the emotional level.

NEXT

Next (Paramount, dir. Lee Tamahori, 2007) was a star vehicle for Nic Cage (although Julianne Moore shared the name above the title credit). Jason Koornick, Todd Gamer, Norm Golightly, Ben Waisbren, Gary Goldman, Graham King, Arne Schmidt and Cage produced. It was co-scripted by Jonathan Hensleigh, Paul Bernbaum and Gary Goldman, who had co-written *Total Recall*. Nic Cage played Cris, a minor Las Vegas magician who has the ability to see into the future – only two minutes into the future, but for some reason (it's lerrrrv, folks!), he can see the love of his life, Liz (Jessica Biel) days or maybe years into the future.

Next was another Philip K. Dick story (*The Golden Man*, 1954) done over as a high budget Hollywood action-adventure movie, constructed within the thriller format. The setting was the present, not the near future (although aspects of the film, such as the vehicles and the FBI's gadgetry, were sleek and hi-tech), and moved from Las Vegas (the hyperreal city beloved of postmodern theorists – yeah, and people who just wanna party!) to an American Indian reservation in the desert, then later a motel near Flagstaff, Arizona, and finally to the City of Lost Angels.

---
[78] By Weller, Jennifer Rubin, Roy Dupuis, Charlie Powell, Andy Lauer and Ron White.

Next contained plenty of expensive set-pieces: the opening chase in the Vegas casino; a car chase; a break-out in downtown L.A.; a hostage scenario; a chase down a hillside with tumbling debris and vehicles; another hostage scene in downtown L.A.; and a big shoot-out at the end, culminating in an atomic bomb explosion.

Because of that, *Next* came across primarily as yet another big, loud action movie (director Lee Tamahori had helmed *James Bond* and *Fast and Furious* movies). And Cris, although he's a Las Vegas performer, turns out to be an action hero capable of beating up bad guys, such as when he unbelievably breaks out of the FBI jail cell (except during the climax, which has Cris walking in amongst the FBI agents, but without a gun – a curiously passive role for a star such as Nic Cage, although he does get to point the FBI agents in the right direction to waste the villains).

Yet there was time for quieter, more reflective (and romantic) scenes in *Next*. The sequence in the Cliffhanger motel,[79] for instance, went on forever, in action movie terms (i.e., it was too talky and too long), before the next action beat kicked in. If there was going to any back-story for the hero or heroine, it would be here, in this romantic interlude. But, as with other Hollywood action movies of the period, back-story and characterization was kept to a minimum.

Next explored the familiar Philip K. Dick theme of seeing into the future. Unfortunately, the plot device of the Russian nuclear device was so hackneyed and predictable. Once again – *yawn* – a bunch of European terrorists had got hold of an atomic bomb from the former Soviet Union and planned to detonate it in America. Yes, the Europeans were vicious and one-dimensional, speaking in French, German and Russian. And, yes, the film addressed a post-9/11 political sensibility with its emphasis on the FBI combating terrorism.

The seeing into the future device had some more intriguing moments, and some humorous moments: the screenwriters could toy with a scene involving a variety of romantic pick-up lines, when Cris first meets Liz in a diner, one chat-up line being replayed after the other (and when Liz's glimpsed for the first time, *of course* she is brightly lit and *of course* ethereal music plays, and *of course* she walks into the diner looking

---

[79] 'Cliffhanger' is of course a movie in-joke – and the film literally plays out a cliffhanger sequence, when Cris leaps off the cliff.

fabulous, and in slow motion. And Jessica Biel's easy on the eye too).[80] But linking Cris's ability to see into the future to the issue of national security was so woefully predictable, down to every plot point and action beat. And that's a pity – although it's also expected from Hollywood.

Next was also, like *Total Recall* and *Minority Report*, a chase movie involving a white romantic American couple on the run from the authorities as well as the bad guys (in a Philip K. Dick movie, the government, FBI and police are often baddies – or at the very least, they're viewed ambiguously. Only towards the end does Cris agree to co-operate with the powers that be – but that was really only after he'd seen the future where he and his beloved die in a nuclear explosion). In these movies, the male star is on the run and encounters a woman along the way (of course she just happens to be beautiful, independent, smart, and unattached).[81]

Although *Next* was an action movie, because of its device of seeing two minutes into the future, it was very much a screenwriter's movie, and a film editor's movie. The cutting (by Christian Wagner) was particularly deft in *Next*, with the editors experimenting with playing scenes out then replaying them with Cris's clairvoyance altering events. That meant that a scene could unfold in a variety of ways, a little like having the rehearsals included in a movie. It also meant that the filmmakers and editors could surprise the audience numerous times throughout the movie. In the opening chase, for instance, Cris's car is hit by a speeding train and demolished – it's great fun to tease the audience by killing off the hero in the first few minutes of a film. But the movie wound back a moment or two (via a complex visual effects shot), and had Cris accelerating in time to miss the train.

Similarly, for the screenwriters, *Next* offered a variety of ways of getting out of scenes: instead of a scene building up to a pay-off or link to

---

[80] A clever piece of scriptwriting had Liz's old boyfriend Kendal turning up in the diner – unusual, but it did explain why a beautiful woman like Liz would be unattached. Hollywood movies are always like that, aren't they? – a fabulous woman appears in the hero's life, and she just happens *not* to be married or in a relationship. It was smart too to have Cris 'rescue' Liz from Kendal, and to add the twist that she doesn't appreciate being saved by a knight in shining armour either. So Cris, seeing into the future, realizes the only way to win Liz's sympathy and attention is to take a slug from Kendal. That's smart scriptwriting – if only the same skill had been applied to the McGuffin of the Russian nuclear bomb.
[81] The screenwriters kept Liz pretty much a regular woman – that is, they resisted the temptation to turn her into a superhero. In *Next*, Liz is what's at stake for Cris – she's his dream girl, literally, the girl who's haunted his dreams. Liz does, though, get to kick one of the villains in the head.

the next scene, a scene could be stopped mid-way through, rewound and started again. OK, it was tiresome after a while, but it was also intriguing from a narrative point-of-view, because the picture could re-invent itself as it went along. The jeopardy and uncertainty was limited, of course – because this is a Hollywood action movie, and the hero always wins and the villains always die. But if the audience knew that Nic Cage would never die and would always be victorious, they didn't know exactly how he would achieve it.

Time travel movies always cheat, of course, favouring the good guys eternally, and *Next* was no different. The entire climactic gun battle in the port and ship turned out to be all foreseen by Cris way back in the Cliffhanger motel. That alternate ending – of Cris being wrong, and the atomic bomb exploding in Los Angeles – had the look of a re-write and a re-shoot (easy to spot such re-shoots, by the way the sequence shifted suddenly from killing the bad guy and rescuing the girl inside the ship to a new scene on the deck, and Cris admitting he'd got it wrong).

So *Next* spooled back to Cris and Liz in the motel, after they'd made love. To be fair to the movie, Cris was able to see much further into the future if it involved the love of his life, Liz, but that whole alternate ending was the usual thing of a Hollywood movie wanting to have it both ways.

IMPOSTOR

Impostor (Dimension Films/ Miramax, directed by Gary Fleder, 2002) starred Gary Sinise, Madeleine Stowe and Vincent d'Onofrio in a feature film based on Philip K. Dick's 1953 short story of the same name. Scott Rosenberg, Caroline Case, Ehren Kruger and David Twohy scripted. Michael Phillips (*The Sting, Taxi Driver, Close Encounters of the Third Kind*) produced. Everything associated with sci-fi cinema and Dick adaptions was in full effect: man on the run story, a slick, hi-tech look, paranoia, urban decay, tons of action beats, stunts, visual fx, and 1000s of additions to

Dick's text.

The prologue was the stand-out sequence in *Impostor*, and contained enough exposition on its own for ten movies: it rapidly evoked a global war, the future, the domes, space battles, the hero and heroine, the hero's back-story, his father, his childhood, and a sex scene. (*Impostor* used footage from other films, including *Starship Troopers* (as did *Serenity*), *Gattaca*, and *Armageddon*, and costumes from *Starship Troopers*. Maybe all movies in the future should be re-edited and re-worked versions of other films – a Dickian concept, in which all movies would be the same movie. Pretty much everything is interchangeable in Hollywood pictures these days anyway).

Performance-wise, *Impostor* featured three actors – Gary Sinise (Olham), Madeleine Stowe (Maya) and Vincent d'Onofrio (Hathaway) – who are always wonderful; d'Onofrio was particularly impressive as the nasty army major Hathaway, sporting an odd ginger crop and an explosive temper. Unfortunately, like other Dick adaptions, the characters were underwritten, and somewhat unappealing.

Part of the problem with *Impostor* was that too much of the film featured Olham and Cale (Mekhi Phifer) running around endless corridors, alleys, tunnels and foyers, always backlit, always at night, always with the cops just around the corner. In a chase movie, all that gets tiresome if you haven't established a really good momentum from the situations, the characters, the relationships, the motives, and the desires. Classic chase pictures sustain interest in a variety of ways – the charisma of the performers, say, or the situations the characters wind up in, or the witty dialogue, or the people they meet along the way, or the force of their desires and goals – but *Impostor* lacked all of those ingredients. It needed the touch of an Alfred Hitchcock or an Orson Welles, or at least filmmakers who could create compelling stories.

Halfway through, you wonder if *Impostor* is going to stick to Phil Dick's 1953 story, and end with the hero blowing himself up. And it does, but adds elements which both twist the story, and create a more upbeat Hollywood ending. Because in the story, Olham turns out to be a bomb sent by aliens, which blows up at the end. The 2002 movie keeps to that ending, but has Olham's wife Maya also being taken over by aliens.[82]

So the bomb inside the robot Olham explodes, and everyone dies. Well, that's a pretty downbeat ending for a number of reasons. First, it means the audience has been rooting for a robot, not a human, and second, he's one of the bad guys, who wants to blow everyone up. In the story, that works; in the movie, it means the audience's identification is scuppered. And not only Olham, but his wife Maya too – both are androids, and both are baddies.

The 2003 film tempers that suicidal ending by introducing a buddy for Olham, Cale (Mekhi Phifer, as with other Phil Dick adaptions – Hollywood movies just can't bear having the hero going on the run on his own). And so *Impostor* does end with the couple together – except not Olham and Maya, but Cale and his now-recovered girlfriend. They sit in the hospital together and watch the real Olham on the TV. Ah, bless, how cute (forget the minor detail that the hospital appeared to be in the city, along with everything else, and would probably have been destroyed by the bomb).

It's the same with *Total Recall*: audiences don't want to think it was all a dream for Arnold Schwarzenegger, or that he was lobotomized at Rekal. And it's the same with *Blade Runner*: making Deckard a replicant means the audiences has been rooting for an android all along. Recent films such as *Bicentennial Man, Star Trek, Star Wars* and *A.I.* have put robots at the centre of the story, and tried to create warm, sympathetic characters. In most sci-fi cinema, though, robots tend to be ambiguous at best (*Alien*), or bad guys (*I, Robot, 2001: A Space Odyssey*).

---

82 When Stowe's Maya is killed, it's a gruesome moment: a woman is shot in the back repeatedly. Forget the fact that a bunch of soldiers are firing at a bomb. *Duh.*

AFTERWORD

Philip K. Dick's stories have formed the basis of some highly entertaining movies, and two solid gold classics of science fiction cinema: *BladeRunner* and *Total Recall*. *Blade Runner* is of course a film in the top ten lists of many filmmakers and fans. It has an afterlife up there with classics like *Singin' In the Rain*, *Bicycle Thieves* or *Jules et Jim*. It's a movie that keeps going on and on.

Some of the Philip K. Dick pictures are distinctly minor – *Next*, *Screamers*, *Paycheck*, *Impostor* – but they are enjoyable for at least one viewing. And a movie such as *Minority Report* is so dense visually it demands repeated screenings. But not every Phil Dick adaption can be a beloved film like *BladeRunner*, like not every new comedy flick can be *Duck Soup* or *The General*.

The adaptions of Philip K. Dick's fiction started out on a very high point – with *Blade Runner*. And the sub-genre shows no sign of slowing up. Indeed, since 2002, the year of *Minority Report* and *Impostor*, versions of Dick's stories keep coming, making him one of the most adapted of sci-fi authors, way ahead of Arthur C. Clarke, Isaac Asimov or Robert Heinlein. (The one sci-fi author I'm eager to see adapted on the big screen in a full-on, mega-budget manner is Ursula Le Guin, for my money the greatest living sci-fi and fantasy author. There's been the wonderful *Tales of Earthsea*, by Studio Ghibli, of course, and the woeful *Earthsea* TV series, but when are we going to see *The Left Hand of Darkness* or *The Dispossessed*?).

On the whole, though, Philip K. Dick has done very well with adaptions of his work (especially if you consider what those films *could* have turned out like, and compared to other sci-fi authors who have been treated less than successfully, to put it politely). It's a pity that Dick didn't get to see *Total Recall*, *Minority Report* or *A Scanner Darkly*, or the completed *Blade Runner*, but one can imagine him enjoying them.

BIBLIOGRAPHY

N. Andrews. *True Myths: The Life and Times of Arnold Schwarzenegger*, Bloomsbury, London, 1995
R. Anobile, ed. *Alien*, Futura, London, 1979
L. Armitt, ed. *Where No Man Has Gone Before: Women and Science Fiction*, Routledge, 1991
—. *Theorising the Fantastic*, Arnold, 1996
J. Arroyo. *Action/ Spectacle Cinema*, British Film Institute, London, 2000
A. Balsamo. "Reading Cyborgs, Writing Feminism", *Communications*, 10, 3, 1988, in J. Wolmark, 1999
—. *Technologies of the Gendered Body: Reading Cyborg Women*, Duke University Press, Durham, NC, 1996
M. Barr, ed. *Future Females, the Next Generation: New Voices and Velocities in Feminism Science Fiction Criticism*, Rowman & Littlefield, Lanham, MD, 2000
R. Barringer: "Skinjobs, Humans and Radical Coding", *Jump Cut*, 41, 1997
J. Baudrillard. *America*, tr. C. Turner, Verso, 1988
—. *Simulacra and Simulation*, tr. S. Faria Glaser, University of Michigan Press, Ann Arbor, 1994
—. "Disneyworld Company", *Liberation*, 4, Mch, 1996
—. *Selected Writings*, ed. M. Poster, Polity Press, Cambridge, 1998
J. Baxter. *Steven Spielberg: The Unauthorized Biography*, HarperCollins, London, 1996
D. Bell & B. Kennedy, eds. *The Cybercultures Reader*, Routledge, 2000
M. Benedikt, ed. *Cyberspace: First Steps*, MIT Press, Cambridge, MA, 1991
C. Berg: "Immigrants, Aliens and Extraterrestrials", *Cine-Action!*, 18, 1989
P. Bizony. *2001: Filming the Future*, Aurum Press, 1994
D. Bordwell & K. Thompson. *Film Art: An Introduction*, McGraw-Hill Publishing Company, N.Y., 1979
—. et al. *The Classical Hollywood Cinema: Film Style and Mode of Production to 1960*, Routledge, 1985
—. *Narration in the Fiction Film*, Routledge, 1988
—. *The Way Hollywood Tells It*, University of California Press, 2006
F. Botting. *Making Monstrous: Frankenstein, Criticism, Theory*, Manchester University Press,

Manchester, 1991
—. *Gothic,* Routledge, 1996
—. *Sex, Machines and Navels: Fiction, Fantasy and History in the Future Present,* Manchester University Press, Manchester, 1999
S. Brewster *et al,* eds. *Inhuman Reflections: Thinking the Limits of the Human,* Manchester University Press, Manchester, 2000
P. Brooker, ed. *Modernism/ Postmodernism,* Longman 1992
A. Brooks. *Postfeminisms: Feminism, Cultural Theory and Cultural Forms,* Routledge, 1997
J. Brosnan. *Future Tense: The Cinema of Science Fiction,* St Martin's, 1978
—. *Primal Screen: A History of Science Fiction Film,* Orbit, 1991
S. Bukatman. "Postcards From the Posthuman Solar System", *Science Fiction Studies,* 55, 1991
—. *Terminal Identity: The Virtual Subject in Postmodern Science Fiction,* Duke University Press, Durham, NC, 1993
—. "The Artificial Infinite", in L. Cooke, 1995
—. *Blade Runner,* British Film Institute, London, 1997
—. "The Ultimate Trip: Special Effects and Kaleidoscopic Perception", *Iris,* 25, 1998
L. Cherny & E.R. Weise, eds. *Wired Women: Gender and New Realities in Cyber-space,* Seal Press, Seattle, 1996
S. Cohan & I.R. Hark, eds. *Screening the Male: Exploring Masculinities in Hollywood Cinema,* Routledge, London, 1993
L. Cooke & P. Wollen, eds. *Visual Display,* Bay Press, Seattle, 1995
B. Creed. "*Alien* and the Monstrous-Feminine", in A. Kuhn, 1990
—. *The Monstrous-Feminine,* Routledge, London, 1993
M. Deeley. *Blade Runners, Deer Hunters and Blowing the Bloody Doors Off,* Faber & Faber, London, 2008
M. Dery, ed. *Flame Wars: The Discourse of Cyberculture,* Duke University Press, Durham, NC, 1994
—. *Escape Velocity: Cyberculture At the End of the Century,* Hodder, 1996
P. Dick. *Minority Report,* Gollancz, London, 2002
J. Dixon & E. Cassidy, eds. *Virtual Futures: Cyberotics, Technology and Post-human Pragmatism,* Routledge, 1998
M. Doel & D. CLark. *From Pastiche To the Screening of the Eye? Or, Geographies of a Diegesis: Postmodernism, Hyperspace and Simulation In the Screening of Blade Runner,* University of Leeds Press, Leeds, 1999
M. Doane. "Technophilia", in J. Wolmark, 1999
J. Donald, ed. *Fantasy and the Cinema,* BFI, 1989
M. Featherstone & R. Burrows, eds. *Cyberspace/ Cyberbodies/ Cyberpunk,* Sage, London, 1995
C. Finch. *Special Effects,* Abbeville, 1984
I. Freer. *The Complete Spielberg,* Virgin Publishing, London, 2001
C. Fuchs: "Death Is Irrelevant: Cyborgs, Reproduction, and the Future of Male Hysteria", *Gender,* 18, 1993
J. Gallagher. *Film Directors On Directing,* Praeger, New York, NY, 1989
K. Gelder, ed. *The Horror Reader,* Routledge, 2000
W. Gibson. *Neuromancer,* Grafton, 1986
F. Glass: "The 'New Bad Future': *Robocop* and 1980s Sci-Fi Films", *Science as Culture,* 5, 1989
L. Goldberg *et al,* eds. *Science Fiction Filmmaking in the 1980s,* McFarland, Jefferson, 1995
J. González. "Envisioning Cyborg Bodies", in G. Gray, 1995
A. Gordon. "Science-fiction and fantasy film criticism: the case of Lucas and Spielberg", *Journal of the Fantastic in the Arts,* 2, 2, 1989
B.K. Grant, ed. *Planks of Reason: Essays on the Horror Film,* Scarecrow Press, N.J., 1984
—. ed. *Crisis Cinema: The Apocalyptic Idea in Postmodern Narrative Film,* Maisonneuve Press, 1993
—. *Film Genre Reader II,* University of Texas Press, Austin, 1995
—. ed. *The Dread of Difference: Gender and the Horror Film,* University of Texas Press, Austin, 1996
C. Gray, ed. *The Cyborg Handbook,* Routledge, 1995
E. Grosz. *Volatile Bodies,* Indiana University Press, Bloomington, 1994
—. *Space, Time and Perversion,* Routledge, 1995
D. Haraway. "A Manifesto For Cyborgs", *Socialist Review,* 15, 2, 1985
—. *Primate Visions: Gender, Race and Nature in the World of Modern Science,* Routledge, London, 1989

—. *Simians, Cyborgs, and Women*, Routledge, London, 1991a
—. "Cyborgs At Large", *Social Text*, 25, 1991b
P. Hardy, ed. *The Aurum Encyclopedia of Science Fiction*, Aurum, 1991
E.R. Helford, ed. *Fantasy Girls: Gender in the New Universe of Science Fiction and Fantasy TV*, Rowman & Littlefield, Lanham, MD, 2000
J. Howard. *The Complete Films of Orson Welles*, Citadel Press, N.Y., 1991
—. *The Stanley Kubrick Companion*, Batsford, 1999
D. Hughes. *The Complete Kubrick*, Virgin, 2000
I.Q. Hunter. *British Science Fiction Cinema*, Routledge, 1999
F. Jameson. *Signatures of the Visible*, Routledge, N.Y., 1990
—. *Postmodernism, or the Cultural Logic of Late Capitalism*, Verso, 1991
—. & M. Miyoshi, eds. *Cultures of Globalization*, Duke University Press, Durham, NC, 1998
S. Jeffords. *Hard Bodies: Hollywood Masculinity in the Reagan Era*, Rutgers University Press, New Brunswick, 1994
G. Jenkins. *Empire Building: The Remarkable Real Life Story of Star Wars*, Simon & Schuster, N.Y., 1997
W. Johnson. *Focus on the Science Fiction Film*, Prentice-Hall, N.J., 1972
S. Jones, ed. *Virtual Culture*, Sage, 1997
M. Kellner et al. "*Blade Runner*", *Jump Cut*, 29, 1984
J. Kerman, ed. *Retrofitting Blade Runner*, Bowling Green State University Popular Press, 1991
G. King. *Spectacular Narratives: Hollywood in the Age of the Blockbuster*, I.B. Tauris, 2000
—. & T. Krzywinmska. *Science Fiction Cinema*, Wallflower, 2000
P. Kolker. *The Altering Eye: Contemporary International Cinema*, Oxford University Press, N.Y., 1983
—. *A Cinema of Loneliness: Penn, Kubrick, Coppola, Scorsese, Altman*, Oxford University Press, N.Y., 1988
A. & M. Kroker, eds. *Body Invaders: Panic Sex in America*, St Martin's Press, N.Y., 1988
—. eds. *The Hysterical Male: New Feminist Theory*, St Martin's Press, N.Y., 1991
—. *Hacking the Future*, New World Perspectives, Montreal, 1996
—. *Digital Delirium*, New World Perspectives, Montreal, 1997
A. Kuhn, ed. *Alien Zone: Cultural Theory and Contemporary Science Fiction*, Verso, London, 1990
—. ed. *Alien Zone 2*, Verso, London, 1999
S. Lefanu. *In the Chinks of the World Machine: Feminism and Science Fiction*, Women's Press, 1988
H. Lightman. "*Blade Runner*", *American Cinematographer*, 1982
J. McBride. *Steven Spielberg*, Faber, London, 1997
D. Menville & R. Reginald. *Future Visions: The New Golden Age of the Science Fiction Film*, Newcastle, CA, 1985
J. Murray. *Hamlet On the Holodeck: The Future of Narrative in Cyberspace*, MIT Press, Cambridge, MA, 1997
D. Neumann, ed. *Film Architecture: From Metropolis to Blade Runner*, Prestel-Verlag, New York, NY, 1996
C. Penley, ed. *Feminism and Film Theory*, Routledge, 1988
—. "Time Travel, Prime Scene and the Critical Dystopia", *Camera Obscura*, 15, 1988
—. et al, eds. *Close Encounters: Film, Feminism and Science Fiction*, University of Minnesota Press, Minneapolis, 1991
—. & A. Ross, eds. *Technoculture*, University of Minnesota Press, Minneapolis, 1991
M. Pierson. "CGI effects in Hollywood science fiction cinema", *Screen*, 40, 2, Summer, 1999
C. Platt, ed. *Dream Makers: Science Fiction and Fantasy Writers At Work*, Xanadu, London, 1986
D. Pollock. *Skywalking: The Life and Films of George Lucas*, Crown, N.Y., 1983, 1990, 2000
E. Rabkin & G. Slusser, eds. *Shadows of the Magic Lamp: Fantasy and Science Fiction in Film*, Southern Illinois University Press, Carbondale, 1985
—. *Aliens: The Anthropology of Science Fiction*, Southern Illinois University Press, Carbondale, 1987
N. Ruddick, ed. *State of the Fantastic*, Greenwood Press, 1992
J. Rusher & T. Frentz. *Projecting the Shadow: The Cyborg Hero in American Film*, University of Chicago Press, 1995
B. Rux. *Hollywood vs. the Aliens*, Frog, Berkeley, 1997
P. Sammon. "Do Androids Dream of Unicorns? The 7 Faces of *Blade Runner*", *Video Watchdog*, 20, Dec, 1993

—. *Future Noir: The Making of Blade Runner*, Orion Media, London, 1996
—. "Bug Bytes: *Starship Troopers*", *Cinefex*, 73, Mch, 1998
—. *The Making of Starship Troopers*, Little, Brown, Boston, MA, 1999
—. *Ridley Scott*, Orion, London, 1999
D. Schaefer & L. Salvato, eds. *Masters of Light*, University of California Press, Berkeley, CA, 1984
P. Schelde. *Androids, Humanoids and Other Science Fiction Monsters*, New York University Press, 1993
G. Schwab: "Cyborgs", *Discourse*, 9, 1987
T. Shone. *Blockbuster: How the Jaws and Jedi Generation Turned Hollywood Into a Boom-Town*, Scribner, London, 2005
K. Silverman. *The Acoustic Mirror: The Female Voice in Psychoanalysis and Cinema*, Indiana University Press, Bloomington, IN, 1988
—. "Back to the Future", *Camera Obscura*, 27, 1991
V. Sobchack. *The Limits of Infinity: The American Science Fiction Film*, A.S. Barnes, N.Y., 1980
—. *Screening Space: The American Science Fiction Film*, Ungar, N.Y., 1987/1993
—. "Cities On the Edge of Time: The Urban Science Fiction Film", *East-West Film Journal*, 3, 1, Dec, 1988
—. *The Address of the Eye: A Phenomenology of Film Experience*, Princeton University Press, N.J., 1992
—. ed. *The Persistence of History: Cinema, Television, and the Modern Event*, Routledge, 1995
C. Springer. "The Pleasure of the Interface", *Screen*, 32, 3, 1991
—. "Muscular Circuitry", *Genders*, 18, 1993
—. *Electronic Eros*, Athlone, 1996
G. Stewart. *Between Film and Screen: Modernism's Photo Synthesis*, University of Chicago Press, Chicago, IL, 1999
Y. Tasker. *Spectacular Bodies: Gender, Genre and the Action Cinema*, Routledge, London, 1993
D. Thomson. *The Alien Quartet*, Bloomsbury, London, 1998
K. Van Gunden. *Fantasy Films*, McFarland, Jefferson, N.C. 1989
—. *Postmodern Auteurs: Coppola, Lucas, De Palma, Spielberg and Scorsese*, McFarland, Jefferson, N.C. 1991
R. van Scheers. *Paul Verhoeven*, Faber, London, 1997
M.C. Vaz. *From Star Wars to Indiana Jones*, Chronicle, San Francisco, 1994
—. & P.R. Duignan. *Industrial Light & Magic*, Virgin, 1996
P. Verhoeven. *Paul Verhoeven: Beyond Flesh and Blood*, Le Cinépage, Cinéditions, Paris, 2001
P. Virilio & S. Lotringer. *War and Cinema*, Verso, 1992a
—. *The Vision Machine*, tr. J. Rose, Indiana University Press, Bloomington, 1994
Walsh. *"Minority Report" Official Strategy Guide*, Brady Games, 2002
P. Warrick: *The Cybernetic Imagination in Science Fiction*, MIT Press, 1980
O. Welles. *Orson Welles: Interviews*, ed. M. Estrin, University of Mississippi Press, Jackson, 2002
D. Wingrove, ed. *Science Fiction Film Source Book*, Longman, 1985
J. Wolmark. *Aliens and Others: Science Fiction, Feminism and Postmodernism*, Harvester Wheatsheaf, 1993
—. ed. *Cybersexualities: A Reader on Feminist Theory, Cyborgs and Cyberspace*, Edinburgh University Press, Edinburgh, 1999
S. Zizek. *Enjoy Your Symptom Jacques Lacan in Hollywood and Out*, Routledge, New York, NY, 1992
—. *Tarrying With the Negative: Kant, Hegel, and the Critique of Ideology*, Duke University Press, Durham, NC, 1993

FILMOGRAPHIES

BLADE RUNNER

Credits for the 1982 production

CAST

Harrison Ford – Rick Deckard
Rutger Hauer – Roy Batty
Sean Young – Rachel
Edward James Olmos – Gaff
M. Emmet Walsh – Bryant
Daryl Hannah – Pris
William Sanderson – J.F. Sebastian
Brion James – Leon Kowalski
Joe Turkel – Dr. Eldon Tyrell
Joanna Cassidy – Zhora
James Hong – Hannibal Chew
Morgan Paull – Holden
Kevin Thompson – Bear
John Edward Allen – Kaiser
Hy Pyke – Taffey Lewis
Kimiko Hiroshige – Cambodian Lady
Bob Okazaki – Howie Lee
Carolyn DeMirjian – Saleslady
Ben Astar – Abdul Ben Hassan
Judith Burnett – Ming-Fa
Leo Gorcey Jr. – Louie - Bartender
Sharon Hesky – Bar Patron
Kelly Hine – Showgirl
Tom Hutchinson – Bartender
Charles Knapp – Bartender
Rose Mascari – Bar Patron
Jirô Okazaki – Policeman
Steve Pope – Policeman
Robert Reiter – Policeman
Alexis Rhee – Geisha #1

CREW

Directed by Ridley Scott
Written by Hampton Fancher and David Peoples
Michael Deeley – producer
Hampton Fancher – executive producer
Brian Kelly – executive producer
Ivor Powell – associate producer
Jerry Perenchio – co-executive producer
Ridley Scott – co-producer
Run Run Shaw – co-executive producer
Bud Yorkin – co-executive producer
Music by Vangelis
Cinematography by Jordan Cronenweth
Film Editing by Marsha Nakashima
Casting by Jane Feinberg, Mike Fenton, Marci Liroff
Production Design by Lawrence G. Paull
Art Direction by David L. Snyder
Set Decoration by Linda DeScenna, Leslie Frankenheimer, Thomas L. Roysden, Peg Cummings
Costume Design by Michael Kaplan and Charles Knode
Shirley Padgett – hair stylist
Marvin G. Westmore – makeup artist
John Chambers – prosthetic makeups
Ana Maria Quintana – script supervisor
Alan Collis – production manager
C.O. Erickson – executive in charge of production
John W. Rogers – unit production manager
Newt Arnold – first assistant director
Morris Chapnick – second assistant director
Peter Cornberg – first assistant director
Donald Hauer – second assistant director
Victoria E. Rhodes – dga trainee
Richard Peter Schroer – second assistant director
Stephen Dane – assistant art director
Mentor Huebner – production illustrator
Tom Southwell – production illustrator

James T. Woods – painting coordinator
John Alvin – poster artist
William Apperson – construction foreman
William Apperson – model maker
Charles Breen – set designer
Marco A. Campos – propmaker
Robert Clark – sculptor
Carmine Goglia – stand-by painter
Peter J. Hampton – production designer: additional scenes
Sherman Labby – production illustrator
Steven Ladish – props
Edward T. McAvoy – scenic artist
Curtis A. Schnell – set designer
Kevin Shanks – drapery man/ floor covering
William Ladd Skinner – set designer
Drew Struzan – poster artist
Michael Taylor – leadman
Gary Zink – carpenter
Gary Zink – propmaker
Terry E. Lewis – property master
Basil Lombardo – standby painter
Syd Mead – visual futurist
James F. Orendorff – construction coordinator
David Q. Quick – assistant property master
John A. Scott III – assistant property master
Arthur Shippee – assistant property master
Bud Alper – sound mixer
Gene Ashbrook – boom operator
Graham V. Hartstone – chief dubbing mixer
Mike Hopkins – dialogue editor
Gerry Humphreys – chief dubbing mixer
Peter Pennell – sound editor
Joel Fein – sound recording mixer
John Hayward – sound re-recording mixer
Nicolas Le Messurier – sound re-recording mixer
Gordon K. McCallum – sound mixer
Brydon Baker III – cable person
Peter Baldock – assistant dialogue editor
Joe Gallagher – assistant sound editor
Greg Curtis – special effects technician
Logan Frazee – special effects technician
Terry D. Frazee – special floor effects supervisor
Steve Galich – special effects technician
Robert Cole – special effects action property foreman
Robert DeVine – special effects
Ken Estes – special effects foreman
Scott Forbes – special effects technician
Michael Backauskas – assistant effects editor: EEG
Tom Cranham – effects illustrator: EEG
Jonathan Seay – visual effects camera
Scott Squires – visual displays: DQI
George Trimmer – model maker
Hoyt Yeatman – visual displays: DQI
Gene Young – model construction
David Dryer – special photographic effects supervisor
Bud Elam – special engineering consultant: EEG
Michael L. Fink – action prop supervisor
Linda Fleisher – action prop consultant
Joyce Goldberg – production office manager: EEG
Robert D. Bailey – matte photography: EEG
David Grafton – special engineering consultant: EEG
Robert Hall – optical photography supervisor: EEG
David R. Hardberger – camera operator: EEG
Alan Harding – special camera technician: EEG
Jack Hinkle – film coordinator: EEG
Richard E. Hollander – computer engineering: EEG
Ronald Longo – camera operator: EEG
Don Baker – camera operator: EEG
Tim McHugh – camera operator: EEG
Gregory L. McMurry – electronic engineering: EEG
Virgil Mirano – still lab: EEG
George Polkinghorne – cinetechnician: EEG
Gary Randall – gaffer: EEG
Philip Barberio – optical line-up: EEG
Richard Rippel – optical line-up: EEG
Robert Spurlock – miniature technician: EEG
Mark Stetson – chief model maker: EEG
David K. Stewart – director of photography: EEG
Tama Takahashi – matte photography: EEG
Douglas Trumbull – special photographic effects supervisor
Patrick Van Auken – key grip: EEG
John C. Wash – animation and graphics: EEG
Evans Wetmore – electronic and mechanical design: EEG
Matthew Yuricich – matte artist: EEG
Richard Yuricich – special photographic effects supervisor
Thomas Baker – motion control camera
Craig Chandler – optical effects
Leslie Ekker – model maker
Bill George – miniature design and construction
Rocco Gioffre – matte artist
Bill Kent – camera operator: special photographic effects
Charles Cowles – camera operator: EEG
Michael McMillen – model maker
Michele Moen – matte artist: EEG
Tom Pahk – model maker
Christopher S. Ross – miniature design and construction
Gary Combs – stunt coordinator
Ray Bickel – stunts
Jeannie Epper – stunts
James M. Halty – stunts
Jeff Imada – stunts
Gary McLarty – stunts
Karen McLarty – stunts
Beth Nufer – stunts
Roy K. Ogata – stunts
Bobby Porter – stunts
Lee Pulford – stunt double: Joanna Cassidy
Ruth A. Redfern – stunts

Janet Brady – stunts
George Sawaya – stunts
Charles A. Tamburro – stunts
Jack Tyree – stunts
Mike Washlake – stunts
Michael Zurich – stunts
Diane Carter – stunts
Ann Chatterton – stunts
Gary Combs – stunt double: Harrison Ford
Gilbert B. Combs – stunts
Tony Cox – stunts
Rita Egleston – stunts
Gary Epper – stunts
Albert Bettcher – camera operator
Dick Colean – camera operator
Stephen Vaughan – still photographer
Michael B. Corbett – lighting technician
Adam Glick – set lighting technician
Dan Greer – assistant camera
Ernest Holzman – film loader
Michael E. Matteson – key grip
James Nordberg – generator operator
Jeff Paynter – second unit focus puller
Peter Santoro – second assistant camera
Bernie Schwartz – grip
Michael Genne – first assistant camera
Haskell Wexler – additional photographer
George D. Greer – second assistant camera
Cary Griffith – key grip
Richard Hart – lighting gaffer
Steven Poster – additional photographer
Steven H. Smith – first assistant camera
Robert C. Thomas – camera operator
Brian Tufano – additional photographer
Winnie D. Brown – costumer: women
Bob E. Horn – costumer: men
James Lapidus – costumer: men
Linda Matthews – costumer: women
Jan Ferris – designer sculptor
Jerry Herrin – costumer supervisor: day crew
Les Healey – first assistant editor
Terry Rawlings – supervising editor
R. William Zabala – assistant editor
Peter Hollywood – additional editing
Gail Laughton – composer: additional music
Vangelis – music: arranged, performed and produced by
Howard Brady Davidson – transportation captain
Mario Simon – transportation
Vickie Alper – production coordinator
Steve Warner – production controller
Brian O. Haynes – production assistant
Jeffrey A. Humphreys – studio utility
Roland Kibbee – voice-over engineer
Michael Neale – location manager
Nancy Ramey – assistant accountant
Jasmine Sabu – horse trainer
Charles A. Tamburro – helicopter pilot
Katherine Haber – production executive
David Scharf – electron microscope photography

Linda Hess – production assistant
Saul Kahan – publicist
Michael Knutsen – craft service
Jerry Perenchio – presenter
Bud Yorkin – presenter
Run Run Shaw – presenter
William S. Burroughs – thanks: for the use of the title "Blade Runner"
Philip K. Dick – dedicated to the memory of

MINORITY REPORT

CAST

Tom Cruise – Chief John Anderton
Max von Sydow – Director Lamar Burgess
Steve Harris – Jad
Neal McDonough – Fletcher
Patrick Kilpatrick – Knott
Jessica Capshaw – Evanna
Richard Coca – Pre-Crime Cop
Keith Campbell – Pre-Crime Cop
Kirk B.R. Woller – Pre-Crime Cop
Klea Scott – Pre-Crime Cop
Frank Grillo – Pre-Crime Cop
Horsford – Casey
Sarah Simmons – Lamar Burgess' Secretary
Eugene Osment – Jad's Technician
Keith Flippen – Tour Guide
Colin Farrell – Danny Witwer
Samantha Morton – Agatha
Daniel London – Wally the Caretaker
Michael Dickman – Arthur
Matthew Dickman – Dashiell
Lois Smith – Dr. Iris Hineman
Tim Blake Nelson – Gideon
George Wallace – Chief Justice Pollard
Ann Ryerson – Dr. Katherine James
Kathryn Morris – Lara Clarke
Tyler Patrick Jones – Older Sean
Dominic Scott Kay – Younger Sean
Arye Gross – Howard Marks
Ashley Crow – Sarah Marks
Mike Binder – Leo Crow
Joel Gretsch – Donald Dubin
Jessica Harper – Anne Lively
Bertell Lawrence – John Doe
Jason Antoon – Rufus Riley at Cyber Parlor
William Mesnik – Cyber Parlor Customer
Scott Frank – Conceited Customer
Peter Stormare – Dr. Solomon Eddie
Caroline Lagerfelt – Greta van Eyck

CREW

Directed by Steven Spielberg
Written by Philip K. Dick, Scott Frank and Jon Cohen
Jan de Bont – producer
Bonnie Curtis – producer
Michael Doven – associate producer
Gary Goldman – executive producer
Sergio Mimica-Gezzan – associate producer
Gerald R. Molen – producer
Walter F. Parkes – producer
Ronald Shusett – executive producer
Music by John Williams
Cinematography by Janusz Kaminski
Film Editing by Michael Kahn
Casting by Denise Chamian
Production Design by Alex McDowell
Art Direction by Ramsey Avery
Set Decoration by Anne Kuljian
Costume Design by Deborah Lynn Scott
Karen Asano-Myers – key hair stylist
Michèle Burke – makeup supervisor
Erica Frauman – post-production supervisor
Sharon Mann – production manager
Sergio Mimica-Gezzan – first assistant director
David Lowery – storyboard artist
Richard Hymns – supervising sound editor
Gary Rydstrom – sound designer
Michael Lantieri – special effects supervisor
Tom Pahk – special effects shop supervisor
Henry LaBounta – visual effects supervisor
Nathan McGuinness – senior visual effects supervisor
Scott Farrar – visual effects supervisor
Brian Smrz – stunt coordinator
Alexandria Forster – costume supervisor
Kenneth Wannberg – supervising music editor
Ana Maria Quintana – script supervisor

TOTAL RECALL

CAST

Arnold Schwarzenegger – Douglas Quaid / Hauser
Rachel Ticotin – Melina
Sharon Stone – Lori
Ronny Cox – Vilos Cohaagen
Michael Ironside – Richter
Marshall Bell – George / Kuato
Mel Johnson Jr. – Benny
Michael Champion – Helm
Roy Brocksmith – Dr. Edgemar
Ray Baker – Bob McClane
Rosemary Dunsmore – Dr. Lull
David Knell – Ernie
Alexia Robinson – Tiffany
Dean Norris – Tony
Mark Carlton – Bartender
Debbie Lee Carrington – Thumbelina
Lycia Naff – Mary
Robert Costanzo – Harry
Michael LaGuardia – Stevens
Priscilla Allen – Fat Lady
Ken Strausbaugh – Immigration Officer
Marc Alaimo – Everett
Michael Gregory – Rebel Lieutenant
Ken Gildin – Hotel Clerk
Mickey Jones – Burly Miner
Parker Whitman – Martian Husband
Ellen Gollas – Martian Wife
Gloria Dorson – Woman in Phone Booth
Erika Carlsson – Miss Lonelyhearts
Benny Corral – Punk Cabbie
Bob Tzudiker – Doctor
Erik Cord – Lab Assistant
Frank Kopyc – Technician
Chuck Sloan – Scientist
Dave Nicolson – Scientist
Paula McClure – Newscaster
Rebecca Ruth – Reporter
Milt Tarver – Commercial Announcer
Roger Cudney – Agent
Monica Steuer – Mutant Mother
Sasha Rionda – Mutant Child
Linda Howell – Tennis Pro
Andy Armstrong – Richter's Henchman
Allan Graf – Harry's Henchman
Peter Kent – Richter's Subway Agent
Joel Kramer – Harry's Henchman
Bennie Moore – Richter's Subway Agent

CREW

Directed by Paul Verhoeven
Written by Philip K. Dick, Ronald Shusett, Dan O'Bannon, Jon Povill, Gary Goldman
Buzz Feitshans – producer
Robert Fentress – associate producer
Mario Kassar – executive producer
Andrew G. Vajna – executive producer
Elliot Schick – associate producer
Ronald Shusett – producer
Original Music by Jerry Goldsmith
Cinematography by Jost Vocano
Film Editing by Carlos Puente, Frank J. Urioste
Casting by Mike Fenton, Valorie Massalas, Judy Taylor
Production Design by William Sandell
Art Direction by José Rodríguez Granada, James E. Tocci
Set Decoration by Robert Gould
Costume Design by Erica Edell Phillips
Rob Bottin – special makeup effects design and creation
Jeff Dawn – makeup department head
Vincent Prentice – lead special makeup effects artist
Peter Tothpal – key hair stylist

Anuar Badin – production manager
Terry Collis – production manager
Vic Armstrong – second unit director & stunt coordinator
Miguel Lima – first assistant director
Kuki López Rodero – first assistant director
Stephen Hunter Flick – supervising sound effects editor
Scott Hecker – supervising dialogue editor
Eric Brevig – visual effects supervisor
Steve Love – music supervisor
Arthur Morton – orchestrator

A SCANNER DARKLY

CAST

Keanu Reeves – Bob Arctor
Robert Downey Jr – James Barris
Woody Harrelson – Ernie Luckman
Rory Cochrane – Charles Freck
Winona Ryder – Donna
Sean Allen – Additional Fred Scramble Suit Voice
Mitch Baker – Brown Bear Lodge Host
Cliff Haby – Voice from Headquarters
Steven Chester Prince – Cop
Natasha Valdez – Waitress
Mark Turner – Additional Hank Scramble Suit Voice
Melody Chase – Arctor's Wife
Alex Jones – Arrested Protester

CREW

Director – Richard Linklater
Written by – Richard Linklater, from the novel by Philip K. Dick.
Producers – Tommy Pallotta, Jonah Smith, Erwin Stoff, Anne Walker-McBay and Palmer West
Co-Producer – Erin Ferguson
Associate Producer – Sara Greene
Executive Producers – George Clooney, Ben Cosgrove, Jennifer Fox, John Sloss and Steven Soderbergh
Film Editor – Sandra Adair
Cinematography – Shane F. Kelly
Unit Production Manager – Susan Kirr
Executive in Charge of Production – Ravi D. Mehta
Original Score – Graham Reynolds
Production Design – Bruce Curtis
Casting – Denise Chamian and Beth Sepko
Set Decoration – Joaquin A. Morin.
Costume Design – Kari Perkins

RIDLEY SCOTT

Films directed by Ridley Scott

1977 *The Duellists*
1979 *Alien*
1982 *Blade Runner*
1985 *Legend*
1987 *Someone to Watch Over Me*
1989 *Black Rain*
1991 *Thelma & Louise*
1992 *1492: Conquest of Paradise*
1996 *White Squall*
1997 *G.I. Jane*
2000 *Gladiator*
2001 *Hannibal*
2001 *Black Hawk Down*
2003 *Matchstick Men*
2005 *Kingdom of Heaven*
2006 *A Good Year*
2007 *American Gangster*
2008 *Body of Lies*
2010 *Robin Hood*
2012 *Prometheus*

VANGELIS

Select filmography

My Brother, the Traffic Policeman (1963)
Five Thousand Lies (1966)
Vortex (1967)
Sex-Power (1970)
Frenitis (1971)
L'apocalypse des animaux (1972)
Hello Jerusalem (1972)
Verve (1973)
Love (1974)
Do You Hear the Dogs Barking? (1975)
Le cantique des créatures: Georges Mathieu ou La fureur d'être (1974)
Le cantique des créatures: Georges Braque ou Le temps différent (1975)
Ace Up My Sleeve (1976)
La fête sauvage (1976)
Death of a Princess (1980)
Defiant Delta (1980)
Chariots of Fire (1981)
Missing (1982)
Blade Runner (1982)
Pablo Picasso Painter (1982)
Nankyoku Monogatari (a.k.a. Antarctica, 1983)
The Bounty (1984)
Sauvage et Beau (1984)
Wonders of Life (1985)
Nosferatu a Venezia (1988)
Francesco (1989)
Mouseio Goulandri Fysikis Istorias (1990)
Bitter Moon (1992)
1492: Conquest of Paradise (1992)

De Nuremberg à Nuremberg (1994)
Kavafis (1996)
Mythodea – Music for the NASA Mission, 2001
Mars Odyssey (2001)
I Hope... (2001)
Alexander (2004)
Perfect Is the Enemy of Good (2005)
El Greco (2007)
The Seven Sages of Antiquity (2010)

CRESCENT MOON PUBLISHING

ARTS, PAINTING, SCULPTURE

The Art of Andy Goldsworthy: Complete Works
Andy Goldsworthy: Touching Nature
Andy Goldsworthy in Close-Up
Andy Goldsworthy: Pocket Guide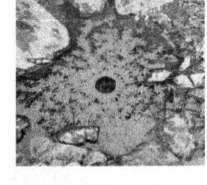
Andy Goldsworthy In America
Land Art: A Complete Guide
The Art of Richard Long: Complete Works
Richard Long: Pocket Guide
Land Art In the UK
Land Art in Close-Up
Land Art In the U.S.A.
Land Art: Pocket Guide
Installation Art in Close-Up
Minimal Art and Artists In the 1960s and After
Colourfield Painting
Land Art DVD, TV documentary
Andy Goldsworthy DVD, TV documentary
The Erotic Object: Sexuality in Sculpture From Prehistory to the Present Day
Sex in Art: Pornography and Pleasure in Painting and Sculpture
Postwar Art
Sacred Gardens: The Garden in Myth, Religion and Art
Glorification: Religious Abstraction in Renaissance and 20th Century Art
Early Netherlandish Painting
Leonardo da Vinci
Piero della Francesca
Giovanni Bellini
Fra Angelico: Art and Religion in the Renaissance
Mark Rothko: The Art of Transcendence
Frank Stella: American Abstract Artist
Jasper Johns
Brice Marden
Alison Wilding: The Embrace of Sculpture
Vincent van Gogh: Visionary Landscapes
Eric Gill: Nuptials of God
Constantin Brancusi: Sculpting the Essence of Things
Max Beckmann
Caravaggio
Gustave Moreau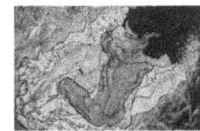
Egon Schiele: Sex and Death In Purple Stockings
Delizioso Fotografico Fervore: Works In Process 1
Sacro Cuore: Works In Process 2
The Light Eternal: J.M.W. Turner
The Madonna Glorified: Karen Arthurs

LITERATURE

J.R.R. Tolkien: The Books, The Films, The Whole Cultural Phenomenon
J.R.R. Tolkien: Pocket Guide
Tolkien's Heroic Quest
The *Earthsea* Books of Ursula Le Guin
Beauties, Beasts and Enchantment: Classic French Fairy Tales
German Popular Tales by the Brothers Grimm
Philip Ullman and *His Dark Materials*
Sexing Hardy: Thomas Hardy and Feminism
Thomas Hardy's *Tess of the d'Urbervilles*
Thomas Hardy's *Jude the Obscure*
Thomas Hardy: The Tragic Novels
Love and Tragedy: Thomas Hardy
The Poetry of Landscape in Hardy
Wessex Revisited: Thomas Hardy and John Cowper Powys
Wolfgang Iser: Essays and Interviews
Petrarch, Dante and the Troubadours
Maurice Sendak and the Art of Children's Book Illustration
Andrea Dworkin
Cixous, Irigaray, Kristeva: The *Jouissance* of French Feminism
Julia Kristeva: Art, Love, Melancholy, Philosophy, Semiotics and Psychoanalysis
Hélene Cixous I Love You: The *Jouissance* of Writing
Luce Irigaray: Lips, Kissing, and the Politics of Sexual Difference
Peter Redgrove: Here Comes the Flood
Peter Redgrove: Sex-Magic-Poetry-Cornwall
Lawrence Durrell: Between Love and Death, East and West
Love, Culture & Poetry: Lawrence Durrell
Cavafy: Anatomy of a Soul
German Romantic Poetry: Goethe, Novalis, Heine, Hölderlin
Feminism and Shakespeare
Shakespeare: Love, Poetry & Magic
The Passion of D.H. Lawrence
D.H. Lawrence: Symbolic Landscapes
D.H. Lawrence: Infinite Sensual Violence
Rimbaud: Arthur Rimbaud and the Magic of Poetry
The Ecstasies of John Cowper Powys
Sensualism and Mythology: The Wessex Novels of John Cowper Powys
Amorous Life: John Cowper Powys and the Manifestation of Affectivity (H.W. Fawkner)
Postmodern Powys: New Essays on John Cowper Powys (Joe Boulter)
Rethinking Powys: Critical Essays on John Cowper Powys
Paul Bowles & Bernardo Bertolucci
Rainer Maria Rilke
Joseph Conrad: *Heart of Darkness*
In the Dim Void: Samuel Beckett
Samuel Beckett Goes into the Silence
André Gide: Fiction and Fervour
Jackie Collins and the Blockbuster Novel
Blinded By Her Light: The Love-Poetry of Robert Graves
The Passion of Colours: Travels In Mediterranean Lands
Poetic Forms

POETRY

Ursula Le Guin: Walking In Cornwall
Peter Redgrove: Here Comes The Flood
Peter Redgrove: Sex-Magic-Poetry-Cornwall
Dante: Selections From the *Vita Nuova*
Petrarch, Dante and the Troubadours
William Shakespeare: *The Sonnets*
William Shakespeare: Complete Poems
Blinded By Her Light: The Love-Poetry of Robert Graves
Emily Dickinson: Selected Poems
Emily Brontë: Poems
Thomas Hardy: Selected Poems
Percy Bysshe Shelley: Poems
John Keats: Selected Poems
D.H. Lawrence: Selected Poems
Edmund Spenser: Poems
Edmund Spenser: *Amoretti*
John Donne: Poems
Henry Vaughan: Poems
Sir Thomas Wyatt: Poems
Robert Herrick: Selected Poems
Rilke: Space, Essence and Angels in the Poetry of Rainer Maria Rilke
Rainer Maria Rilke: Selected Poems
Friedrich Hölderlin: Selected Poems
Arseny Tarkovsky: Selected Poems
Novalis: *Hymns To the Night*
Paul Verlaine: Selected Poems
Arthur Rimbaud: Selected Poems
Arthur Rimbaud: *A Season in Hell*
Arthur Rimbaud and the Magic of Poetry
D.J. Enright: By-Blows
Jeremy Reed: Brigitte's Blue Heart
Jeremy Reed: Claudia Schiffer's Red Shoes
Gorgeous Little Orpheus
Radiance: New Poems
Crescent Moon Book of Nature Poetry
Crescent Moon Book of Love Poetry
Crescent Moon Book of Mystical Poetry
Crescent Moon Book of Elizabethan Love Poetry
Crescent Moon Book of Metaphysical Poetry
Crescent Moon Book of Romantic Poetry
Pagan America: New American Poetry

MEDIA, CINEMA, FEMINISM and CULTURAL STUDIES

J.R.R. Tolkien: The Books, The Films, The Whole Cultural Phenomenon
J.R.R. Tolkien: Pocket Guide
The *Lord of the Rings* Movies: Pocket Guide
The Cinema of Hayao Miyazaki
Hayao Miyazaki: *Princess Mononoke*: Pocket Movie Guide
Hayao Miyazaki: *Spirited Away*: Pocket Movie Guide
Tim Burton
Ken Russell
Ken Russell: *Tommy*: Pocket Movie Guide
The Ghost Dance: The Origins of Religion
The Peyote Cult
Cixous, Irigaray, Kristeva: The *Jouissance* of French Feminism
Julia Kristeva: Art, Love, Melancholy, Philosophy, Semiotics and Psychoanalysis
Luce Irigaray: Lips, Kissing, and the Politics of Sexual Difference
Hélene Cixous I Love You: The *Jouissance* of Writing
Andrea Dworkin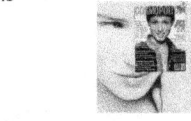
'Cosmo Woman': The World of Women's Magazines
Women in Pop Music
Discovering the Goddess (Geoffrey Ashe)
The Poetry of Cinema
The Sacred Cinema of Andrei Tarkovsky
Andrei Tarkovsky: Pocket Guide
Andrei Tarkovsky: *Mirror*: Pocket Movie Guide
Andrei Tarkovsky: *The Sacrifice*: Pocket Movie Guide
Walerian Borowczyk: Cinema of Erotic Dreams
Jean-Luc Godard: The Passion of Cinema
Jean-Luc Godard: *Hail Mary*: Pocket Movie Guide
Jean-Luc Godard: *Contempt*: Pocket Movie Guide
Jean-Luc Godard: *Pierrot le Fou*: Pocket Movie Guide
John Hughes and Eighties Cinema
Ferris Bueller's Day Off: Pocket Movie Guide
Jean-Luc Godard: Pocket Guide
The Cinema of Richard Linklater
Liv Tyler: Star In Ascendance
Blade Runner and the Films of Philip K. Dick
Paul Bowles and Bernardo Bertolucci
Media Hell: Radio, TV and the Press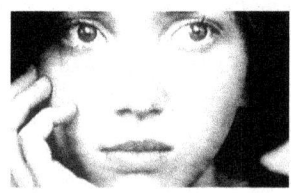
An Open Letter to the BBC
Detonation Britain: Nuclear War in the UK
Feminism and Shakespeare
Wild Zones: Pornography, Art and Feminism
Sex in Art: Pornography and Pleasure in Painting and Sculpture
Sexing Hardy: Thomas Hardy and Feminism

In my view *The Light Eternal* is among the very best of all the material I read on Turner. (Douglas Graham, director of the Turner Museum, Denver, Colorado)

The Light Eternal is a model monograph, an exemplary job. The subject matter of the book is beautifully organised and dead on beam. (Lawrence Durrell)

It is amazing for me to see my work treated with such passion and respect. (Andrea Dworkin)

CRESCENT MOON PUBLISHING
P.O. Box 1312, Maidstone, Kent, ME14 5XU, Great Britain. www.crmoon.com

www.ingramcontent.com/pod-product-compliance
Lightning Source LLC
Chambersburg PA
CBHW070610170426
43200CB00012B/2647